Y0-BCV-657

DAVID GLENN HUNT
MEMORIAL LIBRARY
GALVESTON COLLEGE

New Casebooks

THE MERCHANT OF VENICE

NEW CASEBOOKS

New Casebooks

THE MERCHANT OF VENICE

WILLIAM SHAKESPEARE

Edited by
MARTIN COYLE

St. Martin's Press
New York

DAVID GLENN HUNT
MEMORIAL LIBRARY
GALVESTON COLLEGE

THE MERCHANT OF VENICE

Introduction, selection and editorial matter copyright © 1998 by Martin Coyle

All rights reserved. No part of this book may be used or reproduced in any manner whatsoever without written permission except in the case of brief quotations embodied in critical articles or reviews. For information, address:

St. Martin's Press, Scholarly and Reference Division, 175 Fifth Avenue, New York, N.Y. 10010

First published in the United States of America in 1998

This book is printed on paper suitable for recycling and made from fully managed and sustained forest sources.

Printed in Hong Kong

ISBN 0–312–21689–0 clothbound

Library of Congress Cataloging-in-Publication Data
The merchant of Venice, William Shakespeare / edited by Martin Coyle.
p.   cm. — (New casebooks)
Includes bibliographical references (p.   ) and index.
ISBN 0–312–21689–0
1. Shakespeare, William, 1564–1616. Merchant of Venice.
2. Shylock (Fictitious character)   3. Jews in literature.
4. Comedy.   I. Coyle, Martin.   II. Series.
PR2825.M475   1998
822.3'3—dc21   98–21228
                                                              CIP

Contents

Acknowledgements

The editor and publishers wish to thank the following for permission to use copyright material:

Catherine Belsey, for 'Love in Venice', *Shakespeare Survey*, 44 (1991), 41–53, by permission of Cambridge University Press; Walter Cohen, for '*The Merchant of Venice* and the Possibilities of Historical Criticism', *ELH: English Literary History*, 49 (1982), 765–89, by permission of the Johns Hopkins University Press; John Drakakis, for 'Historical Difference and Venetian Patriarchy' from *The Merchant of Venice*, ed. Nigel Wood (1996), pp. 23–53, by permission of the Open University Press; Kim F. Hall, for 'Guess Who's Coming to Dinner? Colonization and Miscegenation in *The Merchant of Venice*', *Renaissance Drama*, 23 (1992), 87–111, by permission of the Northwestern University Press; Graham Hodlerness, for 'Comedy and *The Merchant of Venice*' from *William Shakespeare: The Merchant of Venice* (1993), pp. vii–xvii. Copyright © Graham Holderness 1993, by permission of Penguin Books; Karen Newman, for 'Portia's Ring: Unruly Women and Structures of Exchange in *The Merchant of Venice*', *Shakespeare Quarterly*, 38 (1987), 19–33, by permission of *Shakespeare Quarterly*; Avraham Oz, 'Transformations of Authenticity: *The Merchant of Venice* in Israel' from *Foreign Shakespeare: Contemporary Performance*, ed. D. Kennedy (1993), pp. 56–75, by permission of Cambridge University Press; Kiernan Ryan, for 'Re-reading *The Merchant of Venice*' from *Shakespeare*, 2nd edn (1995), pp. 17–24, by permission of Prentice-Hall Europe: James Shapiro, for 'Shakespeare and the Jews', The Parkes Lecture (1992), reprinted in *Cultures of Ambivalence and Contempt: Studies in Jewish/Non-Jewish Relations*, ed. S. Jones, A. R. Kushner and S. Pearce, Frank Cass (1997), by permission of the University of Southampton and the author; Alan

Sinfield, for 'How to Read *The Merchant of Venice* without being Heterosexist' from *Alternative Shakespeares: Volume 2*, ed. Terence Hawkes (1996), pp. 122–39, by permission of Routledge.

Every effort has been made to trace the copyright holders but if any have been inadvertently overlooked the publishers will be pleased to make the necessary arrangement at the first opportunity.

General Editors' Preface

The purpose of this series of New Casebooks is to reveal some of the ways in which contemporary criticism has changed our understanding of commonly studied texts and writers and, indeed, of the nature of criticism itself. Central to the series is a concern with modern critical theory and its effect on current approaches to the study of literature. Each New Casebook editor has been asked to select a sequence of essays which will introduce the reader to the new critical approaches to the text or texts being discussed in the volume and also illuminate the rich interchange between critical theory and critical practice that characterises so much current writing about literature.

In this focus on modern critical thinking and practice New Casebooks aim not only to inform but also to stimulate, with volumes seeking to reflect both the controversy and the excitement of current criticism. Because much of this criticism is difficult and often employs an unfamiliar critical language, editors have been asked to give the reader as much help as they feel is appropriate, but without simplifying the essays or the issues they raise. Again, editors have been asked to supply a list of further reading which will enable readers to follow up issues raised by the essays in the volume.

The project of New Casebooks, then, is to bring together in an illuminating way those critics who best illustrate the ways in which contemporary criticism has established new methods of analysing texts and who have reinvigorated the important debate about how we 'read' literature. The hope is, of course, that New Casebooks will not only open up this debate to a wider audience, but will also encourage students to extend their own ideas, and think afresh about their responses to the texts they are studying.

John Peck and Martin Coyle
University of Wales, Cardiff

Introduction

MARTIN COYLE

The present collection of essays is aimed at students who are working on *The Merchant of Venice* and who are looking for new ways of thinking about the play and new ways of thinking about their own practice as critics. More particularly, it should appeal to those who are looking for ways of reading Shakespeare's play that do not depend upon discussing the text in terms of character or theme or the writer's intention. These last three are the traditional approaches which students are taught for making sense of literature, but which leave little room for more searching questions about what is involved in reading, watching and studying a play. By contrast, the purpose of the present collection is to offer a spectrum of the more recent writings on *The Merchant of Venice* that open up its historical, cultural, and political significance, and also serve to demonstrate some of the ways in which contemporary criticism is both based upon critical theory and is also about the practice of criticism. The rest of this introduction is concerned with these issues.

I

Catherine Belsey has made the point that 'there is no practice without theory'.[1] At first sight, her statement says no more than that all criticism and that all critical acts are based on a theoretical position, whether the critic acknowledges it or not. For example, a criticism that focuses upon character takes for granted much of the thinking that underlies liberal humanism; that is, the familiar, common-sense critical thinking that conceives of human nature as essentially unchanging, and, as such, connects the past to the present. We value Shakespeare, in this view, precisely because he was not of an age but for all time, a writer who creates figures with whom we share feelings and ideas regardless of time and history. Such thinking leads on to a number of ideas: that there is a natural coherent order outside the political realm; that it is possible to chart a history of human progress; that the human condition is to be thought of in terms of universals; and that the individual, rather than being, as contemporary criticism would suggest, an effect of language, is the author of meaning and action. Character criticism, however straightforward it may appear, assumes or incorporates some or all of these premises, usually in the form of concentrating on specific individuals without reference to any historical or social or material conditions. Indeed, character criticism is only made possible by the exclusion of such conditions. But the crucial point about character criticism is its investing of character as the origin and destiny of meaning; in such readings, the play is not only essentially but overwhelmingly about character.

In the case of *The Merchant of Venice* it is Shylock who has most often attracted criticism of this kind, with critics divided fairly evenly between those who see him as a tragic figure and those who see him as a monster. The essays that follow do not avoid the question of Shylock, but they do not approach him in terms of this liberal humanist dilemma which restricts the question to his personality without reference to issues of race and politics. The fact that it is now all but impossible to conceive of the play without reference to politics is an indication of the kind of change wrought in criticism over recent years. As Bill Overton suggests in his useful introductory book on the play, it is not possible today to write about *The Merchant of Venice* without recognising the dangers of espousing anti-Semitism and belittling the Holocaust.[2] In much postwar traditional criticism, it has to be said, the Holocaust was passed by and the question of the play's anti-Semitism was overlooked or simply attributed to Elizabethan culture without any sense of the implications of adopting such a stance. As the essays that follow demonstrate, it is here that theory has made the kind of radical difference that Belsey's maxim implies, forcing critics to adjust their practice in the light of broader theoretical thinking about the assumptions that underlie and inform criticism.

A further implication of Belsey's statement, however, is that just as theory underlies practice, so theory is also the product of practice, that what results from critical reading is something other or more than just an interpretation of the text; it is also a reflection on the process and practice of criticism. In this second sense the statement leads us towards a recognition of the primary importance of practice in generating theory rather than the other way round. This is not to say that every piece of textual analysis opens out into critical theory, but it is to suggest that the reading of a text can draw us towards thinking about what it is we are doing when we read a text, about how we might read the text differently, and about what sort of act we are participating in when we read or discuss texts. One of the features of the essays that follow is how often they turn to questions of this kind. Not in any narrow self-reflexive way, but in a self-conscious manoeuvre to highlight their critical position and to consider the implications of what is being said. This self-consciousness is perhaps one of the markers of contemporary critical writing, that it is intensely aware of addressing an audience to persuade, but also to involve us in a different kind of thinking from traditional humanist criticism. Where the latter assumes the text is solidly there, with a clear set of meanings to be found in it, the position of contemporary theory is both more polemical (there is a case to be put about the text), and also more tentative (it questions its own authority as criticism).

This raises two more general points, one simple, the other more complex. One of the assumptions it is easy to pick up as a student is that critical theory – those reading practices involving ideas from feminism, Marxism, deconstruction, new historicism, cultural materialism, psychoanalytic criticism influenced by Lacan, but not limited to these[3] – is a sort of recipe for analysis; that one produces a reading of a text from a certain point of view as a result of having grasped a number of basic pieces of vocabulary. To an extent this may be true. For example, it is possible to arrive at a feminist essay on *The Merchant of Venice* by taking up the ideas of stereotypes, patriarchy, control, ownership and resistance and using them to interrogate and analyse the text. Indeed, this can be a useful starting point for trying new ways of reading: to set up a series of ideas and limits to the analysis. But it is worth remembering that one of the aims of contemporary criticism is to move beyond the fixed, the predetermined, the set, and to recognise and value difference, plurality, change. In other words, there is no need to stay forever within the bounds of a fixed set of ideas as to what, for example, feminist criticism is. Indeed, there are not only different kinds of feminist criticism and critics but also a rich dialogue between feminism and other theoretical positions.

Labels and categories can, then, be misleading and simplifying; they can lead not merely to mechanical approaches to texts – the automatic reading – but to a flattening out of differences, to the loss of subtleties. But they can also lead to the idea that somehow the reading produced suggests that meaning is single and can be pinned down. This is where the second (more complex) general point mentioned above comes in. Contemporary theory, for all its differences and diversity, does share some common features or propositions: it is oppositional criticism (oppositional in the political sense); it is committed to change; it is opposed to the Enlightenment tradition of liberal humanism; it recognises that the individual is not the author of meaning but the effect of it; and that the task of the critic is to foreground what is neglected, demonised, rejected, silenced or denied in the text. But, above all – and this is the more complex point mentioned above – contemporary theory has taken up the poststructuralist perspective that meaning is unstable because language is unstable. In other words, contemporary theory, far from regarding meaning as single, sees meaning as always plural. It is this that distinguishes poststructuralism – by which we generally mean the theory of language and meaning that underpins most contemporary critical writing which sees texts as contradictory, plural, full of gaps, silences – from structuralism. The two are linked in so far as poststructuralism accepts that meaning is a matter of difference, but are separate in so far as poststructuralism rejects the scientific methodology of structuralism and its attempt to formulate meaning onto a grid of rigid structures; such rigidity is rejected in favour of a speculative openness. What we might add is that, whereas structuralism has its roots in linguistics, poststructuralism has its roots in philosophy. More simply, whereas structuralism thinks of meaning and language as something that can be limited and pinned down, poststructuralism and the recent criticism influenced by it see meaning and language as unfixed. It is this new position on language and meaning which connects the different critical voices in the present collection and which informs much of the thinking behind current critical practice, as the next section seeks to explain.

II

As with all accounts of modern critical theory, this one finds itself going back to a series of lectures given by the Swiss linguist Ferdinand de Saussure at the start of the twentieth century. These lectures on linguistics were published in 1915 as the *Course in General Linguistics* and form the theoretical underpinnings to the movement known as structuralism.[4] Saussure argues that meanings are arbitrary: there is no necessary connection between the word 'dog' and what we conventionally understand by that word – the animal that barks; that in simple terms the word dog signifies what it does because it does not signify another concept – for example, cat. Saussure's point is that the signifier 'd g' depends on the relations of difference with other signifiers. For Saussure this gives rise to general rules of intelligibility about the structure of language: that there are organising principles to language, which has a structured system of differences which can be analysed scientifically to arrive at laws about how meaning operates.

It is this rigid structure of language which poststructuralists have challenged and disassembled, especially the French deconstructionist philosopher Jacques Derrida.[5] Briefly, Derrida argues that there are contradictions in Saussure's argument, that while meaning is a matter of difference, meanings are not fixed in binary oppositions but slip; that there is not a total system which can describe language because language is always in play; that if meaning is a matter of difference, then that difference – we know that the word sheep is different from mutton – is not limited to one term but is part of an infinite number of substitutions. He goes on to argue that the signified has no final resting place of meaning, that meaning is both a matter of difference (dog is not cat) and deferral (the word 'dog' does not give us access to an essential single meaning of 'dogness').

Where such thinking has led more recently is to a recognition of how language cannot act as a guarantee of truth or history. Nor can it guarantee the identity or stability of the human subject, for we are similarly subject to flux, change, indeterminacy, to the process itself of language in all its excess. It follows that meaning cannot be contained by the author's intentions, that words spill over, reaching beyond their immediate point and place; the author, whatever his or her intentions, cannot control any more than the critic can the play of language. This does not mean, however, that meaning is subjective, whimsical or private, something utterly individualistic. Indeed, the very reverse is the case: meaning is always public because it consists of the ideas and concepts we share with each other through language. In this sense meaning is conventional: it is what words can mean and have meant.

The implications of these ideas have proved to be far-reaching, for if meaning is plural and language unfixed, then the notion of the final correct reading of the text is rendered impossible; even as criticism tries to reach a settled reading of a text, so other readings are made visible. Put differently, this means that choice is a part of criticism: the choice between ways of reading, of producing one reading rather than another. It is perhaps this more than anything that has caused traditional critic, sm its difficulties with contemporary theory; that where before there seemed only one (natural) way of reading, or perhaps only one kind of reading, there are now many competing readings. In this sense the old stable ego of criticism has gone. But more than this, the implication of all that has been written over the last few years is not that there is a criticism with theory and a criticism without theory, but that theory is inscribed in all practices; that there is, indeed, no practice without theory. Theory comes, as it were, with the language of criticism and is not in this sense an optional extra. Critics who say they want nothing to do with theory are not escaping theory but practising a different kind of theoretical position, one which prefers not to foreground its premises. In a word, you cannot stand outside theory and engage in criticism; to oppose, say, a deconstructionist reading is still to be involved with theory.

The consequence of these recent changes in conceptual thinking is a criticism today that is both diverse and demanding, a criticism that recognises that meaning is not transparent and ready made, and that the literary text does not exist to be unpacked but that criticism is a practice in writing about writing. In the case of drama criticism, there is also a further consideration: this is the text as spoken and as acted and played in different times and places. In these conditions drama perhaps becomes much more complex to deal with than other kinds of literature precisely because of the variations that can be encountered, including such variations as, for example, Arnold Wesker's own *Shylock* play.[6] In traditional criticism there are often sharp divisions between theatre, text and performance, or between history and theatrical adaptations. A further distinguishing mark of contemporary criticism is that it overrides such divisions, dissolving boundaries both between text and text and between disciplines. For example, although I have not included an extract from it, John Gillies' book on *Shakespeare and the Geography of Difference* by its title suggests how concepts of space have come to be seen as important to the literary critic and how ideas from different disciplines can ferment new understandings of texts, opening up their larger significance and problems.[7]

This more open sense of what constitutes criticism and how criticism has changed and is changing should become clearer in the essays collected here. They range from essays that are largely historical to essays that are about appropriations of the play and its place in culture. In the following sections of this introduction there are brief pointers about each essay or a discussion of their theoretical positions as well as some suggestions about threads running through the essays. The sections are not intended to exhaust the essays or pre-empt the reading of them but to indicate some of the reasons for including them and their place in the complex debate about the play. It would be easy enough to give the sections subtitles such as historical criticism, feminist criticism, and political criticism. But subtitles divide and falsify what is a series of arguments and ideas concerning the problems of thinking about the past and its relationship to the present and about the place drama occupies between entertainment and politics, and between radical possibilities and conservativism. It is such issues that are returned to again and again throughout the essays.

III

It should be apparent that the first two essays, by Graham Holderness and Kiernan Ryan, are introductions to these areas of debate. It should also be clear that, like the rest of the essays, they are vexed by what has become for contemporary critics a problem of enormous significance: the problem of history. History, in traditional terms, is what happened when, it is a series of dates and deeds, a record of the past. In essence it is a linear narrative, telling a grand story which runs from the beginning until now. What has undermined the credibility of such a narrative is not only its implicit politics – it is, by and large, a male history that does nothing to challenge the status quo, with women and non-elite groups barely represented – but the recognition of how history is itself constructed through a language that has no inherent fixity. The past is, in fact, just as much a text we read as a Shakespeare play. One consequence of this for some critics is that history has become an almost meaningless idea: that in the postmodern condition in which we live – that is the present age after the age of modernism, the present age after World War II and the Holocaust – there is no grand narrative; indeed, there seems to be only a present which constructs a past. This, however, is only one view. To other theorists the past matters however much we recognise it as a fiction we might construct. Events did happen, though not in any grand narrative, and we should try to engage with history by looking at specific people at specific times.

This is a brief summary of the kind of argument that the problem of history has generated, but it is an important problem that runs through all the essays, about what sort of grip on the past we have, how we interpret it and what we can do with it. Graham Holderness (essay 1) approaches these issues through what might seem an unrelated question of what might be understood by the term comedy. He proceeds to argue that the play, which, given the nature of its subject matter, hardly seems comic much of the time, throws into doubt the neat categories we have for classifying drama by its combination of fairy-tale romantic comedy with the kind of violent enmity characteristic of revenge tragedy, but 'transposed to a real historical place – Venice'.[8] More particularly, Holderness notes that Shylock is not just the stock father figure we might expect in Italian comedy but 'a Jewish moneylender, historically located' in a specific commercial economy.[9] The result, he suggests, is that our response to the play is 'destabilised by our acute awareness of' its racial hatred.[10]

The traditional way of reading the play, Holderness notes, is to see the text as 'firmly located in the past', with Shylock as a convenient device 'for dramatising larger ethical concerns about friendship and enmity, justice and mercy'.[11] By contrast, more recent historical approaches such as new historicism highlight and expose the play's anti-Semitism. Holderness proposes, however, that instead of reading the play as either fixed in history or as foregrounding its contemporary relevance to our own world, criticism needs to be dialectical. That is, it needs to recognise both how the play belongs to a 'very different historical culture' and also to be aware 'of the ways in which subsequent historical developments and modern beliefs may have changed the play's possibilities of interpretation'.[12] In turn this way of reading may lead us towards seeing why the play resists 'simple categorisation' and how it may potentially represent Shylock as a tragic figure who is also the stereotypical Elizabethan Jew, 'that Elizabethan grotesque with the red wig and the artificial nose'.[13]

Holderness, then, sees the text as belonging to more than one context and culture. Kiernan Ryan's essay (2), which offers a vigorous attack on conventional readings, takes this argument on a stage further. Like Holderness, Ryan affirms the need for criticism to be both historical and dialectical and so open to interpretive 'possibilities stored in the text'.[14] Whereas Holderness, however, argues that we should take into account the textual circumstances of the play in history, Ryan argues for a type of criticism that is built on interaction between the past and present perspectives. The aim, he suggests, is to produce an account which recognises the counter-perspective in the text and which undermines the received readings. In particular, Ryan suggests that Shylock's 'Hath not a Jew eyes?' speech not only 'indicts all forms of inhuman discrimination' but 'provokes a sharp shift of emotional allegiance' in the play against the Christians. 'With this speech', Ryan argues, 'there erupts into the play an irresistible egalitarian attitude' which, he suggests, 'transfigures our understanding' of the text.[15]

On a more general level Ryan's analysis is intended to demonstrate some of the ways in which the play achieves a restless subversion of its commitments to racism and capitalism. But not just subversion: this would lead to the sort of ironic reading best seen in A. D. Moody's conventional but acute reading of the play where the Venetians no less than Shylock are held up to scrutiny.[16] Where Ryan differs is in his stress, as in Marxist criticism generally, on the way the text exposes the 'structural social forces' which have made the figures what they are – that is, the 'ruthless priority of money-values over human values' and the 'rights of property' over human rights.[17] At the same time Ryan vigorously defends the bringing to bear on the play present knowledge to discover its oppositional vision. In this sense Ryan's account is a deliberate challenge to the notion of anachronism, to the idea that we must suppress our awareness of the Holocaust and modern politics and somehow read our way back into the past, forgetting all we know of the present. Indeed, the logic of Ryan's case is that it is only by bringing our knowledge of the twentieth century to bear on the text, by taking a 'consciously modern grasp' of the play,[18] that we can release important dimensions of its meaning. 'What *The Merchant of Venice* means today', Ryan therefore contends, 'depends as much on what we are disposed to make of it as it does on Shakespeare's text.'[19]

Ryan's essay was written in 1981 and is followed by Walter Cohen's essay (3) from 1982, a major article on the play and central to much subsequent discussion. It is an essay that, much more than the first two essays, takes us into considerations of theoretical criticism, and in particular Marxist criticism. Underlying Cohen's argument is the premise that literature serves to justify the ruling economic and political conditions in the state. It does this by seeking to 'resolve those contradictions that prove irreconcilable in life'.[20] In the case of *The Merchant of Venice* those contradictions involve the conflict between a dying feudalism and a rising capitalism embodied respectively in Shylock and Antonio which is only resolved through Portia. Her intervention brings about a union of 'aristocratic landed wealth and mercantile capital' which also serves to incorporate whatever threat or fear Shylock poses.[21] As Cohen notes, the effect of this positioning of the text in the economic changes of Renaissance England is not only intended to demystify the play but also the role of the public theatre in early modern England which is seen as helping to promote and legitimate the new social order envisaged in the final scene. In this way Cohen shifts the debate about *The Merchant of Venice* towards a different kind of historical criticism from that of Holderness and Ryan, one much more concerned with the play's significance in the 1590s and the socio-economic implications of its setting in Venice together with the question of usury. Like Holderness and Ryan, however, Cohen is not interested in trying to abstract some kind of 'paraphrasable meaning' from the play or to turn it into a historical document.[22] Rather, like them, he is concerned to demonstrate the problematic nature both of the play and of historical criticism and how we can use them to interrogate one another. To this extent any historical analysis of the text is inevitably only ever a provisional reading, subject to revision and the challenging evidence of the play itself.

IV

The arguments of Holderness, Ryan and Cohen are clearly offered as a response to, and rejection of, the traditional liberal humanist reading of the text that finds its most sustained defender in Lawrence Danson's book, *The Harmonies of 'The Merchant of Venice'* (1978).[23] Danson's discussion itself is part of a long tradition of allegorical or semi-Christian interpretations which see the play in terms of love and law, Old and New Testament, and which seek to establish the text more as myth or parable than as a site of conflicting changes in the early modern period. Paradoxically, such readings – to Danson, we could add the perspectives of Nevill Coghill, Muriel Bradbook, John Russell Brown, C. L. Barber as well as, to a lesser extent, most introductions to most modern editions of the play – while recognising the play's complexity and even its contradictions, argue for an essential unity of idea, usually in terms of 'love's wealth' or the importance of giving and self-sacrifice.[24] Paradoxically, too, such readings, although informed by a detailed knowledge of Elizabethan attitudes to usury and Jews, often see Shylock, as we might expect, in terms of character or comic design. The focus of traditional readings tends to be upon Shylock's humanity or lack of it; or upon the mixed dramatic conventions that seem to shape his role, ranging from the devil in the medieval morality play through the Pantaloon of Italian comedy to the ogre of fairy tale.[25] The traditional critic, that is, looks either at the moral or the dramatic impact of Shylock rather than at the historical or cultural significance of the play's representation of Jews.

It is these historical, cultural and religious questions that are the heart of James Shapiro's ground-breaking essay (4), which follows Cohen's Marxist analysis in this volume, providing a different perspective on the problem of Shylock. In some senses Shapiro's essay is a conventional piece of research, correcting past statements about the 'absence' of Jews in Shakespeare's England. More importantly, however, the essay draws attention to the way in which Jews are central to the play's exploration of cultural identity, including both religious and gender identity. In his reading, Shapiro focuses on how the 'pound of flesh' narrative and its associations with circumcision evoke primitive mythical fears of castration. Shapiro's case, however, goes further than this: his principal claim is that Jews act as the crucial other to English identity in the sixteenth century. Shylock's function, in other words, is not simply that of usurer, murderer, castrator; he is also an alien and stranger who, by his difference, has a pivotal role in questions of identity and race. This is a claim which Shapiro expands on in much more detail in his recent book *Shakespeare and the Jews*, where he argues that 'the English turned to Jewish questions in order to answer English ones ... at a time when their nation was experiencing extraordinary social, religious, and political turbulence'.[26] In this sense the play itself becomes a projection of the fears felt by English (i.e. Christian) men and women as the new nation state under Elizabeth took shape, fears which find their most worrying form in the feminised (because circumcised) figure of Shylock.

Shapiro's essay illustrates an important shift in recent criticism: how history now crosses over into questions of culture and race or, as in Kim Hall's essay (5), into questions of race and gender. Like Shapiro, Hall focuses on the problem of the threat to English identity from 'foreign difference' through commercial trade and exchange.[27] Hall proposes that the play's anxieties are seen not only in the conflict between Jew and Christian but also in the 'silent symbol' of the Moor made pregnant by Launcelot, thus raising the issue of miscegenation.[28] Hall shows how this theme is part of an intricate set of references in the play to food and consumption as well as cannibalism, and how, in turn, this links up with ideas of control and mastery. The Moor's pregnancy, she writes, 'is a reminder of the dangerous result of uncontrolled crossing of borders' into the world of other races, for '[t]he end she promises is a mixed child, whose blackness may not be "converted" or absorbed within the endogamous, exclusionary values of Belmont'.[29] What Hall suggests, then, is how the figure of the pregnant Moor, though she does not appear in the play, serves to disrupt the political project in *The Merchant of Venice*, a project which is intended to eradicate racial difference while gaining new wealth through trade.

Hall's essay begins with an extract from Samuel Purchas's collection of travel narratives and the question of sexual contact between different trading races. The effect of this is to widen the essay's critical focus and suggest links between Shakespeare's play and travel literature. Such an approach might broadly be described as new historicist in so far as the essay is concerned with colonial trade and its imperial attempts to gain mastery over foreign countries and races, but Hall is also interested in drawing out the way in which the female characters 'play key ... roles in the circulation of wealth' in the play.[30] In particular, she examines how both Jessica's and Portia's actions in the end work to support the status quo and oppress outsiders. Despite their transgression through cross-dressing – Jessica escapes her father's house dressed as a page, Portia disguises herself as the lawyer Balthazar – both 'become pliable wives' whose marriages validate the play's resolution and 'repulsion of aliens'.[31] Such a conclusion not only complements Shapiro's analysis of racial difference in the play but also adds to our sense of the way in which, as with the opening essays by Holderness, Ryan and

Cohen, historical readings of the play can serve to open up new areas of interest in the text and force us to reconsider the way in which we read it. But the essay also reveals how there is a much more fluid relationship between theoretical approaches than is sometimes supposed, so that the essay is informed as much by feminist ideas as by a concern with economics and race. Importantly, in this sense it is a reading of the play that suggests how questions of gender in *The Merchant of Venice* cannot readily be separated not only from racial issues and economic issues but also from questions of marriage.

Marriage is, indeed, the subject of Karen Newman's essay (6). The starting point of Newman's analysis is that the action of *The Merchant of Venice* is characterised by 'the exchange of goods', both goods on ships and women as goods.[32] It is these 'structures of exchange' that the essay explores, looking in particular at how, in marriage, women function as 'the most basic of gifts' between men: a woman is given in marriage to one man from another. This exchange, Newman suggests, serves to secure the male homosocial order, for it creates 'alliances and relationships among men' and is directly connected with ideas of power.[33] Here Newman is drawing upon ideas from the French anthropologist Claude Lévi-Strauss who sees the exchange of women as 'at the origin of social life' and so central to the social order. Newman, however, also calls upon recent feminist theory which has shown how such exchanges are part of an entire 'sex/gender system' reflected in, for example, marriage contracts and conduct books.[34] As Newman notes, marriage and the family were commonly represented as a small kingdom in the Renaissance, so that the exchange of women in marriage also involves notions of hierarchy and obedience.

By contrast, Portia's disguise as a male lawyer and gift-giving of her ring in the final scene seem to align her with the 'unruly woman', the woman 'who steps outside her role and function as subservient' and who challenges and overturns male rule through action, language and dress.[35] Newman ends her essay by examining the problem of whether the inversion thus inscribed in Portia's disguise adds up to something more than a temporary carnivalesque. The argument is important since it bears upon the larger question of whether the play reaffirms the status quo, in the way that Cohen, for example, suggests, or whether it is more radical in its questioning. Newman argues that Portia's inversion of roles does not, in fact, reinforce 'the oppositions that ground gender hierarchy' but instead undermines the 'conventional poles of sexual difference' precisely because she is a woman occupying the place of a man.[36] Such a conclusion is in line with Newman's analysis of Portia's speeches elsewhere in the play and their disruption of the sex/gender system and exposure of its contradictory attitudes towards women as both inferior to men but also necessary to the continuation of the social order. More generally, it complements both Shapiro's and Hall's arguments which are similarly concerned with questions of cultural history and identity.

Newman's argument can be usefully brought into relationship with Catherine Belsey's subtle essay (7) about the way in which love in the Renaissance was itself being institutionalised and brought under control, with both its danger and destructive passion slowly being tamed. This 'older understanding of love' as something anarchic, thrilling, hazardous, she suggests, nonetheless 'leaves traces in the text, with the effect that desire is only imperfectly domesticated'.[37] Informing Belsey's analysis here is the Lacanian notion of desire as the endless quest for wholeness, for an object that can neither be held nor found: desire can only be desire to the extent that it remains unfulfilled. In her discussion Belsey goes on to connect this notion of desire with the play's use of riddles which, she suggests, 'are traditionally dangerous because they exploit the duplicity of the signifier, the secret alterity that subsists in meaning'.[38] Like desire, riddles are marked by an excess: they mean more than they say even as desire is more than can be said. In this sense, Belsey suggests, 'riddles could be said to enact at the level of the signifier something of the character of desire, for they entail uncertainty, enigma'.[39]

In a further move in the essay Belsey examines the intricate playfulness of Portia's ring riddles in Act V and how this bears upon her multiple identity, an identity that seems to absorb the meaning of 'friend' into the term 'wife' even as domestic love and marriage was beginning to absorb or replace male friendship.[40] What is thus at stake in the essay is the way the play dramatises a cultural shift in the meaning or meanings of love, a shift which is summed up in Antonio's sadness. He is, Belsey argues, 'in mourning for friendship', for he 'knows things will never be the same' once Bassanio is married.[41] This is not just a matter of the loss of a particular friend but the loss of a culture in which male friendship might rival or co-exist with heterosexual love. The movement in the play is thus towards a more regulated and limited meaning of love.

V

On one level Belsey's essay sums up the way in which criticism of *The Merchant of Venice* has moved away from a concern with its historical situation towards a concern with the play as part of cultural history. It is a movement that not only recognises the play as part of a vanished culture that was different but also sees how any analysis of the text is, in the end, bound to run up against not just particular questions of race or gender or economics but the issue of politics and criticism. This includes both the politics of the play and also the politics of reading; that is, how criticism can intervene in the thinking, values and ideas of the community and either change or reinforce them. But the politics of reading also bears upon the question of the uses to which texts, and especially Shakespeare's texts, are put; it bears upon what purposes and whose interests they serve. This important aspect of modern criticism should be evident in Alan Sinfield's essay (8) on 'How to Read *The Merchant of Venice* without being Heterosexist' which is the first of three essays that are, indeed, as much about how we read the play and how the play is used as they are about its most controversial aspects – homosexuality and anti-Semitism.

As Sinfield notes, there has been a debate about homoeroticism in *The Merchant of Venice* for many years, though often without much progress being made about its significance. That debate has centred on Antonio's sadness at the start of the play and whether he is in love with Bassanio, the position argued by W. H. Auden in an essay in 1962 and taken up by a number of critics subsequently, especially psychoanalytical critics.[42] For some of these, as Sinfield notes, Antonio's bond with Shylock 'is his way of holding on to Bassanio',[43] while Portia's rescue of Antonio and winning of Bassanio's ring 'is purposefully heterosexist',[44] a deliberate strategy to ensure that her husband is bound to her and that married love replaces or displaces male love. Sinfield reformulates the issue not in order to try and settle the question of whether 'Antonio's love is what we call sexual',[45] but rather to examine how the text circulates such issues in our culture. In particular, he questions whether Shakespeare as cultural icon, as symbol of establishment values, merely acts to reconfirm the marginalisation of social groups such as Jews, feminists, lesbians, gays and ethnic minorities in contemporary culture today, or whether, because early modern thinking about such boundaries was different, we can use Shakespeare to construct alternative dissident reading practices. What, then, Sinfield is interested in exploring is how 'readers not situated squarely in the mainstream of Western culture today may relate' to Shakespeare, and how the text throws into question modern thinking about sexuality.[46]

At the same time Sinfield fits *The Merchant of Venice* into a broader framework of discussion of Shakespearean comedies that links back both to Belsey and to Holderness in challenging the assumption that we can read the past through the lens of the present. 'In our societies', he notes, 'whether you are gay or not has become crucial', but it may well be that 'in early modern England same-sex relations *were not terribly important*'.[47] In other words, they were not necessarily seen as abnormal, life-threatening or even incompatible with marriage. Sinfield's argument is that we do not have to conceive of playtexts in narrow generic or cultural limits but rather as 'working across an ideological terrain, opening out unresolved faultlines, inviting spectators to explore imaginatively the different possibilities'.[48] Such a position is very much in line with recent theoretical thinking about Shakespeare's plays as a whole, where the emphasis has fallen not simply on the political, the ideological, but on opening up the possibilities of the text rather than looking for some absolute meaning.

Where Sinfield's essay confronts the question of how to read *The Merchant of Venice* in the light of our contemporary sexual culture and what to make of its significance today, John Drakakis's essay (9) is concerned with the way Shakespeare's text has been used to inscribe an idea of sameness across time – how the play, that is, has been represented as offering timeless moral truths stripped of the historical conditions which produced them. The effect of this blanketing out, Drakakis suggests, is to lead almost inevitably to a mythologising of the play in character terms and an inadvertent dignifying of its anti-Semitism built around Shylock's usury. Drakakis goes on to argue that Shylock's function is altogether more complex than it appears, for he is at once 'in moral and ethical terms, on the margins of the social order', but in political terms 'symbolically central' to Venice's 'operation and self-definition'.[49] His point is that Shylock is both a challenge to Venice but also 'the differential means' by which it constructs its identity.[50] No less important, Drakakis shows how usury is constituted out of 'a web of discourses',[51] including religious, economic, theatrical and gender discourses, so that there is not a simple one-dimensional context but a cluster of ideas that are gathered around Shylock and which construct him both as a threat to the state and an enemy of the theatre, a puritan figure who opposes pleasure and laughter.

There is, however, more to Drakakis's argument than this ideological construction of Shylock as threat. Drakakis notes that in his famous 'Hath not a Jew eyes?' speech, Shylock aligns himself with or imitates Venetian Christian values. In this respect he stands in a complex relationship to Venice as a 'demonisation of its own social and economic practice' – a negative image of its order.[52] His enforced conversion at the end of the play and entry into Christian patriarchy in effect enables the state to overcome an irresolvable problem, of how to reconcile 'Christian participation in usurious practice'. In this reading Shylock is not simply forced into accepting Venice's values but is, in fact, the central part of a process that 'ultimately guarantees the continuation of a Christian patriarchy'.[53] That process is seen in other figures, too, including Antonio, Portia and Jessica who are similarly transformed and brought under control of the dominant Christian domestic economy of the play symbolised in marriage.

Drakakis's essay is the densest piece in the volume. In part this has to do with its argument that *The Merchant of Venice* is a series of historically formulated problems that are constantly in play as the text seeks to resolve the 'insurmountable contradiction' of reconciling Christian patriarchy with the real economic practice of money-lending demonised in Shylock.[54] In part, too, the density of the essay stems from Drakakis's insistence that the business of criticism is not to suppress contradictions by imposing a pattern on the play but instead to open them out. But the essay's difficulty is also produced by its critical discourse: it is presented with few concessions to polite, liberal sentiment about how criticism should be written. In this, the essay can be seen to be taking a deliberate political stance outside the dominant pattern of critical writing in the same way that, for example, Sinfield deliberately draws attention to writing as a gay man. Both critics find in the play an echo of the process of the questioning of ideas and values that they seek to achieve in their own critical work. In their analyses, they do not, however, appear to be imposing their own views on the text; on the contrary, they seem to liberate a more complex sense of the kind of open and unstable effect that is generated in the play. This is one of the paradoxes of recent critical writing on Shakespeare. As against critics who rejected the idea of working from theory, claiming that they were responding to 'the play itself', Sinfield and Drakakis work from theory and from an ideological stance. But, whereas the liberal humanist critics reduced, defined and limited the 'meaning' of the text, the effect of the arguments of Sinfield and Drakakis is just the opposite: they generate and can handle an idea of fluidity and instability of meanings in *The Merchant of Venice*, conveying as they do so a sense of its awkward forcefulness in the Shakespeare canon.

A different kind of political stance emerges in Avraham Oz's essay (10) on *The Merchant of Venice* in Israel which continues the theme of transformation found both in Drakakis's essay and in the opening essay by Graham Holderness. Where Holderness and Drakakis are concerned with various historical appropriations of the play, however, here the topic is modern productions, and the question of 'the legitimacy of theatrical interpretation'.[55] More especially, what Oz examines is not just the gap between any 'hypothetical original intention attributed to the text' and recent productions of the play in Israel but how this stage history relates to the 'developing national consciousness' of the Jewish state.[56] Oz notes that a Hebrew production in 1936, for example, directed by Leopold Jessner, a refugee from Germany, occurred at 'an heroic moment, where national pathos was a standard theme',[57] making any comic potential in the play impossible to stage. With the foundation of the state of Israel in 1948 there began a change of outlook, so that a 1959 revival of the play seems to have tried to shift the performance towards romantic comedy, while a 1972 production again took a 'non-apologetic approach' to the text, presenting Shylock with a 'repellent appearance and mannerisms'.[58]

Not surprisingly, the 1972 production stirred controversy as well as further accusations of Shakespeare's alleged anti-Semitism. It is, however, the 1980 Barry Kyle production that Oz focuses on most, for in his directions to the actor Kyle suggested an association between Shylock and 'the mentality of terrorism',[59] something unacceptable to an Israeli audience. What Oz goes on to argue is that although Shylock does not take hostages he does seek to take over the law for his case and that his actions and language are subversive. In this, continues Oz, he 'manages to bring forth the very target of political terrorism, namely to expose the moral fragility of the dominant ideology'.[60] It is this 'easy transformation of Shylock' from one minority group to another,[61] from persecuted Jew to terrorist, which Oz sees as a way of making the significance of the play's ideological content more general so that it might apply as much, say, to a Palestinian as an Israeli.

Oz's essay, like those of Sinfield and Drakakis, is at once a contribution to the debate about *The Merchant of Venice* and to modern political thinking about Shakespeare. The reservation we might have about Oz's essay is that it might seem to focus rather narrowly on how the political and social context of the production creates a limited interpretation of the play. But what we also need to see is that, like Sinfield and Drakakis, Oz is interested in how the play itself permits a multiplicity of views, in how, because language is unstable, the meaning of the play is plural and shifting. That shifting nature of the play in turn has to do with the interplay between criticism and text. The text, we might argue, provokes criticism, good criticism opens up the text, which opens up criticism, which opens up the text further. It is this two-way exchange and dialogue which the essays in this volume are concerned with, about how we read and respond to *The Merchant of Venice*.

NOTES

1. Catherine Belsey, *Critical Practice* (London, 1992), p. 4: 'But there is no practice without theory, however much that theory is suppressed, unformulated or perceived as "obvious". What we do when we read, however "natural" it seems, presupposes a whole theoretical discourse, even if unspoken, about language and about meaning, about the relationships between meaning and the world, meaning and people, and finally about people themselves and their place in the world.'

2. Bill Overton, *The Merchant of Venice: Text and Performance* (Basingstoke and London, 1987).

3. In many ways the best introduction to critical theory remains Catherine Belsey's *Critical Practice* (London, 1982) together with Ann Jefferson and David Robey (eds), *Modern Literary Theory: A Comparative Introduction* (London, 1986).

4. Ferdinand de Saussure, *Course in General Linguistics* (*Cours de linguistique générale*), trans. W. Baskin (London, 1974).

5. Much of the discussion of Derrida remains obscure, but the following are more accessible: *Structuralism and Since: From Lévi-Strauss to Derrida*, ed. John Sturrock (Oxford, 1979); Christopher Norris, *Derrida* (London, 1987); but also see Derrida, *Positions*, trans. Alan Bass (London, 1987) and *Modern Literary Theory: A Reader*, ed. Philip Rice and Patricia Waugh (London, 1992).

6. Arnold Wesker, *Shylock and Other Plays* (London, 1990). This is a revision of Wesker's original play called *The Merchant* (in *Plays Volume 4* [Harmondsworth, 1980]) written in 1976 and intended as a riposte to Shakespeare. See also Wesker's review of the Jonathan Miller production of *The Merchant of Venice* in the *Guardian* (29 August 1981; reprinted in *Distinctions* [London, 1985]) where he speaks of the play's 'irredeemable anti-Semitism', and a further interview in the *Guardian* (13 April 1994).

7. John Gillies, *Shakespeare and the Geography of Difference* (Cambridge, 1994).

8. See p. 27 below.

9. Ibid.

10. Ibid.

11. See p. 30 below.

12. See p. 34 below.

13. Ibid.

14. See p. 37 below.

15. See p. 38 below.

16. A. D. Moody, *Shakespeare: The Merchant of Venice* (London, 1964).

17. See pp. 39–40 below.

18. See p. 41 below.

19. See p. 42 below.

20. See p. 53 below.

21. See p. 52 below.

22. See p. 58 below.

23. Lawrence Danson, *The Harmonies of 'The Merchant of Venice'* (New Haven and London, 1978).

24. Nevill Coghill, 'The Governing Idea: Essays in the Interpretation of Shakespeare', *Shakespeare Quarterly*, 1 (1948), 9–17, and 'The Basis of Shakespearean Comedy', *Essays and Studies*, 3 (1950) in Anne Riddler (ed.), *Shakespeare Criticism 1935–1960* (London, 1963). For Muriel Bradbrook, 'Moral Theme and Romantic Story', John Russell Brown, 'Love's Wealth and the Judgement of *The Merchant of Venice*', and C. L. Barber, 'The Merchants and the Jew of Venice', see the excellent selection of essays in the original Casebook, *Shakespeare: 'The Merchant of Venice'*, ed. John Wilders (Basingstoke, 1969). For a list of modern editions, see Further Reading below.

25. I am indebted here to the introduction to *The Merchant of Venice* in the New Cambridge Shakespeare, ed. M. M. Mahood (Cambridge, 1987), esp. pp. 9–12.

26. James Shapiro, *Shakespeare and the Jews* (New York, 1996), p. 1.

27. See p. 93 below.

28. See p. 94 below.

29. See p. 109 below.

30. See p. 106 below.

31. See p. 108 below.

32. See p. 117 below.

33. See p. 118 below.

34. See p. 121 below.

35. See p. 127 below.

36. See pp. 132–3 below.

37. See p. 141 below.

38. See p. 143 below.

39. See p. 145 below.

40. See p. 150 below.

41. See p. 155 below.

42. W. H. Auden, 'Brothers and Others', in *The Dyer's Hand* (New York, 1962). See also Coppélia Kahn, 'The Cuckoo's Note: Male Friendship and Cuckoldry in *The Merchant of Venice*', reprinted in *Shakespeare's Comedies*, ed. Gary Waller (London, 1991), pp. 128–37, and Leonard Tennenhouse, 'The Counterfeit Order of *The Merchant of Venice*', in Murray M. Schwartz and Coppélia Kahn (eds), *Representing Shakespeare: New Psychoanalytic Essays* (Baltimore, 1980).

43. See p. 164 below.

44. See p. 165 below.

45. See p. 163 below.

46. See p. 162 below.

47. See p. 168 below.

48. See p. 174 below.

49. See p. 189 below.

50. See p. 191 below.

51. See p. 190 below.

52. See p. 198 below.

53. See p. 204 below.

54. Ibid.

55. See p. 216 below.

56. See p. 218 below.

57. See p. 221 below.

58. See pp. 224, 226 below.

59. See p. 227 below.

60. See p. 230 below.

61. See p. 231 below.

1

Comedy and *The Merchant of Venice*

GRAHAM HOLDERNESS

The Merchant of Venice was clearly understood, when it was originally produced and published, to be a comedy. It appears, under the simple title *The Merchant of Venice*, grouped under the heading 'Comedies' in the first collected edition of Shakespeare's works, the First Folio of 1623. But, to many subsequent readers, critics, actors, directors and playgoers, *The Merchant of Venice* has seemed much more difficult to define straightforwardly in comic terms; on the contrary, it often seems to have read and played more like a 'problem play', or even a tragedy.

> No other Shakespeare comedy before *All's Well that Ends Well* (1602) and *Measure for Measure* (1604), perhaps no other Shakespeare comedy at all, has excited comparable controversy.[1]
>
> (Walter Cohen, 1982)

> *The Merchant of Venice* is, among other things, as much a 'problem' play as one by Ibsen or Shaw.[2]
>
> (W. H. Auden, 1963)

> Indeed, seen from any angle, *The Merchant of Venice* is not a very funny play, and we might gain a lot if, for the moment, we ceased to be bullied by its inclusion in the comedies.[3]
>
> (Graham Midgely, 1960)

> I must include *The Merchant of Venice* among the tragedies, although the frame of the work is a composition of laughing

masks and sunny faces ... as though the poet *meant* to write a comedy.[4]

(Heinrich Heine, 1839)

We have to be careful in our assumptions about what comedy meant to the Elizabethans. Dramatic comedies needn't necessarily, for example, have been particularly funny, though they were likely to contain substantial ingredients of wit and humour. And although modern criticism has largely accepted the other generic definitions proposed by the First Folio – tragedy and history – it is precisely within the category of comedy that problems of theoretical definition have been encountered – even to the point where some plays (*Measure for Measure, All's Well That Ends Well, Troilus and Cressida*) have been disentangled from the comedies group by modern critics and redefined as 'problem plays'.[5] *The Merchant of Venice* has, as W. H. Auden suggested, a lot in common with those generically problematical plays. Perhaps in the sixteenth century the concept of comedy was broader and more elastic than it is today, containing all that we think of as comic, but also incorporating much that we would regard as rather more serious.

COMEDY OR TRAGEDY?

Rough working definitions of genre can, however, be made by comparing the Folio's three categories: comedy, tragedy and history. *The Merchant of Venice* is not a tragedy, we can say with some confidence, because its central character, Antonio (the merchant of the title), is ultimately saved from disaster and death – unlike the hero of Shakespeare's other Venetian drama, *Othello*, which is definitely by all accounts accepted as a tragedy. It is not a history play (although the earliest printed text, the First Quarto of 1600, from which all other texts of the play derive, described it as a 'comicall History'), since its plot is drawn from fictional romance and folk-tale stories rather than from historiographical narratives.

The main thematic and structural elements of the play all seem to belong within the category of romantic comedy rather than elsewhere. The basic action of the play is mobilised by the intertwining of two stories: Bassanio's courtship of the wealthy heiress, Portia of Belmont, which is straightforward romance; and the story of the 'flesh-bond', which was a narrative type of some antiquity, though probably known to Shakespeare through an Italian romance written in the late fourteenth century.[6] What ties the plots together is the friendship or love of Antonio and Bassanio, which becomes the background for a story of hatred and revenge. Bassanio's need for money to support the expenses of his courtship induces him to borrow from Antonio, who in turn has to apply for a loan from the Jewish moneylender, or usurer, Shylock. A member of a racial and religious minority within the predominantly Christian society of Venice, Shylock hates Christians in general, and Antonio in particular, for their racial and economic hostility towards him and his business of moneylending (the 'Christians' do not actually see themselves as Christians, but rather as a normative social group – it is only from the alienated perspective of Judaism that they are regarded as 'Christians'). Seeing an opportunity to gain advantage over Antonio, Shylock proposes the flesh-bond, by means of which Antonio agrees, if the debt is not settled within the agreed term, to permit Shylock to cut off a pound of his flesh. Side by side with the playful glamour of romance we find the implacable enmity and vindictiveness characteristic of revenge tragedy. Counterpoised to the elegant fiction of the three caskets, with its overtones of fairy-tale and magic, appears the grotesque violence of the flesh-bond – a moral or financial debt payable by physical mutilation – which again would not be out of place in a Senecan melodrama like *Titus Andronicus*, or in a Jacobean revenge tragedy.

The courtship plot combines the sophisticated wittiness and verbal playfulness of courtly comedy with the simple emotions and narrative typologies of romance, exemplified in the motif of the three caskets: by the terms of her father's will, Portia is not free to choose her own marriage partner, but must accept the suitor who chooses correctly from the three caskets. Two suitors – the Princes of Morocco and Arragon – choose wrongly and, in the event, the ritual of choice delivers the suitor she herself prefers – Bassanio. The courtship romance operates as smoothly and predictably as a fairy-tale. Two contenders choose wrongly, and success falls to the third: an apparently arbitrary ritual, seemingly based on chance, succeeds perfectly in acquiring the suitor Portia wants and ridding her of various unwanted applicants for her hand and fortune. In the commercial world of Venice, however (so different, at least at face value, from the fairy-tale world of Belmont), reliance on luck does not necessarily produce such gratifying results. Immediately after this resolution of the romance plot, news is delivered that Antonio's ships have been lost, and that he is unable to repay Shylock's loan. The bond is forfeit, and Shylock is legally entitled to take his forfeit from Antonio's body.

Thus the romance narrative precipitates, through the realistic factor of Bassanio's need to borrow money to sustain a gentlemanly lifestyle, Antonio's entering into the dangerous bond with Shylock, which entails his exposure to life-threatening perils. Bassanio's supportive friendship, even when augmented by Portia's wealth, proves powerless to help. The Duke of Venice has to uphold Shylock's right to proceed with his deadly suit against Antonio, since in terms of Venetian law, the moneylender has an unanswerable case. But in winning Portia, Bassanio has not only gained happiness and wealth, he has also acquired the services of someone far more resourceful, enterprising and intelligent than either himself or any of his Venetian companions. Portia quickly disguises herself as a lawyer and defends Antonio's case with masterful legal skill, producing other statutes which not only prevent Shylock from proceeding, but also turn the judicial tables and render Shylock vulnerable to the death penalty for conspiring against Antonio's life. Once Shylock is defeated, the Christian community is prepared to offer him what they regard as a merciful settlement: his life is spared, on condition that he become converted to Christianity, and that half his wealth is handed over to Antonio, who will keep it in trust for the benefit of Shylock's runaway daughter Jessica.

The minor plot involving the abduction of Jessica, Shylock's daughter, by Lorenzo, belongs to another, rather harsher type of comedy – the 'Italian comedy' – which formed the basis for the popular English 'city comedy' of the seventeenth century. This dramatic form, which typically pitted the poor but romantic young against the rich and tyrannical old, consisted of conventional plots and stock characters – the resourceful young hero, the beautiful young heroine, the avaricious father, the scheming servant. Within this generic context, Shylock becomes the miser who serves as an object of ridicule and abuse, while the youthful hero and heroine swindle and desert him, to the unprincipled but unproblematical pleasure of the audience. The whole of the play's last act abandons the dangerously contemporary world of Venice for the fairy-tale retreat of Belmont, and provides the spectator with an unadulterated diet of comic and romantic narrative pleasures – courtly wit-contests, lists of great lovers, romantic reconciliations, clarified misunderstandings, cast-off disguises, music and marriage.

Yet all these characteristics and distinctions of comedy have raised problems for modern criticism of the play. *The Merchant of Venice* is a comedy of ultimate success for Antonio, but a tragic narrative of suffering and loss for Shylock. The story of the flesh-bond was to be found in fiction rather than history, but Shakespeare transposed it to a real historical place – Venice – which represented for sixteenth-century Europeans a highly advanced type of social organisation, with very modern economic and political systems. The Venice of Shakespeare's romantic comedy *The Merchant* must paradoxically have seemed a more accurate representation of a real modern world than the fourteenth and fifteenth-century England of his historical dramas. That teasing interplay of the real and the imaginary, exemplified in the relationship between Venice and Belmont, produces a particularly difficult crux for the modern reader in relation to the figure of Shylock. For Shylock is not simply a stock figure of Italian comedy, or the abstracted persecutor of a timeless folk-tale: he is a Jewish moneylender, historically located into precisely the kind of commercial economy where such people would have been encountered, in Venice or England. It has often seemed to modern readers of the play that it was able to take for granted an attitude towards Jews which would necessarily appear in the modern context as unacceptably racist, or even Fascist in character. When Shylock is placed into a city comedy narrative in which his daughter robs and abandons him to marry a Christian, our responses to the conventions of the genre – which should prescribe simple gratification at the success of the lovers, and mocking delight at the discomfiture of the repressive and miserly father – are destabilised by our acute awareness of the complicating factor of race – which discloses the unpleasant awareness that a dominant, majority culture is seen conspiring to rob and humiliate the representative of a minority ethnic group.

The different moral systems governing Venice and Belmont have often been interpreted in the light of ethical oppositions between Law and Love, Justice and Mercy. But as we watch the dominant Christian community which has been threatened collect its powers and concentrate them into a devastating responsive attack on the member of a minority group, it is distinctly possible for the modern reader's pleasures in comedy to be subverted by a deeper sense of racial and political injustice. It has been suggested that the last act of the play needed to focus so exclusively on the alternative world of Belmont in order to obscure these potential suggestions of injustice:

to drown in soft music the harsh discords of the trial scene, to rinse from the spectator's mouth with a draught of romantic sweetness the bitter taste of Shylock's humiliation and defeat.

TEXT AND HISTORY

There is no direct evidence to indicate how *The Merchant of Venice* was performed on the Elizabethan stage, or perceived by Elizabethan audiences. It may well be, however, that some of its characteristics appeared to resist an easy assimilation into a simple notion of comedy. The descriptive title which appeared in the first printed edition (1600) called it a 'history', and significantly drew attention to features of the play which seem to us in retrospect particularly problematical:

> The most excellent
> Historie of the *Merchant*
> *of Venice.*
> With the extreme crueltie of *Shylocke* the Iewe
> towards the sayd Merchant, in cutting a iust pound
> of his flesh: and the obtayning of *Portia*
> by the choyse of three
> chests.
> *As it hath been divers times acted by the Lord*
> *Chamberlaine his Servants.*
> Written by William Shakespeare

'Historie' here means something closer to our term 'story' than to historiography and since the genre of the history play (very much a new form in the late sixteenth century) was more sharply defined than either tragedy or comedy, 'history' here cannot mean what it meant when applied to *Richard II* or *Henry V*. But it is at least possible that the inclusion here of 'history', meaning a story of a representative or exemplary kind, was used as an indication that the play was not entirely a fictional romance; that it contained disturbing, perhaps even potentially tragic, elements; and that it was designed to be read as in some way 'true' – implying, that is, some form of mimetic relationship between its narrative and the historical conditions of sixteenth-century Europe, or even England. In *The Taming of the Shrew*, a play which has begun fairly recently to appear highly problematical, comedy is defined as 'a kind of history' and the second edition of *The Merchant* substituted 'comical history' for 'historie'.

The title is then extended into what we would now call a 'blurb', a descriptive blend of information and advertising copy. Within it the publisher neatly calls attention to some of those features of the play that happen to have caused modern readers and audiences most problems. The 'extreme crueltie' of Shylock, with its over-tones of revenge drama and its potentiality for a tragic outcome, has often seemed an excessively disturbing action for a comedy. The flesh-bond drama is after all a very close-run thing; it would have needed only a message to miscarry, as in *Romeo and Juliet,* for the plot to resolve itself into a near-comedy rather than a near-tragedy. More importantly, the casting of a Jew ('the Iewe') in the role of revenge villain raises the racial problems suggested earlier: as we shall see, the labelling and addressing of Shylock as 'the Jew', and 'Jew', can prove most disconcerting to modern readings. The refer-ence to the bond and the trial ('a iust pound') focuses on all those difficult questions about law and justice that have dominated sub-sequent critical interpretation of the play. The allusion to Portia's marriage lottery via the fairy-tale motif of the three chests focuses on the problems raised by the play's generic diversity and by the interpenetration of realist and fictional elements within the drama: why do the reassuring guarantees of romance operate so smoothly for Christians, while the Jew's share of the narrative spoils is loss, humiliation, defeat?

There are two ways of looking at this problem. One is to suggest that in *The Merchant of Venice* we have a work which is essentially historical, in the sense of being strictly confined within the ideolo-gical framework, the belief systems and the prejudices of the age in which it was produced; and that the qualities of difficulty, ambiva-lence and internal conflict discovered in the text by modern crit-icism are symptomatic not of the character of the play itself, but only of the extent to which certain attitudes have changed. Thus, if it is assumed that the play embodies, from a modern point of view, an extraordinarily casual view of anti-Semitism, that is explained by the prevalence of anti-Semitic prejudices in its surrounding histori-cal context. Modern interpreters can in turn adopt two different approaches towards this historicist reading: that the proper respons-ibility of critical interpretation is to reproduce an appropriate context for the expression of that strictly limited, historically cir-cumscribed character – in short, to read the play as if we were Elizabethans; or that criticism should acknowledge the deep diver-gences between the ideologies of the past and the culture of the present, and read the play as a document of its time. Differences of interpretation would then arise not from any inherent complexity of the dramatic text, but from the subsequent evolution of cultural differences. Dramatists, readers and playgoers of the 1590s may have shared a basic, unreflective anti-Semitism, but a reader of the later twentieth century, whose views are inevitably coloured by the horrors of the Holocaust, would find it impossible to overlook such a presence within the text of an ideology that has proved in very recent history the source of immense cruelty and suffering.

In that type of reading the ideology of the text is regarded as basically simple, historically conditioned and firmly located in the past. All the complexity, contradiction and ambivalence of modern criticism are produced in retrospective accounts by the facts of historical change. In this school of criticism, which could be called a traditional historicist approach, we should attempt imaginatively to re-enter that past ideology, in order fully to appreciate the drama of that lost culture. In another, typical of certain kinds of poststructuralist criticism such as New Historicism,[7] our responsibility as readers is quite the opposite: we should recognise the past as an enemy, and mobilise our own critical methods in order to confront those questions and problems which we consider to be of paramount importance, although – perhaps even because – writers of the past chose to ignore or minimise their significance. In a traditional historicist reading, we should paradoxically forget the historical specificity of Shylock's racial hatred, and acknowledge his villainy as universal, since the Jewish dimension of the Elizabethan play was only a convenient costume for dramatising larger ethical concerns about friendship and enmity, justice and mercy. In a New Historicist interpretation, the crudity and prejudice of the play need to be highlighted and exposed by a critical method attuned more closely to the concerns of contemporary theory than to the detail of a vanished history. If the play was anti-Semitic, then that should be recognised in a critical account that foregrounds the past and continuing dominance of repressive and exploitative ideologies. We should face up to the anti-Semitism of *The Merchant of Venice* precisely because of an imperative need to identify and combat anti-Semitism and all other forms of racial prejudice in our own contemporary world.

The alternative method of interpretation is to propose that all the complexities discovered by modern criticism were from the outset embodied, or implicitly potential, within the Elizabethan text from the outset. It is always difficult to argue for a simplistic imputation of ideological uniformity to a cultural form like drama, which is by its very nature 'dialogic' – composed by the juxtaposition of different and divergent voices – rather than 'monologic' – expressive of a single authoritative voice enclosing a single ideological perspective. The Elizabethan drama was particularly remarkable for such 'polyphonic' – multiple-voiced – discourse because of its generic heterogeneity: where a single play can contain and synthesise the conventions of comedy, romance, tragedy and even history, it is unlikely to offer itself for simplistic, single-minded readings. If the same dramatic narrative can be experienced as comedy by one individual character or group of characters, romance by another and tragedy by a third, then where is the play's ideological centre? If generic diversity suggests discontinuous fortunes for the characters, would that not be likely to produce divergent reactions from members of an audience and disparate interpretations from different readers?

TEXT AND PERFORMANCE

If we pursue the subsequent history of the play in the theatre rather than in criticism, the evidence points more decisively towards a poststructuralist model of interpretation. By this I mean that changes in the play's theatrical realisation can be linked fairly directly to general changes in the understanding and interpretation of the problems the play represents, particularly to the racial problems associated with Shylock, but also to the very idea of a 'Christian' culture being as dedicated to the uninhibited pursuit of wealth as are Shakespeare's Venetians.

It would almost certainly be true to say that had the villain of this particular narrative not been identified as a Jew – had Shylock been characterised, for example, simply as a miser, distinguished morally rather than racially and ethnically from the Venetian Christians – the play would never have produced the critical and theatrical problems that it has. The discordant elements of *The Merchant of Venice* centre on Shylock, and extend from that central figure across other areas of the play. It is perhaps the peculiarly intractable nature of the play's discords which accounts for the remarkable stage history of *The Merchant*, a history containing some extraordinary transformations. In terms of standard Elizabethan attitudes and conventions,

Shylock can be assimilated to a definite convention – that of the stage Jew, a variant of the medieval dramatic figure of Vice, embellished with the trappings of contemporary anti-Semitism and the uniform of grotesque farce (red wigs and huge artificial noses). This was, presumably, how the play was performed on the Elizabethan public stage some time in the late 1590s, and before James I in the two recorded court performances of 1605. The play seems not to have been especially popular in its own time. By the early eighteenth century its place in the repertory was being reasserted, albeit in the form of extremely free adaptation which was the common method in that period of tailoring Shakespearean texts to the needs of the contemporary theatre. In the course of the eighteenth century we can trace a gradual development of the role of Shylock towards the figure of heroic suffering and tragic dignity that became the Romantic movement's standard interpretation of the Elizabethan Jew. The tendency to see Shylock not as a comic villain, but as someone closer to a hero or hero *manqué*, evidently began much earlier than the twentieth century's experience of Fascism. As early as the eighteenth century the role was treated with some measure of tragic dignity. And in the course of the Romantic movement of the early nineteenth century, a serious re-evaluation and reinterpretation of Shylock appeared on both critical and theatrical agendas. Edmund Kean performed Shylock in 1814 as a tragic figure, marking a significant stage in the rehabilitation of the character's dramatic possibilities. When Kean's production first opened in 1814, the critic William Hazlitt was in the audience to register this profound shift of values. 'We have,' he said:

> formed an overstrained idea of the gloomy character of Shylock, probably more from seeing other players perform it than from the text of Shakespeare. Mr Kean's manner is much nearer the mark ... his Jew is more than half a Christian. Certainly, our sympathies are much oftener with him than with his enemies. He is honest in his vices; they are hypocrites in their virtues.[8]

In order for the audience to be capable of sympathy for Shylock, the actor had to approach the role in a fundamentally sympathetic way. The great actor-manager of the later nineteenth century, Sir Henry Irving, was quite clear that 'Shylock is a bloody-minded monster', but equally confident that the role should not be played on that basis: 'you mustn't play him so, if you wish to succeed; you must get some sympathy with him'.[9] Irving invested in his performance of

Shylock all the virtues of his characteristically 'noble' style of acting, emphasising the background of racial persecution and personal humiliation. According to a contemporary reviewer, Irving 'kept a firm front to the last ... a fine curl of withering scorn upon his lips for Gratiano', as he walked away to die in silence and alone.[10] Irving even interpolated an additional scene, after Jessica's elopement at Act II, scene vi, in which Shylock was seen returning to his own house to find it empty and the door locked against him.

It has often been argued that, in addition to reading the text retrospectively in its history, we should try as spectators to view Elizabethan plays in the context of Elizabethan attitudes and prejudices, avoiding the imposition of our own more tolerant and liberal values. An early theatrical attempt to effect such a shift of attention back towards the play's authentic historical character was William Poel's Elizabethan Stage Society production of 1898, which assumed a radical disjuncture between Elizabethan and modern attitudes. In William Poel's view, the play had gradually been twisted from its basic sixteenth-century structure, in which a vindictive alien threatens the serenity of a pleasure-loving European community, to a modern version of which Shylock is the heroic, martyred and persecuted victim of an oppressive society. The play had become, as Poel ironically adapted the wording of the title-page to show, 'The tragical history of the Jew of Venice, with the extreme injustice of Portia towards the said Jew in denying him the right to cut a just pound of the Merchant's flesh, together with the obtaining of the rich heiress by the prodigal Bassanio'.[11] The production appears to have failed to convince, however, for the obvious reason that Elizabethan conventions of racial stereotyping – Shylock was played in a red wig and artificial nose – had become unacceptable to modern liberal opinion. It was precisely such anachronistic liberalism that Poel was trying to combat, but even as early as 1898 it was clearly impossible to read a play about the persecution of a Jew with detached historical objectivity. More recent events such as the twentieth-century Holocaust – a modern tragedy which seemed to confirm very ancient legends of racial persecution – render such an operation of historical distancing out of the question. The kind of cruel amusement which the educated Elizabethan could apparently direct towards Jews can hardly be revived in a culture where the very names of those Second World War concentration camps in which six million of them were annihilated – Auschwitz, Dachau, Belsen – carry such potent symbolic force.

PAST AND PRESENT

On the other hand, as much recent criticism has convincingly shown, we cannot always be quite so sure as scholars once were of exactly how such 'standard' ideas and prejudices were held by Elizabethan audiences; nor can we confidently attribute those orthodox opinions to Shakespeare or to the plays he wrote. The reading of an Elizabethan play involves both an act of historical imagination – the act of thinking and feeling one's way into a very different historical culture – and an awareness of the ways in which subsequent historical developments and modern beliefs may have changed the play's possibilities of interpretation. Reading in this dialectical way, it becomes possible to recognise within an Elizabethan play potentialities which become fully articulate only in modern interpretation. The modern recognition of Shylock as a tragic figure, which is so incompatible with that Elizabethan grotesque with the red wig and the artificial nose, may be a recognition of possibilities historically inscribed into the play. The pervasive conviction, visible across the whole range of critical approaches, that *The Merchant of Venice* needs to be understood as a problem play or tragicomedy, may simply be a result of those cultural changes that have transformed modern attitudes towards the play and its contents. On the other hand, it may be a recognition that the play was genuinely problematical, authentically resistant to simple categorisation, from the moment of its first production and circulation in the Elizabethan popular theatre of the 1590s.

From Graham Holderness, *William Shakespeare: The Merchant of Venice* (Harmondsworth, 1993), pp. vii–xvii.

NOTES

[Holderness's study of the play, from which this extract comes, is part of the useful Penguin Critical Studies series. Subsequent chapters of the book cover Venice and Belmont, Economics and Sexuality, Jews and Christians, Law and Power, The Elizabethan Stage and 'Endgames', that is, the play's final scene. Throughout Holderness seeks to read the play 'as a document of its time, and by the application of a modern theoretical consciousness, as a text of our own time' (p. 76). His critical position is in this sense the 'dialectical' one he describes in the extract by which he constantly questions and interrogates how we read the text and how we construct its pastness. All quotations are from the New Penguin edition of *The Merchant of Venice*, ed. W. Moelwyn Merchant (Harmondsworth, 1967). Ed.]

1. Walter Cohen, 'The Merchant of Venice and the Possibilities of Historical Criticism', *ELH*, 49:4 (1982), 767. [See essay 3 – Ed.].

2. W. H. Auden, 'Brothers and Others', from *The Dyer's Hand* (1963), quoted from *Shakespeare's Comedies: An Anthology of Modern Criticism*, ed. Laurence Lerner (Harmondsworth, 1967), p. 143.

3. Graham Midgeley, '*The Merchant of Venice*: A Reconsideration', *Essays in Criticism*, 10 (1960), 121.

4. Heinrich Heine, 'Shakespeares Mädchen und Frauen' (1839), quoted from '*The Merchant of Venice*': *A Selection of Critical Essays*, ed. John Wilders (Basingstoke, 1969), p. 29.

5. See E. M. W. Tillyard, *Shakespeare's Problem Plays* (London, 1950).

6. Giovanni Fiorentio, *Il Pecorone*, written in the late fourteenth century, published in 1558. See *The Merchant of Venice*, ed. W. Moelwyn Merchant (Harmondsworth, 1967), pp. 18–19, and *The Merchant of Venice*, ed. John Russell Brown (London, 1955), pp. xxviii–xxx.

7. The term was coined by Stephen Greenblatt, whose *Shakespearean Negotiations* (Oxford, 1988) exemplifies the method. See also, for a consideration of Judaism in Renaissance drama, his essay 'Marlowe, Marx and Anti-Semitism', in Stephen Greenblatt, *Learning to Curse* (London, 1990).

8. William Hazlitt, quoted by John Russell Brown (ed.), *The Merchant of Venice*, p. xxxiv.

9. Henry Irving, quoted by John Russell Brown (ed.), *The Merchant of Venice*, pp. xxxiv–xxxv.

10. Irving's production reviewed in *Blackwood's Magazine* (December, 1879), p. 655.

11. William Poel, quoted in *The Merchant of Venice*, ed. M. M. Mahood (Cambridge, 1987), p. 48.

2

Re-reading *The Merchant of Venice*

KIERNAN RYAN

The crux of *The Merchant* is, of course, Shylock and the significance of his revenge.[1] Conventional criticism has distorted or repressed the full implications of this problem, persisting for the most part in the romantic idealist conception of the play.[2] According to this, *The Merchant* is a tragically tinged but, in the end, delightful romantic comedy, in which the ruling-class Christians triumph, by virtue of their selfless love and merciful generosity, over the threat posed to their happiness by the pitiable but essentially evil Jew. In John Russell Brown's representative view: 'We cannot doubt that Shylock must be condemned. However lively Shylock's dialogue may be, however plausibly and passionately he presents his case, however cruelly the lovers treat him, he must still be defeated, because he is an enemy to love's wealth and its free, joyful and continual giving.'[3]

A telling endorsement of this position was provided several years later by the eminent Shakespeare scholar, Samuel Schoenbaum. Reviewing a whole season of RSC productions, he singled out as the highpoint a production of *The Merchant* which had been 'rapturously received by an audience consisting almost entirely of Shakespeare scholars'. The virtue of the production, in Schoenbaum's eyes, was the director's 'refusal to be seduced by the opposing voice of the play' – the voice, that is, of Shylock. The production is applauded for not being 'sentimental', despite 'the holocaust and the history of European Jewry in this century'. It is acclaimed for its 'courage to be faithful' to what Schoenbaum regards as the historically fixed 'main thrust of the play' against 'the Devil Jew'.[4]

Conventional Marxist interpretations are in complete agreement with this standard view of the play's 'main thrust'. The only real difference is their negative evaluation of the play as the blind tool of whatever they take to be the dominant Elizabethan ideology. Hence Elliot Krieger's *A Marxist Study of Shakespeare's Comedies* reads *The Merchant* as having forged by the end an elaborate resolution designed to consolidate the sway of the aristocracy (Portia and Belmont) over the rising bourgeoisie (Venice and Shylock).[5] While in Christian Enzensberger's long, ambitious study the play is no less reductively diagnosed as an allegory of the triumph of merchant capitalism over the reactionary practice of usury, with Act V as the romantically refracted celebration of a merchant-capitalist utopia. For Enzensberger the text cunningly dramatises and solves a subordinate conflict of the period – mercantilism versus usury – as if it were the main conflict of society. It thus strives to conceal the really central contradiction between a racist capitalism and humanity.[6]

But this contradiction, I would argue, is precisely what the play exposes to the gaze of a fully historical reading. The cited critics are doomed, by their unhistorical idealism or their one-dimensional historicism, to remain deaf to the 'opposing voice' centred in Shylock, and therefore blind to the more valuable possibilities stored in the text. In responding to the play, we should not suppress the awareness we ought to have of 'the holocaust and the history of European Jewry in this century'. Nor should we resist the change in the angle of reception which such a consciousness creates. The extent to which the vision of *The Merchant of Venice* contradicts or corroborates the enlightened viewpoint of the present must be proved first and foremost on the evidence of the text. But we should not fail to take on board too the fact that the conditions of literary production in Shakespeare's time made it possible for his drama to undermine rather than underwrite the governing assumptions of his society. I will say more about this later in the chapter. Suffice it for the moment to suggest that, if one does allow these past and present perspectives to converge upon the text, *The Merchant of Venice* turns out to be dynamised by a profound struggle between conflicting impulses. Its true achievement consists in its subversion of its own conventional commitments.

This process of self-subversion is organised through Shylock. It reaches its first explicit, devastating expression, of course, in his speech rebuking the Jew-baiting Christians on the grounds of their common constitution:

> Hath not a Jew eyes? Hath not a Jew hands, organs, dimensions, senses, affections, passions; fed with the same food, hurt with the same weapons, subject to the same diseases, heal'd by the same means, warm'd and cool'd by the same winter and summer, as a Christian is? If you prick us, do we not bleed? If you tickle us, do we not laugh? If you poison us, do we not die? And if you wrong us, shall we not revenge? If we are like you in the rest, we will resemble you in that ... The villainy you teach me, I will execute, and it shall go hard but I will better the instruction.
>
> (III.i.59–73)

With this speech there erupts into the play an irresistible egalitarian attitude, whose basis in the shared faculties and needs of our physical nature indicts all forms of inhuman discrimination. The speech provokes a sharp shift of emotional allegiance, from which our perception of the Christian protagonists never recovers. Through Shylock, *The Merchant* proceeds to broach a perspective which cracks the received readings wide open and transfigures our understanding of the play.

The key line is the one that defines the rationale of Shylock's revenge: 'The villainy you teach me, I will execute'. The consequences of this line are worth thinking through, for it makes it clear that Shylock's revenge signifies much more than the usual evil threat to the idyllic realm of romance. It explains that Shylock's bloodthirsty cruelty is not simply the result of the Venetians' abuse of him, but the deliberate mirror-image of their concealed real nature. The revenge is a bitter parody of the Christians' actual values, a calculated piercing of their unconsciously hypocritical facade. The whole point of Shylock's demanding payment of 'a pound of flesh', and of Antonio's heart in particular (III.i.127), lies in its grotesque attempt to translate the heartlessness of Venice into reality.[7] Venice is a world where the human heart is literally a quantifiable lump of meat, a world where, as Shylock sardonically remarks,

> A pound of man's flesh, taken from a man,
> Is not so estimable, profitable neither,
> As flesh of muttons, beefs, or goats.
> (I.iii.165–7)

The revenge opens up the covert reality of a money-centred society, which has created Shylock in its own avaricious image in order to project upon him its hidden guilty hatred of itself.

The drive to demystify climaxes in the trial scene. Once again it is a question of unpacking the full implications of the script, of spelling out completely in this case the meaning of Shylock's insistence on his bond, on his acknowledged legal right to his pound of flesh. Castigated by the Christians for his merciless bloodlust, Shylock reminds them that by their own principles, in the eyes of their own law – as they themselves explicitly concede – he is 'doing no wrong'. On the contrary:

> You have among you many a purchas'd slave,
> Which like your assess, and your dogs and mules,
> You use in abject and in slavish parts,
> Because you bought them. Shall I say to you,
> 'Let them be free! Marry them to your heirs!
> Why sweat they under burthens? ...'
> ...   ... You will answer,
> 'The slaves are ours'. So do I answer you:
> The pound of flesh which I demand of him
> Is dearly bought as mine, and I will have it.
> If you deny me, fie upon your law!
>   (IV.i.90–101)

What the established criticism has always repressed here is Shylock's irrefutable demonstration that his 'wolvish, bloody, starv'd, and ravenous' behaviour (IV.i.138) is the very foundation and institutionalised norm of Venice, whose inhumanity is ratified as 'justice' by its laws. The play as romantic comedy has nothing to say in reply that can compensate for this annihilating realisation.

This is not to say that the play ends up justifying or excusing Shylock by turning its sympathy over to him. *The Merchant of Venice* operates at a level beyond the simplistic polarities of such sentimental moralism. To define the play in terms of which party deserves the blame and which the absolution, with readings and productions swinging now to Shylock and now to the Christians, is to miss the point. What is at stake is the deeper recognition that, through the revenge plot and the trial, through the ironies and contradictions they lay bare, an apparently civilised society is unmasked as premised on barbarity, on the ruthless priority of money values over human values, of the rights of property over the elementary rights of men and women. The point lies not in the vindication of the Jew at the expense of the Christians, or of the Christians at the expense of the Jew, but in the critique of the structural social forces which have made them both what they are, for better and for worse.

What is fascinating, moreover, is the way the pressure exerted by this reappraisal of the Shylock plot throws further latent aspects of the text into unexpected relief, and so brings them likewise within the scope of appropriation.

It becomes evident, for example, that the casket-choosing plot at Belmont does more than test the moral competence of Portia's prospective husbands. It underlines the disparity between the visible and the veiled nature of people and things, between supposed worth and actual value: 'All that glisters is not gold,/ ... Gilded tombs do worms enfold' (II.vii.65–9); 'So may the outward shows be least themselves' (III.ii.73). The casket scenes tune us to the frequency of the play's opposing voice. They school our expectations in the logic of inversion that runs through the play, reinforcing the discovery of the Shylock plot that the ruling ethos of this comedy is the shameful reverse of how its heroes and heroines see it.

Or take the intriguing first appearance of Lancelot Gobbo in Act II, scene ii. The clown's monologue presents him as torn back and forth between his conscience's demand that he stay with his master the Jew and the devil's insistence that he abandon him. This apparently inconsequential scene can now be seen to convey more than mere comic relief. As in other plays, especially *King Lear, As You Like It* and *Twelfth Night*, the fool acts as a personified index of the text's evolving viewpoint. Gobbo gives us a condensed comic version of the crisis of allegiance provoked by Shylock throughout *The Merchant of Venice*. What had hitherto lain submerged as no more than a farcical interlude surfaces as a key strategy of estrangement, an internal objectification of the play's tormented subconscious.

We can now begin to decipher too the enigma of Antonio, the merchant of Venice himself. The opening scene fastens at once upon the mystery of Antonio's sadness, writhing itself into a knot of frustrated interrogation which is never untangled. The nominal hero of the play remains to the end a cryptically still and passive presence, the absent centre around which the action of the comedy revolves. But therein lies Antonio's true significance as the embodiment of the void at the heart of Venice. For it is in the play's rebellion against the expectations of its title, in its conspicuous refusal to project the merchant capitalist as hero, that Shakespeare's anguished rejection of the values invading Elizabethan England finds distorted expression.

Once a consciously modern grasp of the Shylock problem has awoken us to the authorised prejudice and inhumanity of Shakespeare's Venice, an equally undisguised concern with sexual injustice allows us to recognise *The Merchant*'s preoccupation with women as the alienated objects of men's vision, choice and possession. As Portia exclaims:

> O me, the word choose! I may neither choose who I would, nor refuse who I dislike; so is the will of a living daughter curb'd by the will of a dead father.
>
> (I.ii.22–5)

For Bassanio, Portia is first and foremost the means 'to get clear of all the debts I owe' (I.i.135). She is 'a lady richly left' (I.i.161), imprisoned as her image in a leaden casket: 'I am lock'd in one of them' (III.ii.40). The freedom of thought, speech and behaviour she displays when alone with her maid Nerissa, or when disguised in male apparel as the lawyer Balthazar, only accentuates the constrictions of her normal identity as obedient daughter and, subsequently, submissive wife: 'Myself, and what is mine, to you and yours / Is now converted' (III.ii.166–7).

Re-examined from this angle, the fifth-act closure in alleged romantic harmony is actually fraught with sinister insinuations. Even the first sweet, moonlit exchange cannot escape the shadow cast across the comedy by what Shylock's tale has taught us. Lorenzo's and Jessica's hymning of their love is infected by a rash of allusions to tragically doomed lovers: Troilus and Cressida, Pyramus and Thisbe, Dido and Aeneas, Jason and Medea (V.i.1–14). In the ensuing banter between the newly wed couples (Portia and Bassanio, Gratiano and Nerissa) disquieting doubts are raised about the quality of the men's love by their failure of the love-test in giving away their rings: 'You swore to me,' protests Nerissa, 'when I did give it you, / That you would wear it till your hour of death' (V.i.152–3). The fact that the men unknowingly returned the rings to the disguised Portia and Nerissa does not override the nagging reproaches in which the women persist for a third of the entire act (V.i.142–246). The discord is amplified by Portia's and Nerissa's teasing threats of revenge through infidelity: 'Lie not a night from home,' warns Portia, 'Watch me like Argus' (V.i.230). And it is on a

note of equivocally contained sexual anxiety that Gratiano ends the
play: 'while I live I'll fear no other thing / So sore, as keeping safe
Nerissa's ring' (V.i.306–7).[8]

Perhaps most unsettling of all, though, is the moment shortly
before this, when Antonio offers to heal the rift between the lovers
by pledging himself once again as surety for Bassanio:

> I once did lend my body for his wealth,
>   … I dare be bound again,
> My soul upon the forfeit, that your lord
> Will never more break faith advisedly.
>   (V.i.249–53)

These lines expose an ominous duplication in the sexual domain of
the triangular financial bond upon whose implications the comedy
has foundered, but with Portia now cast in the role formerly assigned to Shylock. The conscious parallel conveys a subliminal intu-
ition of the symmetries that unite the racial oppression of the Jew
and the sexual oppression of the female.

I have no space to do more than outline these embryonic insights
into the changing meaning of *The Merchant of Venice*, all of which
are confirmable through close textual analysis. The point I want to
stress is that the strategy responsible for these readings is neither arbitrary nor unhistorical. It postulates an historically implanted se-
mantic potential,[9] a determinate range of verifiable readings
genetically secreted by the play. The contexts and angles of the
work's subsequent reception will dictate which veins of meaning
will be mined and which remain undiscerned or neglected. What
The Merchant of Venice means today depends as much on what we
are disposed to make of it as it does on Shakespeare's text. The
account I have privileged is a textually supported option inherent in
the work, objectively encoded in the words that constitute the
edition of the play being used. It is a demonstrably available interpretation, which could not be apprehended within the successive
horizons of the play's previous reception, but which can be seized
and elected to priority within the horizon of its reception now.

For those who share the values that define that horizon, a knowledge of the Holocaust of the Jewish people, and a horror of that
lethal juncture where capitalism and racism intersect, should not be
suppressed as anachronistic or extraneous, as Professor Schoenbaum
suggests. On the contrary, they ought to mark the point of departure for any unclouded engagement with *The Merchant of Venice* at

this point in history, making it inconceivable to evade or refuse the vision which the work offers us today. To accept this vision is to learn that, all along, the play knew more about both its time and the times to come than historicist critics deemed it capable of knowing; that all along it was waiting to reveal uncharted shores of insight to the alien eyes of modern understanding.

From Kiernan Ryan, *Shakespeare*, second edition (Hemel Hempstead, 1995), pp. 17–24.

NOTES

[Like Graham Holderness (essay 1), Kiernan Ryan is interested in the sort of dialogue it is possible to construct between history and modernity, between the text and contemporary critical practice. Unlike a number of other modern Marxist critics, Ryan does not see literature as a conservative force which can only profitably be read against the grain; rather, he argues that Shakespeare's plays constantly push forward new liberating possibilities. In the opening chapter of the book from which this extract comes Ryan seeks to 'work towards a more productive way of reading Shakespeare's plays ... from a progressive modern viewpoint'. To this end he suggests there are certain key questions we need to ask of a play:

> How far, and in what specific way, does the play succeed in challenging the principles of social and sexual relationship governing Shakespeare's world and our own? To what extent, and again by what precise means, does it confirm and reinforce them? Or is the work divided against itself, challenging and confirming on different levels at the same time? And lastly, if the play does question rather than consolidate the status quo past and present, is there any sense in which it foresees more desirable principles of human relationship, sited beyond the horizon of the age in which it was written and perhaps beyond the horizon of our own time too?
>
> (p. 15)

The extract given here is the first example of this vigorous reading practice Ryan demonstrates in the book as a whole. All references are to *The Riverside Shakespeare*, ed. Blakemore Evans (Boston, MA, 1974). Ed.]

1. The unconsidered assumption that the play is anti-Semitic has even led to its being banned from the classroom by school administrations in the United States, a fact which highlights how acutely *The Merchant of Venice* poses the problem of adequate reception. See Samuel Schoenbaum, 'Alternative Shakespeare', *Times Literary Supplement*,

27 October 1978, p. 1262. The Shylock controversy is amply documented in John Gross, *Shylock: Four Hundred Years in the Life of a Legend* (London, 1992) and Harold Bloom (ed.), *Major Literary Characters: Shylock* (New York, 1991).

2. For a concise survey and critique of these readings see A. D. Moody, *Shakespeare: The Merchant of Venice* (London, 1964), pp. 15–21.

3. John Russell Brown, 'Love's Wealth and *The Merchant of Venice*', in *Shakespeare: The Merchant of Venice: A Collection of Critical Essays*, ed. John Wilders (London, 1969), p. 173.

4. Schoenbaum, 'Alternative Shakespeare', pp. 1262–3.

5. Elliot Krieger, *A Marxist Study of Shakespeare's Comedies* (London, 1979), pp. 8–36. See also Frank Whigham, 'Ideology and Class Conduct in *The Merchant of Venice*', in *Shakespeare's Comedies*, ed. Gary Waller (London and New York, 1991), pp. 108–28.

6. Christian Enzensberger, *Literatur und Interesse: Eine politische Ästhetik*, 2 vols (Munich, 1977), II, pp. 15–89.

7. See John Gillies, *Shakespeare and the Geography of Difference* (Cambridge, 1994), pp. 12–37 for further reflections on how 'the confrontation between Antonio and Shylock amounts to a struggle over the political and economic heart of Venice' (p. 129).

8. Complementary and contrasting feminist views of the play can be found in Marianne Novy, *Love's Argument: Gender Relations in Shakespeare* (Chapel Hill and London, 1984), ch. 4: 'Giving and Taking in *The Merchant of Venice*'; Coppélia Kahn, 'The Cuckoo's Note: Male Friendship and Cuckoldry in *The Merchant of Venice*', in *Shakespeare's 'Rough Magic': Renaissance Essays in Honor of C. L. Barber*, ed. Peter Erickson and Coppélia Kahn (Newark, DE, 1985), pp. 104–12; and Carol Leventen, 'Patrimony and Patriarchy in *The Merchant of Venice*', in *The Matter of Difference: Materialist Feminist Criticism of Shakespeare*, ed. Valerie Wayne (Hemel Hempstead, 1991), pp. 59–79.

9. The term is hijacked from Thomas Metscher, 'Literature and Art as Ideological Form', *New Literary History*, 11 (1979), 36 ff.

3

The Merchant of Venice and the Possibilities of Historical Criticism

WALTER COHEN

Traditional historical scholarship has not fared well with many contemporary literary theorists. Jonathan Culler concludes: 'The identification of historical sequences, while an inevitable and indispensable aspect of literary study, is not just open to oversimplification; it is itself an act of oversimplification.'[1] What is rhetorically striking in this passage is the comfortable coexistence of the author's characteristic moderation with the extremity of the position. Under the influence of the work of Louis Althusser in particular and of structuralism and poststructuralism in general, similar doubts have penetrated Marxism, long a bastion of historical interpretation. Terry Eagleton argues that 'Marx initiates a "genealogical" break with any genetic-evolutionist conception of the historical materialist method, and, indeed, of its object – "history" itself.' For Eagleton, 'history is not a classical narrative: for what kind of narrative is it that has always already begun, that has an infinitely deferred end, and, consequently, can hardly be spoken of as having a middle?'[2] Fredric Jameson (although he begins with the injunction 'Always historicise!') is at pains to demonstrate that Marxism 'is not a historical *narrative*'. And his own 'historicising operation' presupposes a fundamental bifurcation:

> we are thus confronted with a choice between study of the nature of the 'objective' structures of a given cultural text (the historicity of its forms and of its content, the historical moment of emergence of its

45

linguistic possibilities, the situation-specific function of its aesthetic) and something rather different which would instead foreground the interpretive categories or codes through which we read and receive the text in question.[3]

In partial opposition to these claims, I hope to show that it is possible to have it both ways, to combine history with structure and to connect 'the historical moment' with 'the interpretive categories' through which that moment has been understood. Such innovative critical strategies as symptomatic reading, metacommentary, and the elucidation of the ideology of form acquire their full force only when explicitly located within the larger framework provided by the Marxist notion of the mode of production. Jameson, in fact, comes close to this position in asserting that 'Marxism, ... in the form of the dialectic, affirms a primacy of theory which is at one and the same time a recognition of the primacy of History itself.'[4] The resulting procedure may also be viewed as a modified version of the approach recently proposed by Robert Weimann.[5] More particularly, the present discussion proceeds from a detailed account of *The Merchant of Venice* to a brief look at broader issues. It concludes by reversing gears and summarily considering not the utility of contemporary theory for the study of Renaissance literature, but the implications of Renaissance literature for the development of theory.

I

The Merchant of Venice (1596) offers an embarrassment of socioeconomic riches. It treats merchants and usurers, the nature of the law, and the interaction between country and city. But since it is also about the relationship between love and friendship, the meaning of Christianity, and a good deal more, a thematically minded critic, regardless of his or her persuasion, may be in for a bit of difficulty. In the most comprehensive and compelling study of the play yet produced, Lawrence Danson attempts to solve this problem by arguing that *The Merchant of Venice* dramatises not the triumph of one set of values over another, but the transformation of conflicts into harmonies that incorporate what at the same time they transcend.[6] Shakespeare's procedure thus resembles both medieval figural and Hegelian dialectics.[7] Because the intellectual and structural design posited by Danson elegantly accommodates not only thematic diversity but also our ambivalent responses to both Shylock and the Christian characters, it is the appropriate object of a scepti-cal scrutiny of interpretation in *The Merchant of Venice*.

Shakespeare needs to be interpreted, it may be claimed, simply because of the antiquity and complexity of his art. Yet far from being ideologically neutral, such an enterprise, by juxtaposing an alternative and richer reality with our own, involves an implicit cri-tique of the present. Even more, we may recall that Shakespeare's plays, despite their elaborateness, appealed to a broadly heteroge-neous primary audience: an achievement that depended on a com-parative social and cultural unity, long since lost, in the nation as well as the theatre. This underlying coherence emerges in the logical and, it would seem, inherently meaningful unfolding of the dramatic plot,[8] a strong example of which is provided by the rigorously inter-locking, causal development of *The Merchant of Venice*. Presumably, then, the best criticism would deepen, rather than overturn, a sense of the play's meaning widely shared in space and in time.[9]

This is, however, precisely what we do not find in discussion of *The Merchant of Venice*. The play has been seen as the unambiguous triumph of good Christians over a bad Jew;[10] as the deliberately am-biguous triumph of the Christians;[11] as the unintentionally ambigu-ous, and hence artistically flawed, triumph of the Christians;[12] as the tragedy of Shylock, the bourgeois hero;[13] and as a sweeping attack on Christians and Jews alike.[14] No other Shakespearean comedy before *All's Well That Ends Well* (1602) and *Measure for Measure* (1604), perhaps no other Shakespearean comedy at all, has excited comparable controversy. Probably the most promising way out of this dilemma is to see the play as a new departure for Shakespeare; as his earliest comedy drawn from the Italian *novelle*; as the first of several not quite successful attempts to introduce more powerful characters, more complex problems of conduct, more real-istic representation, and a more serious vision of life into a tradi-tionally light genre.[15] Such a perspective is not without its drawbacks. Nonetheless, it has the virtue of suggesting that the play is by and large a romantic comedy; that it is partially flawed; that it calls for an unusual set of critical questions;[16] and, most important, that it requires us not so much to interpret as to discover the sources of our difficulty in interpreting, to view the play as a symptom of a problem in the life of late sixteenth-century England.

Critics who have studied *The Merchant of Venice* against the back-ground of English history have justifiably seen Shylock, and espe-cially his lending habits, as the embodiment of capitalism.[17] The last third of the sixteenth century witnessed a sequence of denunciations of the spread of usury. In *The Specvlation of Vsurie*, published during the year Shakespeare's play may first have been performed, Thomas Bell expresses a typical sense of outrage. 'Now, now is nothing more frequent with the rich men of this world, than to writhe about the neckes of their poore neighbours, and to impouerish them with the filthie lucre of Usurie.'[18] Behind this fear lay the transition to capitalism: the rise of banking; the increasing need for credit in industrial enterprises; and the growing threat of indebtedness facing both aristocratic landlords and, above all, small, independent producers, who could easily decline to working-class status.[19] Although the lower classes were the main victims, it may be as inadequate to describe opposition to usury in Shakespeare or elsewhere as popular in character, as it is misleading to argue that 'Elizabethan drama, even in its higher ranges, was not the expression of a "class" culture at all.'[20] Rather, we are confronted with the hegemonic position of the nobility, whose interests the ideology ultimately served. Artisans and peasant smallholders might fall into the proletariat, but once the majority of the traditional ruling class had adapted to capitalism, the issue of usury faded away.

This had not occurred by 1600, however, and *The Merchant of Venice* offers a number of specific parallels to the anti-usury campaign,[21] most notably in its contrasts between usury and assistance to the poor, and between usurers and merchants. Miles Mosse, for example, laments that 'lending upon *vsurie* is growne so common and usuall among men, as that free lending to the needie is utterly overthrowne'.[22] The distinction between merchants and usurers, also of medieval origin, could be drawn on the grounds that only the former operated for mutual benefit, as opposed to self-interest. Or it might be argued, in language recalling Shakespeare's high valuation of 'venturing', that the usurer does not, like 'the merchant that crosse the seas, adventure', receiving instead a guaranteed return on his money.[23]

A number of dubious consequences follow from concentrating too narrowly on the English background of *The Merchant of Venice*, however. From such a perspective, the play as a whole seems unproblematic, non-economic issues unimportant, and related matters like Shylock's religion or the Italian setting irrelevant.[24] Even explicitly economic concerns do not make adequate sense. An emphasis on the difference between trade and usury might imply that Antonio and his creator are resolutely medieval anti-capitalists.[25]

But not only do Shakespeare's other plays of the 1590s show few signs of hostility to capitalism, *The Merchant of Venice* itself is quite obviously pro-capitalist, at least as far as commerce is concerned. It would be more accurate to say that Shakespeare is criticising merely the worst aspects of an emerging economic system, rather than the system itself. In this respect, moreover, he deviates from the anti-usury tracts and from English reality alike. Writers of the period register both the medieval ambivalence about merchants and the indisputable contemporary fact that merchants were the leading usurers: suspicion of Italian traders ran particularly high.[26] It may be that Shakespeare intends a covert parallel between Shylock and Antonio. Yet no manipulation will convert a comedy in which there are no merchant-usurers and in which the only usurer is a Jew into a faithful representation of British economic life.

Similar trouble arises with Shylock, whom critics have at times allegorically Anglicised as a grasping Puritan.[27] The identification is unconvincing, however, partly because it is just as easy to transform him into a Catholic[28] and, more generally, because he is too complex and contradictory to fit neatly the stereotype of Puritan thrift. It is also unclear what kind of capitalist Shylock is. The crisis of the play arises not from his insistence on usury, but from his refusal of it. The contrast is between usury, which is immoral because it computes a charge above the principal from the moment of the loan, and interest, which is perfectly acceptable because it 'is never due but from the appointed day of payment forward'.[29] Antonio immediately recognises that Shylock's proposal falls primarily into the latter category, and he responds appropriately, if naïvely: 'Content in faith, I'll seal to such a bond, / And say there is much kindness in the Jew.'[30]

In addition, the penalty for default on the bond is closer to folklore than to capitalism: stipulation for a pound of flesh, after all, is hardly what one would expect from *homo economicus*. To be sure, Shakespeare is literalising the traditional metaphorical view of usurers.[31] Moreover, Shylock's desire for revenge is both motivated by economics and possessed of a large degree of economic logic (e.g. I.iii.39–40; and III.i.49, and 117–18). But when the grasping moneylender refuses to relent in return for any repayment – 'No not for Venice' – he goes beyond the bounds of rationality and against the practices of a ruthless modern businessman (IV.i.226).[32] In short, although it is proper to view *The Merchant of Venice* as a critique of early British capitalism, that approach fails even to account for all of the purely economic issues in the work. Can tolerable sense be made of the play's economics, or was Shakespeare merely being fanciful? To answer these questions, we need to take seriously the Venetian setting of the action.

To the English, and particularly to Londoners, Venice represented a more advanced stage of the commercial development they themselves were experiencing. G. K. Hunter's telling remark about the predilections of the Jacobean theatre – 'Italy became important to the English dramatists only when "Italy" was revealed as an aspect of England' – already applies in part to *The Merchant of Venice*.[33] Yet Venetian reality during Shakespeare's lifetime contradicted almost point for point its portrayal in the play. Not only did the government bar Jewish usurers from the city, it also forced the Jewish community to staff and finance low-interest, non-profit lending institutions that served the Christian poor. Funding was primarily derived from the involuntary donations of Jewish merchants active in the Levantine trade. The Jews of Venice thus contributed to the early development of capitalism not as usurers but as merchants involved in an international, trans-European economic network. Ironically, elsewhere in the Veneto, the public Christian banks on which the Jewish loan-houses of Venice were modelled drew most of their assets from interest-bearing deposits by the late sixteenth century.[34]

From a longer historical view of Italy and Venice, however, *The Merchant of Venice* assumes a recognisable relationship to reality. Between the twelfth and the early fourteenth centuries in Italy, international merchant-usurers were often required by the church to make testamentary restitution of their profits from moneylending. Thereafter, this occupation decomposed into its constituent parts. Without changing their financial transactions, the merchants experienced a sharp rise in status, eventually evolving into the great philanthropical merchant princes of the Renaissance. The other descendants of the earlier merchant-usurers, the small, local usurer-pawnbrokers, suffered a corresponding decline in social position. This latter group, the main victim of ecclesiastical action against usury in the fifteenth and sixteenth centuries, increasingly consisted of immigrant Jews.[35]

Jewish moneylenders benefited the Venetian Republic in two principal ways. They provided a reliable, lucrative source of tax revenues and forced loans to finance the state's military preparations; and they also drove down interest rates for private citizens, rich and poor, underselling the Christian usurers, whom, consequently, they gradually replaced. The Christian banks referred to above, founded beginning in the late fifteenth century, were designed not only to assist the poor but also to eliminate Jewish moneylenders by providing cheaper credit. Although never established in Venice itself, the *Monti di Pietà*, as they were called, were soon widespread in the cities and towns of the Republican mainland. They rarely succeeded in completely replacing Jewish pawnbrokers, however.[36]

This, then, is the other, Italian historical background to *The Merchant of Venice*. None of Shakespeare's probable sources refers to any prior enmity between merchant and usurer, much less to a comparable motive for the antagonism. English discussions of Italy, on the other hand, regularly mention both Jewish usury and Venetian charity,[37] while Bell, among others, speaks of the *mons pietatis*, a bank where the poor can 'borrow money in their neede, and not bee oppressed with usury'.[38] From this point of view, the hostility between Antonio, the open-handed Christian merchant, and Shylock, the tight-fisted Jewish usurer, represents not the conflict between declining feudalism and rising capitalism, but its opposite. It may be seen as a special instance of the struggle, widespread in Europe, between Jewish quasi-feudal fiscalism and native bourgeois mercantilism, in which the indigenous forces usually prevailed.[39] Both the characterisation and the outcome of *The Merchant of Venice* mark Antonio as the harbinger of modern capitalism. By guaranteeing an honourable reputation as well as a secure and absolute title to private property, the exemption of the Italian merchant-financier from the stigma of usury provided a necessary spur to the expansion of the new system.[40] Shylock, by contrast, is a figure from the past: marginal, diabolical, irrational, archaic, medieval. Shakespeare's Jacobean tragic villains – Iago, Edmund, Macbeth, and Augustus – are all younger men bent on destroying their elders. Shylock is almost the reverse, an old man with obsolete values trying to arrest the course of history.[41]

Obviously, however, the use of Italian materials in *The Merchant of Venice*, for all its historicity, remains deeply ideological in the bad sense, primarily because of the anti-Semitic distinction between vindictive Jewish usurer and charitable Christian merchant.[42] Shylock's defence of usury is not so strong as it could have been,[43] nor was Shakespeare's preference for an Italian merchant over a Jewish usurer universally shared at the time.[44] Indeed, the very contrast between the two occupations may be seen as a false dichotomy, faithful to the Renaissance Italian merchant's understanding of himself but not to the reality that self-conception was designed to justify.

We can understand the apparently contradictory implications of British and Italian economic history for *The Merchant of Venice* as a response to the intractability of contemporary life. The form of the play results from an ideological reworking of reality designed to produce precisely the intellectual and structural pattern described at the beginning of this discussion. The duality we have observed, especially in Shylock, is absolutely necessary to this end. Briefly stated, in *The Merchant of Venice* English history evokes fears of capitalism, and Italian history allays those fears. One is the problem, the other the solution, the act of incorporation, of transcendence, toward which the play strives.

A similar, if less striking, process of reconciliation is at work with Antonio, whose social significance varies inversely to Shylock's. As a traditional and conservative figure, he nearly becomes a tragic victim of economic change; as the embodiment of progressive forces, he points toward the comic resolution. But Antonio cannot be too progressive, cannot represent a fundamental rupture with the past. Giovanni Botero attributed his country's urban pre-eminence partly to the fact that 'the gentleman in *Italy* does dwell in Cities',[45] and indeed the fusion in the towns of nobility and bourgeoisie helped generate the Renaissance in Italy and, much later, in England as well. The concluding tripartite unity of Antonio, Bassanio, and Portia[46] enacts precisely this interclass harmony between aristocratic landed wealth and mercantile capital, with the former dominant. A belief that some such relationship provided much of the social foundation of the English monarchy accounts for Shakespeare's essentially corporatist defence of absolutism in the 1590s.

A brief consideration of Marx's views on Jews, on usurers, on merchants, and on *The Merchant of Venice* will enable us to restate these conclusions with greater theoretical rigour and to point toward additional, related issues. In the 'Contribution to the Critique of Hegel's *Philosophy of Right*: Introduction', Shylock is an exploiter of the lower classes. Characterising the German historical school of law, Marx comments: 'A Shylock, but a servile Shylock, it swears upon its bond, its historical, Christian-Germanic bond, for every pound of flesh cut from the heart of the people.' The second part of 'On the Jewish Question' basically equates Judaism with capitalism, a position that Volume One of *Capital* reasserts in a discussion of the efforts of nineteenth-century British manufacturers to force children to work long hours. 'Workmen and factory inspectors protested on hygienic and moral grounds, but Capital answered: "My deeds upon my head! I crave the law, / The penalty and forfeit of my bond." This Shylock-clinging to the letter of the law ... ,' Marx adds, 'was but to lead up to an open revolt against the same law.' But the extended discussion of usury in Volume Three of *Capital* implicitly reaches a very different conclusion. Usurer's capital, Marx claims, arises long before the capitalist system itself, its parasitic action weakening the pre-capitalist model of production off which it lives. But unassisted it cannot generate a transition to capitalism. When that transition does occur, however, usury inevitably declines, partly as a result of the determined opposition of mercantile capital. Finally, commercial capital itself is, like usury, an early and primitive form of capital and, as such, ultimately compatible with pre-capitalist modes of production. Thus, Marx's comments in effect recapitulate our entire argument on the economics of *The Merchant of Venice*.[47]

In one instance, however, they lead beyond that argument. Up to now, we have been primarily concerned to show how dramatic form, as the product of an ideological reworking of history, functions to resolve those contradictions that prove irreconcilable in life. But, of course, many critics have been unable to feel a final coherence to *The Merchant of Venice*. In Volume One of *Capital*, after showing how industrial capital endangers the worker, 'how it constantly threatens, by taking away the instruments of labour, to snatch from his hands his means of subsistence', Marx quotes Shylock's reply to the Duke's pardon: 'You take my life / When you do take the means whereby I live.'[48] The passage implies exactly the opposite of what is suggested by the lines previously cited from the same volume. There, Shylock was identified with capital, the Christians with labour; here, the Christians represent capital, Shylock labour. Such a reversal cannot be assimilated to the dualisms we have already discussed: instead, Marx's use of selective quotation succeeds in capturing Shylock as both victimiser and victim.

As many critics have observed, the fact that Shylock is grand as well as pitiable does not in itself imply any structural flaw in *The Merchant of Venice*. Shakespeare needed an antagonist possessed of sufficient, though perhaps not 'mythical', stature to pose a credible threat.[49] The sympathy elicited by the Jewish usurer, often a consequence of his mistreatment by Christian characters who resemble him more than they would admit, also serves a plausible formal purpose in the overall movement towards mercy and harmony. In fact, by the end of the trial scene most of the Christian characters have fairly settled accounts with Shylock.[50] The trouble is that Christianity has not. Although the Christian characters in the play are better than Shylock, the Christian characters *not* in the play are not. In his famous 'Jew' speech and in his declamation on slavery to the court, Shylock adopts the strategy of equating Christian with Jew to justify his own murderous intentions (III.ii.47–66, and IV.i.89–103). But by the end of Act IV, his analogies are strictly irrelevant to most of the Christian characters in the play. They have either given up the practices that Shylock attributes to them, or they have never been guilty of them at all: certainly, we meet no Christian slaveholders in *The Merchant of Venice*. Yet Shylock's universalising accusations are never challenged in word by his Christian auditors, nor can they be sufficiently answered in deed by the individual charitable acts with which the trial concludes. The devastating judgements, particularly of the second speech, are allowed to stand; and they tell us that although Shylock is defeated and then incorporated in the world of the play, in the world beyond the play his values are pervasive.

This bifurcation is a consequence of the fundamental contradiction in Shakespeare's social material. English history requires that the threat embodied in Shylock be generalised; Italian history, that it remain localised. Yet if Shakespeare had fully responded to both imperatives, *The Merchant of Venice* would have lapsed into incoherence. If the play revealed that merchants were as exploitative as usurers, that they were in fact usurers, then its entire thrust toward harmonious reconciliation could only be understood as a fiendishly oblique instance of ironic demystification. But if instead Shakespeare intended the movement toward transcendent unity to be taken at least as seriously as the dangers of nascent capitalism, he needed to present the latter in a way that would not undermine the former. He needed to transform materialist problems into idealist ones (Antonio cannot very well give up commerce, but he can learn to be more merciful) or to project them harmlessly away from the Christian characters in the play (some Christians whom we do not meet own and mistreat slaves). To achieve a convincing resolution, Shakespeare had to begin with a partly imaginary dilemma. But only partly. For had his premise been wholly imaginary, his treatment could easily have been relatively free of contradiction. That it is not is a testimony to both his strengths and his limitations.

Such a perspective enables us to understand and in a sense to justify the opposed responses to *The Merchant of Venice*, to see in its flaws not signs of artistic incompetence but manifestations of preformal problems. It also suggests answers to the questions with which we began. We need to interpret this play particularly because its formal movement – dialectical transcendence – is not adequate to the social conflict that is its main source of inspiration and one of its principal subjects. Some of the merit of *The Merchant of Venice* ironically lies in the failure of its central design to provide a completely satisfying resolution to the dilemmas raised in the course of the action. We have seen that one purpose of the form is to reconcile the irreconcilable. Similarly, one effect of interpretive methods that view explication as their primary end is a complicity of silence with the play, in which the ideology of the form is uncritically reproduced and the whole, *The Merchant of Venice* as we have it, is replaced by the part, Shakespeare's possible intention.

These inferences may be related to the debate on organic form and artistic totality that has troubled Marxist criticism since the 1930s. It would seem that the above argument aligns itself with those theories that see in the sense of closure or wholeness sometimes produced by a work of art an analogue to reactionary corporatist ideologies designed to suppress awareness of class conflict. An anti-organicist orientation, however, must deny in principle the possibility that the realm of aesthetics can deliver an experience of a contradictory totality or, for that matter, of demystification followed by retotalisation.[51] Few plays if any completely accomplish so much: the achievement of *The Merchant of Venice* is oblique and partial. But it would be a mistake to overgeneralise from a single example: some of the greatest works of the early seventeenth-century theatre, most notably *King Lear*, do in fact approach this elusive ideal.

Nonetheless, our consideration of the ideology of form in *The Merchant of Venice* from the vantage point of economic history has primarily constituted an act of demystification. An exclusive preoccupation of this sort fails to do justice to the play, however. To locate the merit of the work in Shakespeare's inability to accomplish precisely what he intended hardly corrects the deficiency; it merely betrays the critic's wish that *The Merchant of Venice* were *The Jew of Malta*. The positive value of Shakespeare's comedy naturally includes the significant concerns that it voices, a prominent example of which is the problem of usury. But at least as important is the utopian dimension of the play: what may seem escapist from one perspective, from another becomes liberating. Although the effort of art to transcend the constraints of its time is not necessarily apparent, in *The Merchant of Venice* much of this tendency is right on the surface. For instance, the play persistently attempts to establish a congruence between economic and moral conduct, between outer and inner wealth; to depict a society in which human relationships are not exploitative. Such a vision, quite literally a fantasy, simultaneously distracts us from the deficiencies of our lives and reveals to us the possibility of something better. Utopian mystification and liberation are always inseparable and often, as here, strictly identical.

Similar lines of analysis could be extended to the other major issues in the play. Here, however, we need only suggest the outlines of such an inquiry. The suppression of justice by mercy, of the letter by the spirit, and of the Old Law by the New in the trial that occupies Act IV at once reveals the fairness of the legal system and the ethical premises of the entire plot.[52] Shakespeare's demonstration that the principle of equity is inherent in the rigour of the law is rooted 'in the adjustment of the common law to the practice of Equity in the Court of Chancery' during the sixteenth century.[53] Beginning in the 1590s, however, the officials of the old, comparatively popular common law courts and their counterparts on the newer, royally dominated courts like Chancery entered into a struggle that ultimately resulted in the common lawyers joining the militant opposition to the crown.[54] In this respect Shakespeare's ideological project represents an anticipatory and, in the event, futile attempt to reconcile absolutist values with popular, traditional, but ironically revolutionary institutions, so as to prevent civil war.[55] Another version of this compromise is implicit in Shylock's demand of his bond from the Duke: 'If you deny it, let the danger light / Upon your charter and your city's freedom!' (IV.i.38–9). On the one hand, the case acquires such political reverberations because Shakespeare assumes a feudal conception of law, in which justice is the central peacetime conduit of aristocratic power. On the other, Shylock's threat becomes so grave because the trial is based on a bourgeois commitment to binding contracts. Portia's integrative solution reveals the compatibility of rigour and freedom, of bourgeois self-interest and aristocratic social responsibility. But the profound allegiance to contractual law can make this ideological yoking seem either unjust or precarious, responses that indicate the tension between the limits of reality and the promises of utopia in *The Merchant of Venice.*

The relationship between country and city, perhaps the other major, overtly social issue raised by the action, situates the play in the tradition of Renaissance pastoral, a literary and theatrical reaction by the nobility to the two dominant trends of the age – the rise of capitalism and the partly complementary growth of absolutism. The construction of the pastoral world resolves the intractable dilemmas of aristocratic life in the city or at court: the form ideologically reconciles the socially irreconcilable.[56] Rather than representing a species of escapism, however, this enterprise is transformed into a fully conscious process in *The Merchant of Venice*. The strictly causal logic of the action, noted earlier, is identical to the interplay between Belmont and Venice. Because the multiple plot extends the social range of representation, the traditional ruling class, ensconced in the second or 'green' world, is tested and validated by its ability to master the deepest conflicts of the first world. Shakespeare's goal is thus, once again, to rebind what had been torn asunder into a new unity, under aristocratic leadership. The symbolic repository of value is the great country house, home not of reactionary seigneurial barons but, especially in England, of a rising class increasingly dependent for its revenues on capitalist agriculture and soon to align itself against the monarchy. The play, of course, remains oblivious of these developments: no one does any work at Belmont; there is no source of Portia's apparently endless wealth; and all comers are welcome to a communism of consumption, though not of production.[57] The aristocratic fantasy of Act V, unusually sustained and unironic even for Shakespearean romantic comedy, may accordingly be seen as a formal effort to obliterate the memory of what has preceded.

The treatment of love is also socially hybrid. The fairy-tale-like affair between Bassanio and Portia is constrained by the harsh will of a dead father, is motivated by a concern for property, and is premised upon the traditional sexual hierarchy. But largely for these very reasons, it produces a love match in which virtue counts for more than wealth or beauty, and the wife is, in practice at least, the equal of her husband. Shakespeare's typical synthesis here represents a response to the unsettled position of the late sixteenth-century aristocracy, whose practices and ideology were in the process of transition from a feudal to a bourgeois conception of marriage.[58] The striking characteristic of love in *The Merchant of Venice*, however, is that it is not unambiguously primary. For Leo Salingar, Shakespeare's comedies regularly enact an unresolved conflict in their author's mind 'over the claims of love and the claims of law in Elizabethan society'.[59] But in this play the controlling intellectual pattern requires what is partly a romantic and personal solution to a social problem. From this perspective, however, Act V may also be viewed as a playful and graceful effort by the aristocratic heroine to carry out the serious business of re-establishing the bourgeois assumptions of her marriage, assumptions endangered by the very romantic solution to a social problem that she has just provided.[60]

Since our discussion has been designed to complicate and at times to challenge a Christian interpretation, it is appropriate to conclude by examining directly the religious dimension of the action. The problem is not particularly the tendency of some critics to overemphasise the allegorical meaning of the plot's unfolding,[61] although attempts to incorporate such moments as Shylock's anguished response to Jessica's sale of his ring or his forced, as opposed to his daughter's voluntary, conversion may seem a bit strained.[62] It is rather the difficulty of transforming the play into a paraphrasable meaning of any kind. Founding his argument upon the critical controversy over *The Merchant of Venice*, Norman Rabkin has questioned 'the study of meaning' and the 'bias towards rationality' in general, pronouncing 'all intellection ... reductive' because of 'its consistent suppression of the nature of aesthetic experience'.[63] Although Rabkin's position is obviously opportunistic in its reliance on a notoriously hard case, it is quite true that 'aesthetic experience', especially when induced by more than words alone, cannot be adequately converted into argumentative meaning. At any rate, religious interpretation has proven symptomatically incapable of understanding the play as a comedy, except to the limited extent, suggested above, that romantic comedy and Christian myth share a common ritual movement. On the other hand, as part of an effort to elucidate the overall significance of the work,[64] including its aesthetic value, a demystification of allegorical reading can specify the comic side of *The Merchant of Venice*, in its integral relationship to the popular tradition in the theatre.

Allegory may be viewed as a utopian drive to assimilate alien experience, to create or restore unity where only incoherence and fragmentation are felt, to confer meaning upon a secular existence that seems intrinsically meaningless.[65] Shakespeare's intermittently quasi-allegorical mode in *The Merchant of Venice*, in its moving revelation of the correspondence between human agency and divine plan, represents the most profound version of the Christian

Neoplatonism that flourished especially in the pastoral tragicomedy of the Counter Reformation court.[66] The providential pattern of Neoplatonism in turn moralises the intrigue, a dramatic genre that at times confirms the Russian Formalist insistence on the primacy of form. When the intrigue serves as an end in itself, rather than merely as a means, issues are raised and then dropped not for their cognitive importance, but for their contribution to the plot, whose elegance is meant to point only to the playwright's ingenuity.[67] Ideologically, the intrigue, unlike Shakespearean comedy, proclaims that people are not responsible for their conduct, that social rules have no consequences, that things will work out, that the status quo is secure. But the intrigue itself actually domesticates a still more anarchic impulse toward misrule and liberation that returns us to the root of comedy. Today, literature often censors some fantasy about work;[68] in the Renaissance, however, when hierarchy was more open and alienated labour not yet the norm, dramatic form often submerged an aspiration toward freedom from social convention and constraint. Shakespeare's own religious interpretive strategy in *The Merchant of Venice* thus simultaneously constitutes an act of humane sophistication and a process of repressive concealment.

But the repression is incomplete, and the internal distancing produced by the subversive side of the play justifies our transformation of the learned surface, a comedy mainly in the Dantean sense, into a deep comic structure with affinities to popular festivity, folklore, and ritual. In general, Shakespeare's synthetic enterprise in an age of transition ran a considerable risk: the ultimately anti-absolutist implication, invisible to the playwright, of even a qualified allegiance to the country or to the common law is an obvious example. But these conflicts mainly concern the upper classes, and much of the material that we have considered and still more that could be cited place the work within the neoclassical literary and dramatic tradition. To understand the tensions generated within the synthesis by the popular heritage, to explore the consequences of what we will later identify as the inherent contradiction between artisanal base and absolutist superstructure in the public theatre for which Shakespeare wrote, we must attend to matters of stage position and of dramatic speech, to deviations from the norms of blank verse and Ciceronian prose.[69]

It is easy to demonstrate that the clown, Launcelot Gobbo, has an integral role in *The Merchant of Venice*, that, for example, his abandonment of Shylock for Bassanio foreshadows and legitimates Jessica's similar flight from Jew to Christian.[70] Nonetheless, his physical, social, ideological, and linguistic proximity to the audience comically challenges the primary mimetic action and intellectual design. Launcelot's function may first be illustrated by his penchant for malapropism. In seeking service with the understandably bewildered Bassanio, the socially mobile clown explains that 'the suit is impertinent to myself' (II.ii.130). Having somehow obtained the job, he revisits his old employer to invite him to dinner with his new one: 'I beseech you sir go, my young master doth expect your reproach'; to which Shylock replies, 'So do I his' (II.v.19–21). Shylock's recognition that the apparent misuse of 'reproach' for 'approach' is at some level intentional points to the linguistically and socially subversive connotations of young Gobbo's double meanings, to the 'impertinent' quality, again in two senses, of his speech and conduct.

In his final major appearance, Launcelot begins by expressing his theological concern for Jessica: 'I speak my agitation of the matter: therefore be o' good cheer, for truly I think you are damn'd, – there is but one hope in it that can do you any good, and that is but a kind of bastard hope neither' (III.v.4–7). The confusion of 'agitation' and 'cogitation', the proposed response of 'good cheer' to the prospect of damnation, the ironic play on bastardy – all hopelessly jumble and thus demystify the serious religious issues of the plot. Later in the same scene the clown systematically and wittily misconstrues Lorenzo's apparently straightforward order that the kitchen staff 'prepare for dinner' (III.v.43). His quibbling replies range from an aggressive assertion that the servants, too, are hungry ('they have all stomachs!') to a pretended retreat into deferential humility ('I know my duty' [III.v.44 and 49]). In general, then, from his very first appearance, significantly in soliloquy, when 'the devil himself' prompts him to run from his master 'the Jew ... the very devil incarnation' (II.ii.25–6), Launcelot provides an alternative perspective on the related matters of Christian orthodoxy and social hierarchy. On the one hand, his nonsense parodically demystifies; on the other, it uniquely combines archaic memories and utopian vistas.

This complex vision is compatible with the disturbingly ambiguous implications of Shylock, himself a figure with important ancestors in the popular tradition.[71] Like the vice, he is associated with the devil; is the leading manipulator of the action; elicits from the audience fascination as well as revulsion, laughter as well as terror;

functions as both homiletic foe of Christianity and incisive critic of Christian society; and, accordingly, ranges linguistically from rhetorically polished, mimetic dialogue to popular, self-expressive monologue. Thus, insofar as *The Merchant of Venice* combines a formally dominant, Christian, aristocratic ideology with that ideology's qualification by the alternative and partly oppositional conduct and values of other social classes, the play escapes standard categories of interpretation while strikingly embodying the central creative tension of Shakespearean drama.

II

The preceding comments rest on a number of assumptions that have not been explicitly stated. It may be useful, then, to sketch in some of the mediations between drama and society that make it plausible to think of *The Merchant of Venice* as a response to a conflict between two modes of production. I propose to move from the play to the form of romantic comedy; from there to the theatre as an institution; and from there, finally, to the larger contours of late Tudor England and of Renaissance Europe in general.

Any attempt to assimilate *The Merchant of Venice* to a conventional generic category like romantic comedy is bound to be problematic, however. The work stands apart from Shakespeare's other comedies of the 1590s, romantic or not, and, in addition, from most other comedies of the period, both in the gravity of its subject and in its socio-economic emphasis. Yet the play is entirely typical of comedy in its movement toward resolution and reconciliation, and typical of specifically romantic comedy in its reliance on married love as a means to those ends. Indeed, it is on the embattled terrain of the love-marriage that the ideological significance of the form of romantic comedy is to be located. On the one hand, married love represented a progressive step for women and men alike, consequent upon the relative liberation of women – at least in the realm of ideas – during the age of the Renaissance. On the other, the concluding matrimony of many a comedy may be viewed as a transference, defusing, or suppression of conflict. Romantic comedy, firmly founded on marital love, its climactic weddings presided over by great lords, dramatises the adaptation of the nobility to a new social configuration, an acceptance of change inextricable from a reassertion of dominance.

The form carries out this function in self-consciously theatrical fashion. First, the characters' frequent recourse to disguise or acting is in part a response to the simultaneous instability and rigidity of the aristocracy's position. The improbable situations confronted by the protagonists are at once signs of uncertainty and insecurity, and preferred alternatives to the imposed constraints of daily life. Pastoral, intrigue, lower-class disguise, acting, the atmosphere of holiday or of release – all testify to a utopian impulse toward freedom and an extended range of self-expression. In the end, playing and pretence often help resolve the problems of the action: the main characters forego masquerade and return to the common conduct of a class whose collective sense of purpose has been renewed and reformed by their experience. Yet the conventional resolutions do not entirely negate the liberating moments that have preceded. From this perspective, it is possible to understand a distinctive feature of the form: that its power primarily resides not in social mimesis but in the representation of comic, anarchic freedom issuing in an ideal solution. It is from here, moreover, that its most enduring social criticism usually derives. As a rule, the festive side of a play is inversely proportional to both the social seriousness of the subject and the prominence of other, potentially antagonistic classes. Hence, *The Merchant of Venice*, by its very atypicality, reveals the formal and ideological limits of Renaissance romantic comedy.

At least in England, most such plays were performed in the permanent, public, commercial theatres that emerged in the last quarter of the sixteenth century. What was the character of this new institution? The monarchy, the nobility, the clergy, and the bourgeoisie all crucially shaped the cultural, political, social, and economic functioning of the theatre industry. Yet on matters of immediate production and consumption – actors and companies, stages and playhouses, playwrights and audiences – popular influences were paramount.[72] More precisely, the theatre combined widespread commercialisation, relative absence of a proletariat, and extensive regulation of the conditions of production. It most closely approximated, in other words, the post-feudal, pre-capitalist, fundamentally artisanal mode of economic organisation known to some historians as petty commodity production.

As such, the public theatre constituted part of both the base and the superstructure, and its function in one conflicted with its role in the other. However aristocratic the explicit message of a play might be, the conditions of its production introduced alternative, lower-class effects. For members of the audience, a trip to the theatre was a festive occasion, a species of escape, a form of aspiration, an embodiment of an ideal. Romantic comedy in particular could evoke recollections of popular pagan ritual and thus inspire often legitimate upper-class fears of religious heterodoxy. The same interaction of dramatic form and theatrical mode of production generated socially subversive effects from the recurrent use of lower-class disguise as a means of aristocratic validation; yet stage performance also rationalised and contained such implications, not only by the specific resolution of the plot, but also by the channelling of anarchic instincts that is an inherent part of attendance at a play. The public theatre in this respect offered communal affirmation and social ratification, a means of confronting fear and anger in a manner that promoted reassurance about the existence and legitimacy of a new order. The theatre within the nation, like theatricality within the play, at least in part served to restore a stratified social unity.

That unity was ultimately guaranteed by an incomplete but stable absolutist state that had temporarily abandoned centralising efforts after the unrest of the middle of the century and the still earlier era of initial national consolidation. Like the public theatre, though on a far grander scale, the monarchy both reinforced and depended on the relative cultural homogeneity of town and country, of upper class and lower. Its social basis was thus at least as complex as the stage's. We might note in particular the presence of an increasingly powerful ensemble of capitalist classes, whose crucial influence is unmistakable everywhere from the broadest issues of national policy to the narrowest details of a play such as *The Merchant of Venice*. But in the end, emphasis on the bourgeoisie or analogies between the state and the theatre are profoundly misleading. In England as elsewhere in Europe, absolutism served the interests of the neofeudal aristocracy against those of all other classes, in the epoch of western Europe's transition from feudalism to capitalism.[73] *The Merchant of Venice* is of a piece with this international pattern of development. An English play with an Italian setting, it attempts to come to terms with a stage in the process by which western Europe was undergoing an internal transformation that was soon to make it the dominant power on earth.

III

At this point, it may reasonably be asked what guarantees of validity are possessed by the interpretive categories and procedures that govern the present discussion. Metacommentary, for example, can obviously be turned against itself, opening up a process of infinite regress. The primacy claimed for models of production would seem to be vulnerable to a similar, if not quite identical, challenge. The reply to these objections, such as it is, is the traditional one: the validity of the overall argument offered above depends on that argument's explanatory power. Put another way, the organising hypotheses are designed to provide a paradigm for, and thus to risk falsification across, the range of European drama of the sixteenth and seventeenth centuries, from Ariosto to Racine. Yet explanatory power is hardly a neutral or independent concept, inextricably bound as it is to such questions as what sort of knowledge is being sought and why. And the answers to these questions will ultimately be determined by the critic's sense of what matters most. The founding premise of this essay is – to quote Fredric Jameson once again, this time apparently contradicting his opposition between Marxism and historical narrative – that 'the human adventure is one; ... a single great collective story; ... for Marxism, the collective struggle to wrest a realm of Freedom from a realm of Necessity'.[74]

Finally, if we attempt to use *The Merchant of Venice* to interrogate literary theory, rather than the other way around, it will be evident from what already has been said that the play imposes upon us, in a particularly forceful fashion, the need to account for both its familiarity and its otherness. But it seems more profitable to ask instead what problems the work raises for the specific perspective adopted here. We may approach this matter by noting that Renaissance dramatic theory was fundamentally incapable of grasping the nature or significance of Renaissance dramatic practice, at least in England. This failure was largely a consequence of an inability to theorise the social heterogeneity, and especially the popular elements, that gave the drama its distinctive quality and that have always made it an attractive subject for a radical, activist-oriented criticism. Yet the distance between Renaissance and Marxist theory may not be as great as this formulation suggests. In both instances, the problem is the gap between theory and practice. Marxist theory, whatever its intentions, will tend to reproduce the defects of Renaissance theory whenever it remains isolated, as it currently does, from a now scarcely existent,

larger, contemporary movement for social and political transformation capable of once again uniting learned and popular culture, and
thereby both justifying a theoretical project like the present one and
providing Shakespearean drama with its most resonant context at
least since the early seventeenth century.

From *English Literary History*, 49 (1982), 765–89.

NOTES

[Walter Cohen's essay was followed, in 1985, by his book *Drama of a
Nation: Public Theater in Renaissance England and Spain* which contains a
similar wide-ranging discussion of the drama. Cohen's stance is clearly that
of the Marxist critic; what, therefore, he is interested in is the class society,
values, symbols and ideas that form the context of Shakespeare's play, and
also the material conditions under which the play was produced – the
theatre, the economic system, the real conditions of life that have a direct
bearing upon the production of all goods. In this sense Cohen is interested
in the two main structural features of society described by Marxists as the
base and superstructure, although, as the essay indicates, modern Marxist
criticism is much more subtle than this simple analytical model. In the essay
Cohen quotes from Marx's own essay 'On the Jewish Question' of 1843
which focuses on issues of finance and also political issues, on how the state
and religion are related. Marx argues, briefly, that the basic problem in the
state is the split between self-interest and fellow-feeling, a split leading to
alienation which can only be overcome when need is humanised. In many
ways *The Merchant of Venice* would seem to lend itself almost too readily to
a Marxist reading of this kind unless we recognise the issues inherent in
such a reading, as Cohen clearly does at the end of his essay where he discusses what problems the play raises for the practice and theory of criticism.
All quotations are from the Arden edition of *The Merchant of Venice*, ed.
John Russell Brown (London, 1955). Ed.]

1. Jonathan Culler, *The Pursuit of Signs: Semiotics, Literature,
   Deconstruction* (Ithaca, NY, 1981), p. 65.

2. Terry Eagleton, *Walter Benjamin: Or, Towards a Revolutionary
   Criticism* (London, 1981), pp. 64 and 70.

3. Fredric Jameson, *The Political Unconscious: Narrative as a Socially
   Symbolic Act* (Ithaca, NY, 1981), pp. 9, 139, and 9, respectively.

4. Ibid., p. 14.

5. Robert Weimann, *Structure and Society in Literary History: Studies in
   the History and Theory of Historical Criticism* (Charlottesville, VA,
   1976).

6. Lawrence Danson, *The Harmonies of 'The Merchant of Venice'* (New Haven, CT, 1978).

7. For figural interpretation, see Erich Auerbach, 'Figura', in *Scenes from the Drama of European Literature*, trans. Ralph Manheim (New York, 1959), pp. 11–76. The dialectics of the trial scene are stressed by Danson, *Harmonies*, p. 70; the more general 'dialectical element in Shakespeare's comic structure' is noted by Northrop Frye, *A Natural Perspective: The Development of Shakespearean Comedy and Romance* (New York, 1956), p. 133.

8. For the social and ideological implications of the well-made plot in the novel, see Jameson, 'Metacommentary', *PMLA*, 86 (1971), 12–13. Sigurd Burckhardt, *Shakespearean Meanings* (Princeton, NJ, 1968), pp. 206–36, offers a symbolic modernist, self-referential analysis of the rigours of the plot in *The Merchant of Venice*.

9. For this argument, see Richard Levin, 'Refuting Shakespeare's Endings – Part II', *Modern Philology*, 75 (1977), 132–58.

10. See C. L. Barber, *Shakespeare's Festive Comedy: A Study of Dramatic Form and Its Relation to Social Custom* (Princeton, NJ, 1959), pp. 163–91. Frank Kermode, 'The Mature Comedies', in *Early Shakespeare*, ed. John Russell Brown and Bernard Harris, Stratford-upon-Avon Studies, no. 3 (New York, 1961), pp. 220–4; and Paul N. Siegel, 'Shylock, the Elizabethan Puritan, and Our Own World', in *Shakespeare in His Time and Ours* (Notre Dame, IN, 1968), pp. 337–8.

11. Danson's argument is a sophisticated version of this approach.

12. See Madeleine Doran, *Endeavors of Art: A Study of Form in Elizabethan Drama* (Madison, WI, 1954), pp. 318–19, 347, and 362–4.

13. Auerbach, *Mimesis: The Representation of Reality in Western Literature*, trans. Willard S. Trask (Princeton, NJ, 1953), pp. 314–15, 316, 320, 325, and 328, offers elements of this reading, though also acknowledging that the resolution of the play precludes a tragic interpretation. The stage tradition described by Brown, 'The Realization of Shylock: A Theatrical Criticism', in *Early Shakespeare*, ed. Brown and Harris, pp. 187–209, seems to fall primarily into this category.

14. Anselm Schlösser, 'Dialectic in *The Merchant of Venice*', *Zeitschrift für Anglistik und Amerikanistik*, 23 (1975), 5–11; Marc Shell, 'The Wether and the Ewe: Verbal Usury in *The Merchant of Venice*', *Kenyon Review*, ns 1 (1979), 65–92; Burton Hatlen, 'Feudal and Bourgeois Concepts of Value in *The Merchant of Venice*', in *Shakespeare: Contemporary Critical Approaches*, ed. Harry R. Garvin (Lewisburg, 1980), pp. 91–105; and René Girard, '"To Entrap the Wisest": A Reading of *The Merchant of Venice*', in *Literature and Society*, ed. Edward W. Said, Selected Papers from the English Institute, 1978, NS 3 (Baltimore, MD, 1980),

pp. 100–19. For a more detailed discussion of this debate over the play, see Danson, *Harmonies*, pp. 1–18.

15. Leo Salingar, *Shakespeare and the Traditions of Comedy* (Cambridge, 1974), pp. 298–325.

16. For a theoretical statement and practical application of this argument, see Ralph W. Rader, 'Fact, Theory, and Literary Explanation', *Critical Inquiry*, 1 (1974), 249–50 and 258–61.

17. John W. Draper, 'Usury in *The Merchant of Venice*', *Modern Philology*, 33 (1935), 37–47; E. C. Pettet, '*The Merchant of Venice* and the Problem of Usury', *Essays and Studies*, 31 (1945), 19–33; and Siegel, 'Shylock'.

18. Thomas Bell, *The Specvlation of Vsurie* (London, 1596), A2r. For similar statements, see Thomas Lodge, *An Alarum Against Vsurers* (London, 1584), E1r, and Roger Fenton, *A Treatise of Vsurie* (London, 1611), B1r.

19. R. H. Tawney, Introd. to *A Discourse Upon Usury by Way of Dialogue and Orations, for the Better Variety and More Delight of All Those That Shall Read this Treatise* (1572), by Thomas Wilson (New York, 1925), pp. 1–172. See also Lawrence Stone, *The Crisis of the Aristocracy, 1558–1641* (Oxford, 1965), pp. 158, 183, and 541–3.

20. L. C. Knights, *Drama and Society in the Age of Jonson* (London, 1937), p. 11. The same assumption governs Knights's comments on usury, pp. 127–30, 164–8, and passim.

21. Some of these are pointed out by Draper, 'Usury', pp. 45–6, and Pettet, 'Problem of Usury', pp. 26–7.

22. Miles Mosse, *The Arraignment and Conviction of Vsurie* (London, 1595), C3v. See also H. A. [Henry Arthington?], *Provision for the Poore, Now in Penurie* (London, 1597), C2v, and Philip Caesar, *A General Discovrse Against the Damnable Sect of Vsurers* (London, 1578), the title page of which refers to '*these/later daies, in which, Charitie being ba-/nished, Couetousnes hath got/ten the vpper hande*'.

23. *The Death of Vsvry, or the Disgrace of Vsvrers* (London, 1594), E1r. The contrary valuation of merchant and usurer may also be found in Nicolas Sanders, *A Briefe Treatise of Vsurie* (Lovanii, 1568), D1r, and in Lodge and Thomas Greene's *A Looking Glasse for London and England* (1590), ed. Tetsumaro Hayashi (Metuchen, NJ, 1970), I.iii. and III.i. A sympathetic view of merchants is taken for granted – a position impossible at the time with regard to usurers – in John Browne, *The Marchants Avizo* (London, 1591), and in *A True Report of Sir Anthony Shierlies Journey* (London, 1600).

24. Draper, 'Usury', pp. 46–7; Pettet, 'Problem of Usury', pp. 19, 29, and 32; and Siegel, 'Shylock', pp. 249 and 252.

25. Draper, 'Usury', p. 39, and Pettet, 'Problem of Usury', pp. 19, 22, 23, 27, and 29.

26. Bell, *Specvlation of Vsurie*, B4v and C3v, is again representative. Medieval attitudes toward merchants are surveyed by Tawney, *Religion and the Rise of Capitalism: A Historical Study*, Holland Memorial Lectures, 1922 (New York, 1954), pp. 20–39. *A Discovery of the Great Svbtiltie and Wonderful Wisedom of the Italians* (London, 1591), B1r, partly attributes Italy's success in economically exploiting other nations to the country's vigorous trade.

27. Siegel, 'Shylock', and A. A. Smirnov, *Shakespeare: A Marxist Interpretation* (New York, 1936), p. 35.

28. Danson, *Harmonies*, pp. 78–80, and T. A., *The Massacre of Money* (London, 1602), C2v.

29. Mosse, *Arraignment*, F2r. Tawney, *Religion*, pp. 43–4, elaborates on this point, and W. H. Auden, *The Dyer's Hand and Other Essays* (New York, 1968), pp. 227–8, notes that Shylock does not demand usury.

30. The Arden edition of *The Merchant of Venice*, ed. Brown (London, 1955), I.iii.148–9. Subsequent references are noted in the text.

31. Barber, *Shakespeare's Festive Comedy*, p. 169; *Whartons Dreame* (London, 1578), A3r; and for a striking theatrical anticipation, Robert Wilson, *The Three Ladies of London* (1581), ed. John S. Farmer (1911), D4v.

32. Stephen J. Greenblatt, 'Marlowe, Marx, and Anti-Semitism', *Critical Inquiry*, 5 (1978), 291–307, emphasises Shylock's irrationality, even madness. My discussion of *The Merchant of Venice* is generally indebted to this essay.

33. 'English Folly and Italian Vice – The Moral Landscape of John Marston', in *Jacobean Theatre*, ed. John Russell Brown and Bernard Harris, Stratford-upon-Avon Studies, No. 1 (London, 1960), p. 95. For reservations about conflating late Elizabethan and Jacobean Italianism, see pp. 91–4. For comments on Venetian trade, see Robert Johnson's translation of Giovanni Botero, *Relations of the Most Famovs Kingdoms and Common-weales thorovgh the World* (London, 1611), Gg2v–Gg3v, and George Sandys, *A Relation of a Journey* (London, 1615), B1r.

34. Brian Pullan, *Rich and Poor in Renaissance Venice: The Social Institutions of a Catholic State, to 1620* (Oxford, 1971), pp. 538–621, and Fernand Braudel, *The Mediterranean and the Mediterranean World in the Age of Philip II*, trans. Siân Reynolds (London, 1973), II, 817 and 823. Fynes Moryson, *Shakespeare's Europe: A Survey of the Conditions of Europe at the End of the Sixteenth Century: Being*

Unpublished Chapters of Fynes Moryson's 'Itinerary' (1617), ed. Charles Hughes, 2nd edn (1903; rpt. New York, 1967), p. 488, gives a reasonably accurate picture of the position of Italian Jews.

35. Benjamin N. Nelson, 'The Usurer and the Merchant Prince: Italian Businessmen and the Ecclesiastical Law of Restitution, 1100–1550', *Journal of Economic History*, Supp. 7 (1947), 104–22, an essay deeply aware of the parallels to *The Merchant of Venice*.

36. Pullan, *Rich and Poor*, pp. 431–537.

37. Wylliam Thomas, *The Historye of Italye* (London, 1549), U4v–X1r, Y2v and Y3v; Lewes Lewkenor's translation of Gasparo Contarini, *The Commonwealth and Gouernment of Venice* (London, 1599), T2r; and Moryson, *An Itinerary* (London, 1617), H1v–H2r.

38. D4v. See also Fenton, *Treatise*, P4v, and, for background, Tawney, Introd. to *A Discourse*, pp. 125–7, and *Religion*, p. 53; Draper, 'Usury', pp. 45–6; and Nelson, *The Idea of Usury: From Tribal Brotherhood to Universal Otherhood*, 2nd edn (Chicago, 1969), p. 73 n. 2. Greenblatt seems to be the only critic to suggest a parallel between Antonio and the Monti di Pietà.

39. For fiscalism versus mercantilism, see Immanuel Wallerstein, *The Modern World-System: Capitalist Agriculture and the Origins of the European World-Economy in the Sixteenth Century* (New York, 1974), pp. 137–8 and 149. For possible problems with this hypothesis, as applied to Italy, see Pullan, *Rich and Poor*, p. 451. Greenblatt employs Wallerstein's paradigm to help explain *The Merchant of Venice*, but he does not seem aware that his argument consequently contradicts the position of those scholars, whom he also cites, who rely on the anti-usury tracts. See his n. 5.

40. Nelson, 'The Usurer and the Merchant Prince', 120–2.

41. For similar perceptions, see Barber, *Shakespeare's Festive Comedy*, p. 191, and Frye, *Natural Perspective*, p. 98.

42. Curiously, Brown, Introd. to his edition of *The Merchant of Venice*, p. xxxix, denies that the play is anti-Semitic.

43. Danson, *Harmonies*, pp. 148–50, argues that Shakespeare allows Shylock a fairly strong case, but Draper, 'Usury', pp. 43–4, seems more persuasive in taking the opposite position.

44. See, for example, *Three Ladies*, D3v.

45. Robert Peterson's translation of Botero, *A Treatise, Concerning the Causes of the Magnificencie and Greatnes of Cities* (London, 1606), 13v.

46. Danson, *Harmonies*, p. 55.

47. Marx's remarks may be found in 'Contribution to the Critique of Hegel's *Philosophy of Right*: Introduction', in *The Marx–Engels Reader*, ed. Robert C. Tucker, 2nd edn (New York, 1978), p. 55; 'On the Jewish Question', in the *Marx–Engels Reader*, pp. 47–52; *The Process of Capitalist Production*, trans. Samuel Moore and Edward Aveling, vol. 1 of *Capital: A Critique of Political Economy*, ed. Frederick Engels (New York, 1967), pp. 287–8; and *The Process of Capitalist Production As a Whole*, vol. III of *Capital*, ed. Engels (New York, 1967), pp. 593–610 and 32ȝ–38.

48. *Capital*, I, 487.

49. The term is from Brents Stirling, Introd. to his edition of *The Merchant of Venice*, in *William Shakespeare: The Complete Works*, gen. ed. Alfred Harbage (Baltimore, MD, 1969), p. 213.

50. This position is most fully developed by Danson, *Harmonies*. See especially pp. 123–5.

51. For an early and crucial stage of this debate, see Ernst Bloch, Georg Lukács, Bertolt Brecht, Walter Benjamin, and Theodor Adorno, *Aesthetics and Politics*, trans. and ed. Ronald Taylor, Afterword by Jameson (London, 1977). Contemporary positions appear in Louis Althusser, 'The "Piccolo Teatro": Bertolazzi and Brecht', in *For Marx*, trans. Ben Brewster (London, 1977), pp. 129–51; Terry Eagleton, *Criticism and Ideology: A Study in Marxist Literary Theory* (London, 1976), pp. 102–61; and Pamela McCallum, 'Ideology and Cultural Theory', *Canadian Journal of Political and Social Theory*, 3 (1979), 131–43.

52. A recent attempt to define the meaning of the plot in terms of Act IV is Alice N. Benston's 'Portia, the Law, and the Tripartite Structure of *The Merchant of Venice*', *Shakespeare Quarterly*, 30 (1979), 367–85. See also Brown, Introd., p. li, and Danson, *Harmonies*, pp. 82–96 and 118–25. On the relationship between trial and drama, see Herbert Lindenberger, *Historical Drama: The Relation of Literature to Reality* (Chicago, 1975), pp. 21–3.

53. W. Gordon Zeeveld, *The Temper of Shakespeare's Thought* (New Haven, CT, 1974), pp. 141–2. Other discussions of the play against the background of common law and Chancery include Maxine MacKay, '*The Merchant of Venice*: A Reflection of the Early Conflict between Courts of Law and Courts of Equity', *Shakespeare Quarterly*, 15 (1964), 371–5; George Williams Keeton, *Shakespeare's Legal and Political Background* (New York, 1967), pp. 132–52; and E. F. J. Tucker, 'The Letter of the Law in *The Merchant of Venice*', *Shakespeare Survey*, 29 (1976), 93–101. For a general review of commentaries on the legal situation in the play, see O. Hood Phillips, *Shakespeare and the Lawyers* (London, 1972), pp. 91–118.

54. Stone, *The Causes of the English Revolution* (London, 1972), pp. 62, 75, 97–8, 103–5, and 114.

55. Zeeveld, *Temper of Shakespeare's Thought*, p. 154 n. 20, and Tucker, 'Letter of the Law', pp. 98–101, both emphasise that Portia's argument and solution occur wholly within the canons of common law. But this particular integration of letter and spirit would have been impossible without Chancery's influence. For the popular pre-feudal bases of English law, see Perry Anderson, *Passages from Antiquity to Feudalism* (London, 1974), p. 160, and *Lineages of the Absolutist State* (London, 1974), pp. 115–16.

56. Noël Salomon, *Recherches sur le thème paysan dans la 'comedia' au temps de Lope de Vega* (Bordeaux, 1965), passim, esp. pp. 167–96, 222–3, and 451–73; Raymond Williams, *The Country and the City* (New York, 1973), pp. 18–21; and Elliot Krieger, 'The Dialectics of Shakespeare's Comedies', *Minnesota Review*, 7 (1976), 85–8.

57. Stone, *Causes*, pp. 105–8, and Williams, *Country and City*, pp. 22–34.

58. Stone, *Crisis*, pp. 589–671.

59. Salingar, *Traditions of Comedy*, p. 312.

60. On the special role of love in this play, see R. F. Hill, '*The Merchant of Venice* and the Pattern of Romantic Comedy', *Shakespeare Survey*, 28 (1975), 75–87. For the problem of marriage in Act V, see Shell, 'The Wether and the Ewe', pp. 86–7.

61. This is the case in Barbara K. Lewalski's distinguished essay, 'Biblical Allusion and Allegory in *The Merchant of Venice*', *Shakespeare Quarterly*, 13 (1962), 327–43.

62. See Danson's efforts, *Harmonies*, pp. 136–9 and 164–9.

63. 'Meaning and Shakespeare', in *Shakespeare 1971: Proceedings of the World Shakespeare Congress Vancouver, August 1971*, ed. Clifford Leech and J. M. R. Margeson (Toronto, 1971), pp. 89–106. The quoted passages appear on p. 100.

64. This distinction is pursued, for different purposes, by E. D. Hirsch, Jr, 'Introduction: Meaning and Significance', in *The Aims of Interpretation* (Chicago, 1976), pp. 1–13.

65. Jameson, 'Metacommentary', p. 10, and 'Criticism in History', in *Weapons of Criticism: Marxism in America and the Literary Tradition*, ed. Norman Rudich (Palo Alto, CA, 1976), pp. 41–2.

66. Louise George Clubb, 'La mimesi della realtà invisibile nel dramma pastorale italiano e inglese del tardo rinascimento', *Misure Critiche*, 4 (1974), 65–92.

67. On the intrigue, see Laura Brown, 'The Divided Plot: Tragicomic Form in the Restoration', *ELH*, 47 (1980), 67–79.

68. Jameson, 'Metacommentary', p. 17.

69. For Shakespeare and Ciceronian prose, see Jonas A. Barish, *Ben Jonson and the Language of Prose Comedy* (Cambridge, 1960), pp. 1–40. Brian Vickers, 'Shakespeare's Use of Rhetoric', in *A New Companion to Shakespeare Studies*, ed. Kenneth Muir and S. Schoenbaum (Cambridge, 1971), pp. 83–98, demonstrates that classical rhetoric informs the language of high and low characters alike. The remainder of the present discussion is primarily indebted to Robert Weimann's *Shakespeare and the Popular Tradition in the Theater: Studies in the Social Dimension of Dramatic Form and Function*, ed. Robert Schwartz (Baltimore, MD, 1978).

70. Geoffrey Bullough, *Narrative and Dramatic Sources of Shakespeare*, I (London, 1957), 457, and Frye, *Natural Perspective*, p. 97.

71. Frye, *Natural Perspective*, p. 93, sees the affinity between the two characters, though in somewhat different terms. Bernard Spivack, *Shakespeare and the Allegory of Evil: The History of a Metaphor in Relation to His Major Villains* (New York, 1958), generally tends to exclude Shylock from the vice tradition, but he neglects most of the relevant evidence.

72. Although this conclusion rests on the work of a number of contemporary scholars, most of the relevant data may still be found in E. K. Chambers, *The Elizabethan Stage*, 4 vols (Oxford, 1923).

73. Anderson, *Lineages of the Absolutist State*.

74. Jameson, *The Political Unconscious*, p. 19.

4

Shakespeare and the Jews

JAMES SHAPIRO

Roughly a hundred years have passed now, since the Anglo-Jewish Historical Exhibition of 1887, and the founding of the Jewish Historical Society of England in 1893, landmark events in history of scholarship about Shakespeare and the Jews. From the archival work of Lucien Wolf, Cecil Roth, Edgar Samuel, and many others, a picture of the small Jewish community of early modern England has gradually come into focus, a community that existed, for the most part in London, between the expulsion of the Jews in 1290 and the so-called 'readmission' under Oliver Cromwell in 1656. No longer can scholars insist – though, surprisingly, many on both sides of the Atlantic still do – that there were no Jews in Shakespeare's England. Perhaps a hundred or more Jews might have jostled Shakespeare in the crowded streets of London, and we know from Spanish Inquisition records and the complaints of various Catholic ambassadors, that Jewish holidays like Passover and Yom Kippur were celebrated in England in the late sixteenth century.

Virtually all those Jews practised their faith in secret – since most were of Spanish or Portuguese descent, *marranos*, they surely had had enough experience with disguising their beliefs because of their experience of the Inquisition, far harsher than any repression they might face in England. A Londoner in early Stuart England, curious about what the word '*marrano*' meant, might have turned for help to John Florio's dictionary, *Queen Anne's New World of Words* (London, 1611), where the term is described as 'a nick-name for Spaniards, that is, one descended of Jewes or Infidels and whose Parents were never christened, but for to save their goods will say they are Christians'. But Florio's definition seems to raise more questions than it resolves: is this a nickname for all Spaniards? Were the *marranos* simply dissimulators or did they hold any religious beliefs at all? Were they Jews, infidels, or Christians? Lapsed Jews? Fake Christians? How could one know for sure, after all, since to save their goods they 'will say they are Christians' anyway? We have here some glimpse of the problem that Jews caused for the emerging categories of social, national, racial, and religious difference in early modern England.

Had Shakespeare wished to speak with someone who had converted from Judaism to Christianity he could have done so easily enough: there was a converts' house in London, the *Domus Conversorum*, which was in existence on Chancery Lane from 1232, when it was founded by King Henry III as a home for poor Jewish converts to Christianity. Throughout the sixteenth century, with the exception of the years 1551–1578, there were always a tiny handful of residents there. One of the residents, Nathaniel Menda, had been publicly converted at All Hallows Church, Lombard Street, London, in 1577 by John Foxe, more famous for his *Book of Martyrs*. We learn from Foxe's *Sermon Preached at the Christening of a Certain Jew, at London* (London, 1578), that Menda had lived in London as a Jew before his conversion, having been 'transported from out the uttermost parts of Barbarie into England, and conversant amongst us, by the space of five whole yeeres', before his baptism. The sermon is a remarkable document for what it says about Christian beliefs about Jews in Elizabethan London. In his long discourse Foxe addresses the 'circumcised Race' directly, decrying their 'intolerable Scorpionlike savagenes, so furiously boyling against the innocent infants of the Christian Gentiles: and the rest of your haynous abominations, insatiable butcheries, treasons, frensies, and madnes'.

For his part, Menda dutifully added his *Confession of Faith, which Nathaneal a Jewe borne, made before the Congregation in the Parish Church of Alhallowes in Lombard Street at London* (London, 1578), which was 'written first by him selfe in the Spanish tongue and now translated into English for the more benefite of the godlie Reader'. In his *Confession* Menda promises: '[I will] utterly forsake my former wayes and the steps that my nation walketh in, leaving with them not only that false looking for an other Christ, but my name also which was given me at my circumcision (being Iehuda) though in it selfe it be honourable: desiring that as I have received a new gift from the Lord, so in token thereof I may be called Nathaneal.' The sermon and confession, bound together, were popular enough to be cited a half-century later.

There were other Jews as well in London, including Dr Roderigo Lopez, Elizabeth's personal physician, put to death in 1594 for allegedly conspiring to poison the Queen. And Roger Prior has recently described how a smaller Jewish group of Italian descent, the Lupos, Comys, and Bassanos, brought over by Henry VIII around 1540, were court musicians. Predictably, Jews, usually converted ones, could also be found teaching Hebrew at Oxford and Cambridge, or helping Bodley with the Hebrew catalogue at the University Library. One of the more interesting Jews – in part because he was unwilling to deny his Judaism – was Joachim Gaunse, a mining expert from Prague who lived openly as a Jew until his run-in with a Protestant minister in Bristol in 1589. Outraged with Gaunse's evasive response to Christ's authority – 'What needed the almightie God to have a sonne, if he is not almightie?' – the Reverend Curtys and the mayor and alderman of Bristol referred the dangerous matter to the Privy Council, and Gaunse, despite his earlier service to the state and his participation in Raleigh's Roanoke expedition, was probably hustled out of the country – for that is the last we hear of him.

The lives of many other, anonymous Jews in England will necessarily remain unrecorded – we have just glimpses of a few, like the Jew that Sir John Lancaster took with him from London to serve as his translator in his East Indies expedition; or the unnamed Jew asked to assist in translating a letter sent to Queen Elizabeth from Constantinople, concerning Hugh Broughton's efforts to convert the Jews. By the end of the sixteenth century, years before the full-fledged philosemitism of the early seventeenth century, so ably described by David Katz, Richard Popkin, and Jonathan Israel,[1] interactions between Jews and the English were more and more frequent, not simply in London, but in the foreign ports in Morocco and Turkey where English merchants were trading, and on the Continent as well, especially Antwerp and Amsterdam, where Jewish communities were flourishing.

Frustratingly, the findings of these Anglo-Jewish historians have yet to find their way into mainstream histories of England. Gavin Langmuir, a Scot and something of an outsider in the matter, has surveyed what he calls 'Majority History', and has concluded that having inherited 'a historiographic tradition hostile toward or ignorant of Jews, or both, and writing for a society little interested in Jewish history or more or less hostile to Jews, historians of the majority have been little attracted to Jewish history'.[2]

One would have hoped that the 'new historicism' (popularised in the United States for the past decade or so by Stephen Greenblatt and his followers), an historical approach dedicated in large measure to writing the history of the Other in the Renaissance, would have compensated for the relative silence of the mainstream historians of early modern English culture when they came to the matter of the Jews. Disappointingly, this has not occurred. Though the new historicists have rediscovered virtually every marginalised Other imaginable in early modern England – including witches, hermaphrodites, Moors, cross-dressers, Turks, sodomites, criminals, prophets, and vagabonds – they have steered carefully around the Other of Others in the Renaissance, the Jews (all the more strange, perhaps, because so many of these scholars are themselves of Jewish descent). Greenblatt himself has written that 'there is no "Jewish Question" in Marlowe's England', and that the Jews in their real historical situation are finally incidental in works like Marlowe's *The Jew of Malta*.[3]

I have not come here today with any new discovery that Shakespeare might have known Jews personally, nor have I any new Jews to add to the lists compiled – and still being enlarged – by Anglo-Jewish scholars. I am a literary and cultural historian, and the kinds of questions I'm interested in exploring have largely been ignored by both Anglo-Jewish and mainstream British historians. Simply put, *how* and *why* were the English so obsessed with Jews in the sixteenth and seventeenth centuries? The Elizabethan obsession with Jews is far out of proportion with their actual presence and role in late sixteenth-century English social and political life. Yet when we turn to Tudor and Stuart drama, the chronicles of English history, travel literature, and sermons, let alone the various discourses of trade, millenarianism, usury, magic, race, gender, and nationalism we find an unusual and persistent interest in the Jews. What, ultimately, defines the difference of the Jews? Were they a nation or still a nation in their diaspora (John Donne calls them 'a whole nation of Cains, fugitives, and vagabonds')? Some Englishmen even believed that after the expulsion from England the Jews had gone to Scotland (why else, they argued, were the Scots so frugal and hated blood pudding). The international-nation of Jews clearly complicated the emerging notion of the 'nation' in early modern England.

Alternatively, were the Jews, as the Spanish believed, a separate race, one that could contaminate the blood lines of Christians? Or were the Jews defined simply by their religious practices? If this were so, what happened when radical Puritans, seeking to emulate Old Testament rituals, began to resemble Jews? Anne Curtyn, for example, was committed to New Prison at Clerkenwell in 1649 'for being a professed Jew and causing children to be circumcised', though she was clearly a Christian and a follower of John Traske. While Curtyn was released from prison, Traske himself was not so fortunate: we learn from John Chamberlain's letter of 14 February 1618 that Traske had been stamped with the letter *J* on his forehead 'in token that hee broached Jewish opinions'. In Traske's case insult was added to injury: 'William Hudson, a treatist of the Court, adds that [Traske] was also ordered to eat swine's flesh whilst in prison, an admirable example from Hudson's point of view of the Star Chamber's habit of making the punishment fit the crime where possible.' *Who*, or *what* then, for the confused Elizabethans, was a Jew?

Clearly, even as the Elizabethans have something to tell us about the Jews, their obsession with Jews tells us even more about the Elizabethans. The kind of Anglo-Jewish history that remains to be written is one that explains why such powerful myths as those of ritual murder and the wandering Jew originated in Medieval England, with bloody historical consequences throughout Europe in ensuing centuries. Ultimately, it is not the raw number of Jews in early modern England that is of interest as much as the kind of cultural preoccupation they became, the way that Jews complicated a great range of social, economic, legal, political, and religious discourses, and turned other questions into Jewish questions as well.

In trying to redress these omissions, and in trying at the same time to explain how the problems posed by 'Jews' were central to English conceptions of both difference and of national identity, I focus upon how these cultural negotiations are worked out in Shakespeare's *The Merchant of Venice*. In its resituation of the Jew in terms of various cultural myths, as well as within the nascent discourses of nation, gender, and race, Shakespeare's play explores what may be described as a cultural identity crisis, an insistence on difference that ends by undermining the very terms of identity by which that difference is affirmed: male, Christian, English.

I

In exploring the Jews as source and site of cultural anxiety in *The Merchant of Venice* I focus today even more specifically on 'the pound of flesh' narrative and its relationship to the myth – still current in Shakespeare's day (and indeed, still promulgated in England as late as the 1930s by Arnold Spenser Leese) – that Jews committed ritual murder. How this myth passed into history, and from history into literature and back into history (with terrible consequences for the Jews persecuted for this alleged crime in Europe) is part of the larger context of my talk. The basic narrative of this myth is familiar enough and can be dated back to its English origins in 1144, in Thomas of Monmouth's account of William of Norwich. By the late fifteenth century, with the invention of the printing press, the myth spread rapidly through Europe, disseminated in works like Hartmann Schedel's *Nuremberg Chronicle*, which recounts and gruesomely illustrates the ritual slaughter of Simon of Trent, until a master narrative emerged: the accusations generally included the abduction of a Christian boy by the Jews around Easter time, followed by his circumcision, then execution, the blood being used, often cannibalistically, for a range of mysterious purposes, ranging from the preparation of matzot, to anointing rabbis, as part of the circumcision rite, stopping menstrual bleeding, and to paint the bodies of the dead.

The various connections between *The Merchant of Venice* and the discourse of ritual murder extend beyond the physical act of taking the knife to Christian flesh to encompass its setting at Easter-time, cannibalism and abduction. Given the recurrent emphasis on Christ's crucifixion and the cannibalistic use of Christian blood, it is no accident that accusations of blood-libel repeatedly occurred during Easter week. Notably, the only specific mention of the time of year in *The Merchant of Venice* is to this holiday: Launcelot, Shylock's servant, says that it 'was not for nothing that my nose fell a-bleeding on Black Monday last at six a'clock i' th' morning'. Black Monday was Easter Monday, so called in commemoration of the freezing cold Easter of 1360. While Launcelot's superstitious remark offers only the slightest connection to the popular myth of ritual murder, it may have called to mind the set of popular beliefs associated with Easter. The most prominent was the annual abduction of a Christian boy. Another, stemming from the period before the expulsion of the Jews from England, had to do with Christians like

Launcelot who were servants to Jews. D'Blossiers Tovey records in *Anglia Judaica* (Oxford, 1738) an unusual royal proclamation 'against Christian Women's entring into Service with Jews', in response to alleged Jewish mistreatment of Christian wet-nurses at Easter. He explains that

> The Reason of which Prohibition (particularly with Relation to their being Nurses) is mention'd by none of our Historians. But I suspect it to have been that foolish Custom, which at this time prevail'd amongst the Jews, of obliging them to milk themselves into a Privie, for three Days after Easter-Day; for fear that the Body and Blood of Jesus Christ, which all Christians were oblig'd to receive upon that Holy Festival, shou'd, by Incorporation, be transfus'd into their Children.

Christ's sacrifice, physically embodied in the Eucharist, was central to the Easter celebration. And the celebration, which involved the taking and eating of the blood and body of Christ, finds its inversion in the Jewish devouring the blood of Christian children. Trace elements of Jewish cannibalism are to be found in Shakespeare's play, where Shylock is repeatedly described as feasting upon his Christian enemies' bodies. We learn in his first appearance that he 'will feed fat the ancient grudge' he bears Antonio, and he later adds that he'll 'go in hate, to feed upon / The prodigal Christians'. When asked by Salerio what possible use he could have for Antonio's flesh Shylock replies, 'To bait fish withal; if it will feed nothing else, it will feed my revenge.' And Gratiano, calling Shylock 'wolfish, bloody, starved, and ravenous', compares him to a predatory wolf who has fed on human flesh and is 'hanged for slaughter'.

Yet another example whereby features of the myth of ritual murder recur in inverted form in Shakespeare's play concerns the abduction of the innocent male child. Where in the traditional accusations of ritual murder it is the Jew who steals away the Christian child, in *The Merchant of Venice* it is the Christian Lorenzo who, in Antonio's words, 'lately stole [Shylock's] daughter'. In this reversal the abducted Jewish child '[b]ecome[s] a Christian'. The connection to the blood ritual plot is strengthened when Jessica acknowledges that she is 'transformed to a boy' when leaving her father's house, giving her cross-dressing a significance that has to do with multiple discourses, gendered and religious. Launcelot underscores the dark undercurrent of ritual murder accusations and the ensuing relations against Jews when he punningly warns Jessica in the proverbial jingle: 'There will come a Christian by / Will be worth a Jewes eye.'

Lorenzo is indeed the Christian for whom Jessica waits; but the 'worth' of the proverb has less to do with the value of a lover than the revenge exacted upon the Jewish community.

Tovey offers an anecdote that draws together the various strands of such revenge and threatened circumcision, set in motion by the abduction of a Jewish daughter in the year 1260, when

> all the Jews in England were commanded by this King [Henry III], to change their Religion; having their Children, under six years of Age, taken from them, and brought up Christians: which he says was occa-sion'd by the Marriage of a Christian Priest with a Jewish Woman, whom he was desperately in Love with, but cou'd obtain from her Parents on no other Condition than Circumcision; which so enrag'd the Populace, that they wou'd have burnt all the Jews alive, if the King, to pacify them, had not given the aforementioned Orders.

And Act IV of *The Merchant of Venice* reproduces a number of key features of ritual murder accusations and trials, the most striking of which is its visual representation of the secret and unobserved (except in pictures or plays) bloody rituals of the Jews. We actually watch Shylock sharpen his knife, as Antonio stands with his bosom bared, prepared to meet his fate at the hands of a murderous Jew. The trial in this scene also moves the conflict to a courtroom, the site of legit-imate (though contested) legal jurisdiction so crucial to the blood-libel cases. At the same time it reproduces the Jewish strategy of insistently refusing to provide motives for the murderous intent. Finally, it offers the retribution brought upon the Jew for threatening the life of a Christian. In covering this ground Act IV of *The Merchant of Venice* offers a fantasy solution to some of the pressing social, political, and economic contradictions of early modern European society: a world in which usury was balanced against the need for venture capital; where emerging nationalism was threatened by the internationalism of groups like the Jews who were a 'nation' and yet scattered over the world, especially in the economic sphere; where local authority was pitted against central control; where social anxieties about religious faith could be exorcised by the conversion of the Jew.

II

My particular interest today, is on that unusual aspect of the myth of ritual murder: that Jews took the knife to Christians, circumcis-ing, and in some cases, castrating, their Christian foes. When my undergraduates, reading *The Merchant of Venice* for the first time, learn of Shylock's desire to exact 'an equal pound' of Antonio's 'fair flesh, to be *cut off* and taken / In what part of your body pleaseth me', they often wonder just what part of Antonio's body Shylock has in mind. Those of you all too familiar with the play may easily forget that it is not until the trial scene in Act IV that this riddle is solved and we learn that Shylock intends to cut Antonio's 'breast' near his heart. But why, my students then ask, is Antonio's breast the spot most pleasing to Shylock? And why, the more literal wonder, would one cut 'off' and not 'out' a pound of flesh from 'nearest his heart'? Often, one of my students who has not read through to the trial scene will wonder whether Shylock, in exacting that pound of flesh, intends to castrate Antonio – and his or her classmates laugh nervously.

I want to follow up on that line of thought, since for Elizabethans, no less than for modern audiences familiar with theories of castration anxiety, the phrase 'cut off' could easily suggest taking the knife to a male victim's genitals. In fact, the judgement read to convicted male traitors and felons in Shakespeare's day includes the decree that 'at the place of execution ... you are to be hanged by the neck, and being alive cut down, *and your privy-members to be cut off*'. Moreover, the word 'flesh' was the standard euphemism for penis, not only in the various Elizabethan Bibles, but in popular writing as well: the extended play on male erection and tumescence in Sonnet 151, culminating in the lines 'flesh stays no farther reason, But rising at thy name doth point out thee', is typical. Castration is never far from the centre of the sexual anxieties that pervade *The Merchant of Venice*; allusions to it occur not only in Antonio's description of himself as 'a tainted wether', that is, a castrated ram, but also in Salerio's joke about Jessica having Shylock's 'stones [or testicles] upon her', and Gratiano's comment about 'mar[ring] the young clerk's pen [or penis]'.

I want to distinguish my argument (which is an historical one) from earlier psychoanalytic, feminist, and philosophical ones that point at similar conclusions. It was Freud who first argued that '[c]ircumcision is unconsciously equated with castration', and it was Freud's most Jewish disciple, Theodore Reik, who applied this insight to *The Merchant of Venice*, and proposed that Shylock threatened Antonio with such a cut.[4] That similar readings have been proposed by the feminist scholar Marjorie Garber and the philosopher Stanley Cavell in the context of broader arguments about gender and identity in Shakespeare suggests that Shylock's threat is a site of multiple signification – and is situated at the heart of the cultural anxiety explored – and produced – in the play.

These psychoanalytic insights dovetail with my historical argument about ritual murder. Thus, Samuel Purchas, drawing upon the notes of John Selden, can write in 1626 of 'One cruell and (to speake the properest phrase) *Jewish crime* was usuall amongst them, every yeere towards Easter, though it were not always knowne ... to steale a young boy, *circumcise him*, and after a solemn judgment, making one of their owne Nation a Pilate, to crucifie him out of their divellish malice to Christ and Christians.' So pervasive was the belief that Jews circumcised their victims – retailed by enormously influential writers like John Foxe the martyrologist in his account of Hugh of Lincoln, whom the Jews 'first had circumcised, & then deteined a whole yeere in custodie, intending to crucifie him' – that Menasseh ben Israel, the Dutch Rabbi who sought from Cromwell the readmission of the Jews in 1656, had to dwell at considerable length in his *Vindiciae Judaeorum* at refuting this claim; after all, Menasseh argued, since circumcision signified conversion to Judaism, it doesn't make any sense for Jews first to turn a boy into a Jew and then kill him. Nonetheless, William Prynne, Menasseh's most stalwart adversary, continued to insist in the 'Second Part' of his *Demurrer to the Jews* (London, 1656) that the Jews of England had engaged in 'circumcising and crucifying Christian children'.

The English chronicles that Prynne drew upon for his information – chronicles that circulated widely in late sixteenth-century England – were full of such accounts. One of the more remarkable concerns a circumcision that turned into a total castration: D'Blossier Tovey, who also drew upon these sources, describes how during the reign of King John the Jews 'began soon, again, to be calumniated, as Crucifyers of Children, false coiners, and Emasculators; so far that, in the fourth year of this King, one Bonefand a Jew of Bedford was indicted, not for Circumcising, but tota[l]ly cutting off the Privy Member of one Richard, the Nephew of Robert de Sutton.' For the record, Bonefand, we learn, 'pleaded not guilty, and was very honourably acquitted', raising the interesting question of how, given the medical evidence, the case could ever have been successfully prosecuted.

When we turn to one of Shakespeare's main sources for the 'pound of flesh' narrative we find a clear precedent for the argument that a Jew considers the possibility of castrating the Christian.

In Alexander Silvayn's *The Orator*, translated into English in 1596, we read of 'a Jew, who would for his debt have a pound of the flesh of a Christian': asking *what a matter were it then, if I should cut of his privie members, supposing that the same would altogether weigh a just pound?'*

The threat embodied in these lines proved far too disturbing for the Victorian editor H. H. Furness to reproduce in his important Variorum edition of *The Merchant of Venice*. In a deliberate act of textual castration, Furness changes the line from 'cut off his privie members' to 'cut of his [head], supposing that the same would weigh a just pound'. This makes little sense, no matter how light-headed his victim might be, since in the very next sentence the Jew continues, 'Or else his head'. Furness's textual intervention immediately influenced subsequent editions of the play and its sources; a year after his Variorum was published, for example, Homer Sprague would write 'head' (without Furness's brackets) in his popular school edition of the play. Disturbingly, the bowdlerisation of this source had deflected critical attention away from that part of the play that touches upon alleged ritual Jewish practices.

For Shylock to take the knife to Antonio's privy members would be to threaten circumcision (and symbolically conversion) since it is a ritual whose complex function is to separate Jew from non-Jew, and Jewish men from Jewish women. Only through the male could this covenant be transmitted, which helps explain why Jewish daughters like Jessica and Abigail can so easily cross the religious lines that divide their fathers from the dominant Christian community; their difference is not physically inscribed in their flesh. Given Antonio's anxious assertion of difference in terms of both gender and faith a potential circumcision is understandably threatening.

Before turning to what Elizabethans thought about circumcision, it is worth indicating what their actual experience of it was. With the exception of a handful of infants circumcised by the radical Puritan group led by John Traske around 1620, there is no evidence that circumcisions took place in early modern England. Nor would there have been many opportunities, at home or abroad, for Elizabethans to see a circumcised penis. This did not mean that they were not curious. Contemporaries of Shakespeare, in particular some of the intrepid Elizabethan travellers, expressed considerable interest in observing this ritual, and several of their detailed accounts survive. It is unlikely that Shakespeare ever witnessed this rite, though he could have been familiar with all aspects of this practice not only through biblical injunctions, but also from redactions in contemporary sources, such as *Purchas His Pilgrimage* (London, 1613), or the stories in circulation that led to the publication of such accounts.

Those Elizabethans who did witness circumcisions have left accounts that emphasise the child's transition from his mother to the community of men. Fynes Morison thus observes that at 'the dore, the wemen [were] not permited to enter, [and] deliverd the Childe to the Father'. And Thomas Coryate observes that the final act of the ritual is a presentation of the foreskin to the mother, symbolising the cut between her and her son as he enters the community of men: the 'prepuce that was cut off was carried to the Mother, who keepeth it very preciously as a thing of worth'. Both Morison and Thomas Coryate are struck by the practice of *mezizah*, in which the circumciser sucks the blood from the penis of the circumcised infant. Moryson writes that 'the Rabby cutt off his prepuce, and (with leave be it related for clearing of the Ceremony) did with his mouth sucke the blood of his privy part, and after drawing and spitting out of much blood, sprinckled a red powder upon the wounde'. In a comment that reveals just how complex the gendering of Jewish circumcision was, Morison is clearly uncomfortable with describing *mezizah* – 'with leave be it related' – a practice for which he can find no biblical authority.

Thomas Coryate, who had long sought to observe a circumcision, finally had his wish granted in Constantinople, at the 'house of a certaine English Jew, called Amis, borne in the Crootched Friers in London, who hath two sisters more of his owne Jewish Religion, Commorant in Galata, who were likewise borne in the same place'. He expresses no surprise, it might be noted, that Amis was a Jew who had spent thirty years in a London that many scholars assume was free of Jews. Coryate's description is worth quoting at length:

> [D]ivers Jewes came into the room, and sung certain Hebrew Songs; after which the child was brought to his Father, who sate downe in a chaire, and placed the child being now eight days old in his lap. The whole company being desirous that we Christians should observe the ceremonie, called us to approach neere to the child. And when we came, a certaine other Jew drawing forth a little instrument made not unlike those smal [sic] Cissers that our Ladies and Gentlewomen doe much use, did with the same cut off the Prepuce or fore-skinne of the child, and after a very strange manner, unused (I beleeve) of the ancient Hebrewes, did put his mouth to the child's yard, and sucked

up the bloud. All his Privities (before he came into the roome) were besprinkled with a kind of powder, which after the Circumciser had done his businesse, was blowed away by him, and another powder cast on immediately. After he had dispatched his worke, the same also after his worke was done, he tooke a little strong wine that was held in a goblet by a fellow that stood neere him, and powred it into the child's mouth to comfort him in the middest of his paines, who cried out very bitterly; the paine being for the time very bitter indeed, though it will be (as they told me) cured in the space of foure and twentie houres. Those of any riper yeeres that are circumcised (as it too often commeth to passe, that Christians that turne Turkes) as at fortie or fiftie yeeres of age, doe suffer great paine for the space of a moneth.

Circumcision was usually identified as a Jewish (or Turkish) custom, though Elizabethans who travelled to Africa were also aware that other cultures practised this rite; Samuel Purchas, for example, argued strenuously that the practice of circumcision by the Egyptians predated the Jews. While the anthropological interest of explorers like Purchas and Jobson helped demystify the practice as an exclusively Jewish one, for many if not most Christian men the act was still seen as one that marked men as Jewish. Thomas Thorowgood's *Jews in America* (London, 1660) is representative. In arguing that native Americans were Jewish, having descended from the Ten Lost Tribes, Thorowgood's first evidence is that they practise circumcision:

> I begin with Circumcision, and justly, for it is the mainest point of Jewish Religion, saith Bishop Montague ... [after citing many testimonies to his effect he concludes that] it will doubtless seem probable also, that many Indian Nations are of Judaicall race, seeing this frequent and constant Character of Circumcision, so singularlie fixed to the Jews, is to be found among them.

It comes as no surprise that Jews would be prosecuted for this act alone, not simply as part of a more complex ritual murder. Tovey recounts in *Anglia Judaica* 'the famous Trial of Jacob of Norwich, and Accomplices, for Stealing away, and Circumcising, a Christian child':

> The Case was this. As a Boy, of five Years old, was playing in the Street, several Jews seiz'd, and convey'd him to the House of the aforesaid Jacob; where they kept him a Day and a Night; and then binding his Eyes with a Napkin, cut off his Foreskin, which they put

> into a Bason, and covered with Sand; after which, blowing the Sand
> with their Mouths, till they found it again, (the Person, who first dis-
> cover'd it being call'd Jurnepin,) the Boy, from him, was order'd to
> be call'd Jurnepin, and declar'd a Jew.

Of particular interest in this story is the question of the reversibil-
ity of the act, since circumcision is seen as determining the male
child's religious identity. At the trial 'one Maud ... depos'd, that,
after the Boy was taken Home again, several Jews came to her, and
bade her have a care how she gave him any Swines Flesh to eat, for
he was a Jew.' Popular interest in the case stemmed from the de-
nouement: the boy's foreskin 'by some Art or other, had been made
to grow again'. So complex were the religious and political implications of this action that the authorities were at loss to determine
proper jurisdiction: 'The Matter therefore appearing doubtful; and
the Bishops protesting, that, as Baptism and Circumcision were
Matters of Faith, the Cause ought to be tried in their Courts, the
Parliament consented to part with it.' For Elizabethans, circumcising
fell into the same category as baptism (which replaced it) in determining one's religious identity. As Samuel Purchas put it, through
circumcision one 'is thus made a Jew'.

One of the most widely circulated and humorous identifications
of circumcision with castration can be found in the dedicatory
poems prefaced to Thomas Coryate's *Coryates Crudities*, published
in 1611. These poems were apparently inspired both by Coryate's
narrative and by one of the several scenes depicted on the title page
which depicts a Jew, knife in hand, in hot pursuit of the fleeing
Coryate. While this woodcut no doubt relates to Coryate's celebrated escape from a crowd of hostile Jews of Venice whom he had
sought to convert, there is no evidence anywhere in the text that
these Jews bore weapons against him. Evidently, the woodcut is
based either on the artist's imagination or on Coryate's no doubt
embellished personal account; in either case the prefatory poems
return to this image repeatedly. The knife-wielding Jew, however,
threatens not death but circumcision, for Laurence Whitaker:

> Thy Cortizan clipt thee, ware Tom, I advise thee,
> And flie from the Jewes, lest they circumcise thee.

Hugh Holland writes in a similar vein (comparing Coryate to
Hugh Broughton, the great Elizabethan Hebraist and converter of
Jews):

He more prevaild against the'excoriate Jewes
Than Broughton could, or twenty more such Hughs.
And yet but for one pettie poore misprison,
He was nigh made one of the Circumcision.

And in another couplet Holland again draws attention to the
danger to Coryate's foreskin:

Ulysses heard no Syren sing: nor Coryate
The Jew, least his praepuce might prove excoriate.

Given the absence of textual evidence for a Jew wielding a knife
threatening to attack Coryate, let alone circumcise him, it is at least
worth considering whether the memory of Shylock, knife in hand,
threatening Antonio, coloured either the artist's rendition or these
poets' commendatory descriptions of the woodcut.

III

Two other and interconnected aspects of circumcision found in early
modern English texts cast additional light on Shylock's threatened cut
of Antonio's flesh. The first concerns why, if this is indeed a threatened circumcision, Shylock ultimately chooses to cut the pound of
flesh from near Antonio's heart. An explanation for this shift can be
found in a series of Old and New Testament discussions of circumcision and the commentary and sermon literature that grew out of them.

John Donne's sermon on the 'Feast of the Circumcision' clarifies
how the circumcised *heart* of the Christian has replaced the circumcised *penis* of the Jew. For Donne, quite simply, 'the principall
dignity of this Circumcision, was, that it ... prefigured ... that
Circumcision of the heart'; the 'Jewish Circumcision was an absurd
and unreasonable thing, if it did not intimate and figure the
Circumcision of the heart'. To circumcise a penis was, frankly, too
'obscene a thing, to be brought into the fancy of so many Women,
so many young Men, so many Strangers to other Nations, as might
bring the Promise and Covenant it selfe into scorne'. So strong was
the Christian revulsion against circumcision (which some radical
Protestants on the Continent and in England began to practise) that
Martin Luther would angrily observe 'I hope I shall never be so
stupid as to be circumcised. I would rather cut off the left breast of
my Catherine and of all women.'

John Donne, who apparently believed in a version of the myth of ritual murder, writes elsewhere of his belief that Jews observed a 'barbarous and inhumane custome' of 'always keep[ing] in readiness the blood of some Christian, with which they anoint the body of any that dyes amongst them, with these words, "if Jesus Christ were the Messias, then may the blood of this Christian availe thee to salvation"'. For Donne, with the coming of Christ the thing signified – 'the spirituall Circumcision of our hearts' – happily replaced the 'mutilation' of the Jews' crude signifier. Viewed in light of this familiar exegetical tradition, Shylock's decision to cut a pound of flesh from near Antonio's heart could be seen as the height of the literalism that informs all of his actions in the play, a literalism that when imitated by Portia leads to his demise. Shylock will literally circumcise his Christian adversary in that part of his body where Christians are figuratively circumcised: their hearts.

Donne's sermon also provides insight into a related issue: 'uncircumcision'. At the conclusion of his sermon Donne demands of his congregation that they ask of themselves 'whether those things which you heard now, have brought you to this Circumcision, and made you better this yeare than you were the last, and find you not under the same uncircumcision still'. This concept of 'uncircumcision' is also grounded in the notion that in a post-Judaic world, circumcision is to be understood metaphorically, an act of self-renewal. After Shylock's circumcising threat against Antonio fails, the punishment Antonio begs of the court for his enemy – baptism – becomes, ironically, an act of uncircumcision performed upon the Jew.

The threat to cut Antonio's 'flesh' also suggests that Shylock, like Bonefand (mentioned above), is a Jewish 'emasculator', one who somehow threatens to transform Antonio from a man to something other and less than a man. The principle of inversion or substitution that operates throughout the play obtains here as well. The threatened feminisation occurs within a larger context in which the dominant early modern Christian culture projected its fear of feminisation by investing the Jewish male with female qualities. A good example occurs in Edwin Sandys's *A Relation of the State of Religion* (1605), where, writing about religion in Italy, Sandys draws an analogy between Jews and female prostitutes, who 'sucke' on those of lesser social station, only to be 'sucked' by those more powerful.

Still others advanced the peculiar argument that Jewish men menstruated (a belief that seems to have derived from assertions about *foeder Judaicus*, the awful smell of the Jew, addressed most directly in Sir Thomas Browne's essay on whether Jews stink). While there are a number of such accounts in sixteenth-century Spanish writers, there are fewer in English texts. One example appears in Thomas Calvert's *Diatriba of the Jews' Estate*, where Calvert causally relates Jewish male menstruation to the practice of 'Child-Crucifying among the Jews'. Calvert reports third-hand that the Jews 'can never bee healed of this shamefull punishment wherewith [they] are so vexed, but onely by Christian blood. This punishment so shameful they say is, that Jews, *men*, as well as females, are punished *curso menstruo sanguinis*, with a very frequent Bloud-fluxe.' Not entirely convinced, Calvert chooses to 'leave it to the learned to judge and determine by writers or Travellers, whether this be true or no, either that they have a monthly Flux of Blood, or a continuall mal-odoriferous breath'.

The Jewish male body was, then a leaky body, and as such a suspect one. Again and again the Jewish man was constructed as a creature of the bodily fluids: spitting, stinking, menstruating, smearing faeces on Christian symbols, constantly falling into privies. In their androgyny, monstrosity, implication in local and unsolvable crimes, apostasy, secret rituals, 'Sabbath', and interest in sorcery and magic, the Jews resembled the other great marginal and threatening social group of the early modern period: witches. Indeed, some of the earliest individuals prosecuted for sorcery in England were Jews. There may well be a relation between the banishment of the Jews from England at the close of the thirteenth century and the emergence of witch prosecutions shortly thereafter; certainly, there is a common thread in monstrous allegations, torture, and executions to which both groups were subjected in early modern Europe.

IV

The social anxieties that circulated through Shakespeare's play have had an afterlife over the course of the next four centuries, in large measure because the play continues to give voice to recurrent cultural problems of nation, race, and gender. The anxieties I am describing are not merely English ones, and as Shakespeare's popularity spread over the next two centuries we find *The Merchant of Venice* intervening in other cultural and national crises. I described in my lecture earlier this week – 'Shakespeare and the "Jew Bill" of

1753' – how *The Merchant of Venice* entered into English political discourse during the heady days of the Jewish Naturalisation Act. In this century there are many more examples to choose from. For example, shortly after Kristallnacht in 1938, *The Merchant of Venice* was broadcast for propagandistic ends over the German airwaves; productions of the play followed in Lubeck (1938), Berlin (1940), Vienna (1943), and elsewhere, in Nazi territory. Of course, while the sinister aspects of a usurious Shylock were appealing to the Nazis, the successful intermarriage of Jessica and Lorenzo was not. The play has frequently been altered to accommodate different kinds of national and religious beliefs in this century. Barry Kyle's 1980 production of *The Merchant of Venice* in Israel, for example, completely omitted Shylock's conversion to Christianity. And in the United States, the play has been long banned from many high school curricula, and is the source of controversy virtually every time it is staged.

The cultural anxieties, the deep, disturbing myths about Jews, about otherness, that Shakespeare raises in the play, continue to trouble us. As long as cultural 'difference' – of race, of gender, of religion, of nationality – continues to be the basis of social antagonism and prejudice, *The Merchant of Venice* will ironically fulfil that dictum, that Shakespeare's plays 'were not of an age, but for all time'.

From James Shapiro, 'Shakespeare and the Jews', The Parkes Lecture (University of Southampton, 1992).

NOTES

[James Shapiro's essay, which examines the history of the Jews in Renaissance England, offers an incisive reading of Shylock's bond and its meanings. At the same time the essay touches on a number of themes common in recent Shakespeare criticism – the trope of the body, the effeminisation of men, and the fear of other races and practices. As noted in the Introduction, Shapiro's book *Shakespeare and the Jews* (1996) takes up this network of ideas and explores them in much more historical detail – it is concerned with 'myths and misconceptions about who and what was a Jew', about 'notions of Jewish criminality', especially the 'alleged "Jewish crime" in which Jews reputedly abducted, circumcised, then ritually murdered Christians' (p. 1), about religious identity and political and racial attitudes. The book is at once a combination of scholarship and cultural criticism, while Shapiro's strength as a writer lies in his recognition of the complexity of the material he is dealing with. A useful supplement to Shapiro's work can be found in the excellent introduction to Annabel Patterson's edition of *The Most Excellent Historie of The Merchant of Venice* for the Shakespearean Original series (Hemel Hempstead, 1995) dealing with racial stereotyping and the play's history up until the Civil War. Ed.]

1. David S. Katz, *Philo-Semitism and the Readmission of the Jews 1603–1655* (Oxford, 1982); *The Jews in the History of England* (Oxford, 1994); Richard Popkin, 'Jewish-Christian Relations in the Sixteenth and Seventeenth Centuries: The Conception of the Messiah', *Jewish History*, 6 (1992), 163–77; Jonathan Israel, *European Jewry in the Age of Mercantilism, 1550–1750* (Oxford, 1989).

2. I might add that a number of exciting essays are forthcoming on this subject in *The Jewish Heritage in British History: Englishness and Jewishness*, ed. Tony Kushner (London, 1992).

3. Stephen Greenblatt, 'Marlowe, Marx, and Anti-Semitism', *Critical Inquiry*, 5 (1978), 291, rpt. in *Learning to Curse: Essay in early Modern Culture* (New York, 1990).

4. Theodore Reik, 'Jessica, My Child', *American Imago*, 8 (1951), 3–27.

5

Guess Who's Coming to Dinner? Colonisation and Miscegenation in *The Merchant of Venice*

KIM F. HALL

I

Samuel Purchas introduces his popular collection of travel narratives, *Purchas His Pilgrimes* (the 1625 sequel to Richard Hakluyt's *Principal Voyages*), by recounting the virtues of trade. He equates the benefits of navigation with Christian charity and leads his reader into the collection proper by envisioning a world converted to Protestantism:

> ... and the chiefest charitie is that which is most common; nor is there any more common then this of Navigation, where one man is not good to another man, but so many Nations as so many persons hold commerce and intercourse of amity withall; ... the West with the East, and the remotest parts of the world are joyned in one band of humanitie; and why not also of Christianitie? Sidon and Sion, Jew and Gentile, Christian and Ethnike, as in this typicall storie? That as there is one Lord, one Faith, one Baptisme, one Body, one Spirit, one Inheritance, one God and Father, so there may be thus one Church truly Catholike, One Pastor and one Sheepfold?[1]

Charity may not begin at home, but it certainly ends up there, as the charitable cause of conversion redounds to the economic benefit of the English world. The initial ideal of 'commerce and intercourse of amity' among many types of men is replaced by a vision of global unity that denies difference just as Purchas's own language does. (The singular construction ['one Lord, one Faith'] subsumes difference when it replaces the 'and' that allows differences to exist simultaneously ['Jew and Gentile'].) English trade, rather than fostering a mixing of cultures, will eradicate religious differences, as well as cultural and gender differences, under one patriarchal God.

Purchas's glorified version of the end of English colonisation similarly serves to efface the multivalent anxieties over cross-cultural interaction that permeate English fictions of international trade. In uniting economics and Christian values, Purchas highlights the fact that colonial trade involves not only economic transactions, but cultural and political exchange as well. The anthropologist Gayle Rubin notes in her influential feminist critique of Lévi-Strauss, 'Kinship and marriage are always parts of total social systems, and are always tied into economic and political arrangements'.[2] Likewise, the exchange of goods (or even the circulation of money) across cultural borders always contains the possibility of other forms of exchange between different cultures. Associations between marriage, kinship, property, and economics become increasingly anxiety-ridden as traditional social structures (such as marriage) are extended when England develops commercial ties across the globe. Extolling the homogenising influence of trade suggests that English trade will turn a world of difference into a world of Protestant similitude. However, it leaves unspoken the more threatening possibility – that English identity will be subsumed under foreign difference.

It is this problem of 'commerce and intercourse', of commercial interaction inevitably fostering social and sexual contact, that underlies representations of miscegenation in the early modern period.[3] In addition to addressing domestic anxieties about the proper organisation of male and female (particularly about the uncontrolled desires of women), the appearance of miscegenation in plays responds to growing concerns over English national identity and culture as England develops political and economic ties with foreign (and 'racially' different) nations. This essay will draw on Purchas's dual sense of the all-encompassing nature of trade encounters and colonialism's alleged homogenising power to suggest the significance of a brief instance of miscegenation in Shakespeare that has been insistently ignored by critics.

Although the most central – and most commented on – problem of difference and trade in *The Merchant of Venice* is between Jew and Christian, more general anxieties about the problem of difference within economic exchange are encapsulated in an instance of miscegenation never staged. In Act III, the audience witnesses a joking interchange between Shylock's servant, Launcelot, and Lorenzo and Jessica about their mixed marriage:

> **Jes.**   Nay, you need not fear us Lorenzo, Launcelot and I are out, – he tells me flatly that there's no mercy for me in heaven, because I am a Jew's daughter: and he says that you are no good member of the commonwealth, for in converting Jews to Christians, you raise the price of pork.
>
> **Lor.**   I shall answer that better to the commonwealth than you can the getting up of the negro's belly: the Moor is with child by you Launcelot!
>
> **Laun.**   It is much that the Moor should be more than reason: but if she be less than an honest woman, she is indeed more than I took her for.
>
> (III.v.28–39)

The Arden edition of *Merchant* helpfully notes that 'this passage has not been explained' and suggests, 'Perhaps it was introduced simply for the sake of the elaborate pun on Moor/more'.[4] Their joking conversation no doubt parodically reflects the investment of the commonwealth in sexual practices. Nonetheless, it also begs the question of the difference between Lorenzo's liaison with a Jew and Launcelot's with a Moor. The Renaissance stage abounds with jokes about bastards: if Launcelot's fault was merely the getting of another, there would be no reason to emphasise that this invisible woman is a Moor. In his *Black Face, Maligned Race*, Anthony Barthelemy notes that this exchange reflects ideas of the licentiousness of the black woman typical of the time.[5] However, it may be that this pregnant, unheard, unnamed, and unseen (at least by critics) black woman is a silent symbol for the economic and racial politics of *The Merchant of Venice*. She exposes an intricately wrought nexus of anxieties over gender, race, religion, and economics (fuelled by the push of imperial/mercantile expansion) which surrounds the various possibilities of miscegenation raised in the play.

II

Before moving into the play itself, I would like to sketch out some of these anxieties over miscegenation by examining one of the play's possible 'sub-texts'.[6] In 1596, despite her earlier support of English piracy in the slave trade, Queen Elizabeth expressed concern over the presence of blacks in the realm. She issued a proclamation to the Lord Mayor of London which states her 'understanding that there are of late divers blackmoores brought into this realme, of which kinde of people there are allready here to manie'[7] and demands that blacks recently brought to the realm be rounded up and returned. This effort was evidently not very successful, as she followed up that proclamation with another order of expulsion:

> ... whereas the Queen's Majesty, tendering the good and welfare of her own natural subjects greatly distressed in these hard times of dearth, is highly discontented to understand the great numbers of Negars and Blackamoors which (as she is informed) are crept into this realm since the troubles between Her Highness and the King of Spain, who are fostered and relieved here to the great annoyance of her own liege people that want the relief which those people consume; as also for that the most of them are infidels, having no understanding of Christ or his Gospel, hath given especial commandment that the said kind of people should be with all speed avoided and discharged out of this Her Majesty's dominions. ... And if there shall be any person or persons which are possessed of any such Blackamoors that refuse to deliver them in sort as aforesaid, then we require you to call them before you and to advise and persuade them by all good means to satisfy Her Majesty's pleasure therein; which if they shall eftsoons willfully and obstinately refuse, we pray you then to certify their names unto us, to the end Her Majesty may take such further course therein as it shall seem best in her princely wisdom.[8]

While such critical attention as has been paid to this document concentrates on the attempt to discharge Moors from the realm and uses the attempt itself to prove the existence of a viable black presence in England,[9] the terms of the proclamation demand special attention. The image of large numbers of Moors having 'crept into this realm' suggests that they suddenly appeared of their own volition (despite having been 'fostered and relieved' here by unnamed residents).[10] The proclamation then lays the fault of this invasion at the foot of Spain, a country already suspect for its past history of interracial alliance.[11] The rest of the document is concerned to prevent contact between these 'creeping' invaders and 'her own liege' people despite its contradictory contention that Elizabeth's own subjects are the ones 'possessed' of blackamoors to the detriment of the state.

Although chronic food shortages occurred throughout Elizabeth's reign and certainly seemed to be a goad to plantation and exploration, her naming of 'these hard times of dearth' suggests that both of the expulsions occurred in the context of very immediate state concerns. England from 1594 to 1597 saw dramatic declines in grain harvests (the staple of the lower-class diet), culminating in the famine of 1597. Indeed, much of northern Europe (although, interestingly, not Italy) suffered from famine and starvation from 1595 to 1597. Although the famine in England hit hardest in the northwestern parishes, its effects were felt throughout the realm, as Andrew Appleby notes, 'It is abundantly clear, however, that the grain harvest was the heart of the English economy ... and that its malfunctions were felt, with disastrous results, throughout the kingdom'.[12] Private citizens, the Privy Council, and the general public showed concern over the unavailability of bread even in the earliest of those years. These 'dear years' carried with them a range of other social dislocations: a reduction in baptismal and marriage rates, a rise in mortality and civil unrest, and, significantly, the unemployment of servant classes. Key government measures were issued in proximity to both expulsions and indicate that the famine generated a degree of class conflict. Elizabeth's order to make starch from bran rather than grain needed for food was issued in the same month as the first order of expulsion. Another proclamation, ending price-fixing and compelling the landed classes to remain in the counties because 'her majesty had thus determined for relief of her people to stay all good householders in their countries, there in charitable sort to keep hospitality',[13] was issued a few months later.

Equally important in the expulsion order is the reference to the religion (or lack of religion) of the Moors, which is based on the supposition that they are a logical group to cut off from state resources because they have 'no understanding of Christ or his Gospel'. In this time of crisis Christianity becomes the prerequisite for access to limited resources. Certainly, Elizabeth's evocation of the religious difference of the Moor would seem to support the common view that religion, not race, is the defining mark of difference in early modern England.[14] I would argue, however, that even though religion is given as a compelling reason for excluding Moors, emphasising religious difference only clouds the political reality that the Moors' visibility in the culture made them a viable target for exclusion. In other words, it is their physical difference *in association with cultural differences* (a combination that is the primary basis for the category 'race') that provokes their exclusion – not just their religion.

In Elizabeth's proclamation we see what may be a source of the threat posed by Launcelot's Moor. In times of economic stress, visible minorities very often become the scapegoat for national problems. The proclamation shares with *Merchant* an alarm over unregulated consumption. Launcelot's evocation of the scarcity of food through his jesting over the rising price of pork reveals a similar unease over limited resources. Thus, famine, one of the more specific rationales for English colonial plantation and expansion, becomes here associated with the black woman. Ultimately both texts draw on and reproduce the same racial stereotype. Just as the image of the black female as consumer of state resources in the twentieth-century United States is statistically inaccurate but politically powerful, so may the black presence have been a threat (albeit small) to white European labour, which is magnified by its very visibility.[15] This sense of privation produces an economic imperative in the play, which insists on the exclusion of racial, religious, and cultural difference. With the finite resources of a Venetian (or Elizabethan) society reserved for the wealthy elite, the offspring of Launcelot and the Moor presents a triple threat that in this world is perceived as a crime against the state. Their alliance is perhaps even more suspect than the ominous possibility of a marriage between Portia and the prince of Morocco, since it would produce a half-black, half-Christian child from the already starving lower classes who threatens to upset the desired balance of consumption. The pun on 'Moor/more' further supports this image of the black woman as both consuming and expanding and is particularly striking in a play where the central image is the literal taking of flesh and where Christian males worry throughout about having 'less'.

The acute sense of privation amid plenty is signalled through *Merchant*'s ubiquitous images of starvation that are interwoven with the incessant eating in the play. Walter Cohen sees Launcelot as integral to the play and notes in particular the way he 'systematically and wittily misconstrues Lorenzo's apparently straightforward order that the kitchen staff "prepare for dinner!"'.[16] Launcelot's first move is to remind Lorenzo of the servants' hunger: 'they all have stomachs' (III.v.44). Earlier, he claims that he is starving in Shylock's employ: 'I am famish'd in his service. You may tell every finger I have with my ribs' (II.ii.101–3). Shylock's version, 'The patch is kind enough, but a huge feeder' (II.v.45), may reinforce the idea that these outsiders literally starve rightful citizens, yet it also suggests a Christian appetite out of control. Bassanio, describing his poor finances, suggests bulk without sustenance in saying that he lost wealth, 'By something showing a more swelling port / Than my faint means would grant continuance' (I.i.124–5). Finally, Antonio, in reminding Solanio of Venice's strict commercial laws, laments, 'These griefs and losses have so bated me / That I shall hardly spare a pound of flesh / Tomorrow, to my bloody creditor' (III.iii.32–4).

The associations with eating and starvation link outsiders, particularly Shylock, with one of the most compelling tropes of colonialist discourse: the cannibal.[17] Cannibalism was a source of as much anxiety as fascination for the traveller; it seemed to be one of the final lines drawn between the savage Other and the civilised self.[18] The reasons given for imperial plunder by Bertoldo in Philip Massinger's *The Maid of Honour* suggest that much of this obsession springs from a sense that the dividing line is not as clear as one might like:

> Nature did
> Designe us to be warriours, and to breake through
> Our ring the sea, by which we are inviron'd;
> And we by force must fetch in what is wanting,
> Or precious to us. Adde to this, wee are
> A populous nation, and increase so fast,
> That if we by our providence, are not sent
> Abroad in colonies, or fall by the sword,
> Not *Sicilie* (though now, it were more fruitfull,
> Then when 'twas stil'd the granary of great *Rome*)
> Can yeeld our numerous frie bread, we must starve,
> Or eat up one another.
>
> (I.i.202–13)[19]

In specifically ascribing to the English an aggression and ferocity that are the essence of European definitions of the cannibal,[20] Bertoldo hints at the tentativeness of that division. The movement of the passage also suggests a blurring of boundaries: the opening image of the breach of England's geographic insularity which releases the energies of a warlike nation rapidly moves into an evocation of violent, desperate want which could easily turn in upon itself. Massinger skates a fine line between identity and difference in allowing his character to suggest that imperial expansion is the only thing separating the civilised Englishman from the cannibal and that the dangers of cannibalism lie on either side of England's borders.

His metaphor is similar to an earlier and more specific reference to English want in Richard Hakluyt's *Discourse of Western Planting*. In this attempt to persuade Elizabeth to adopt a plantation policy, Hakluyt associates cannibalism with another marginalised group – the unemployed. He warns Elizabeth:

> But wee for all the Statutes that hitherto can be devised, and the sharpe execution of the same in poonishinge idle and lazye persons for wante of sufficient occasion of honest employmente cannot deliver our common wealthe from multitudes of loyterers and idle vagabondes. ... [W]e are growen more populous than ever heretofore: So that nowe there are of every arte and science so many, that they can hardly lyve one by another, nay rather they are readie to eate upp one another.[21]

The troping of cannibalism links actual shortages of food with the need to promote colonial trade in a way that also provides a compelling metaphor for the loss of communal identity in such trade. The desire to make contact with and to exploit Others always carries with it the possibility of engulfment. Such fears of erasure are embedded in metaphors of eating, but the figure of the cannibal specifically locates such fears within a framework of colonial trade and religious difference.

The language of eating in *The Merchant of Venice* situates Shylock within this framework by merging images of cannibalism with older accusations of blood libel. He claims, 'But yet I'll go in hate, to feed upon / The prodigal Christian', and Gratiano describes him, 'thy currish spirit / Govern'd a wolf, who hang'd for human slaughter –' (IV.i.133–5).[22] According to Maggie Kilgour, feeding from (or eating with) the Other is a perilous involvement which carries the risk of being eaten by the Other:

> To eat in a country is potentially to be eaten by it, to enter into a false identification by being absorbed by a foreign culture – what we call 'going native' – and so be prevented from returning to a place of origin in which one is truly at home. The opposite of returning to one's own hearth is ultimately to be subsumed totally by a hostile host.[23]

Shylock's reluctance to eat with the Christians displays the fear of 'be[ing] subsumed ... by a hostile host', but in terms that ratify the reciprocal Christian fear of being consumed by a guest/alien who has been allowed into the home/country. Economic exchanges with an outsider like Shylock open up Venice to sexual and commercial intercourse with strangers; this breach brings with it the threat of economic upheaval and foreign invasion. Social activities such as eating and marriage resonate because of the already permeable borders of the Venetian economy. In defending his insistence on the completion of a legal bond, Shylock comments on the assumed rights of the Venetians to 'bond' and to preserve their racial purity in a speech laden with references to problematic communal activities:

> You have among you many a purchas'd slave,
> Which (like your asses, and your dogs and mules)
> You use in abject and in slavish parts,
> Because you bought them, – shall I say to you,
> Let them be free, *marry them to your heirs?*
> Why sweat they under burthens? let their beds
> Be made as soft as yours, and let their palates
> Be season'd with such viands?
> (IV.i.90–7; emphasis added)

Rhetorically, Shylock exposes the fears of a chauvinist culture by revealing the Venetians' problematic economic position, suggesting that, in such an open system, the slaves among them may just as well become sons-in-law.[24] The passage may also tie the problem of eating with colonial trade in the reminder ('let their palates / Be season'd with such viands') that the search for spices for aristocratic palates provided much of the momentum for foreign trade. His questions allow for a provocative glance at Queen Elizabeth's dilemma. Producers of labour are also consumers, and the blacks that she wants to exile are a presence precisely because of the increased economic expansion she supported.

As critics have often noted, the language of commerce and trade permeates the Venetian world. This mercantile vocabulary is tied to an erotic vocabulary in much the same way as Titania's description of her Indian votress in *A Midsummer Night's Dream* links the pregnant maid and Indian trade. Like his companion, Bassanio, Antonio begins the play in a melancholy mood; Solanio attributes his sadness not to love, but to the possibility of economic disaster: 'Believe me sir, had I such a venture forth, / The better part of my affections would / Be with my hopes abroad' (I.i.15–17). Echoing the eroticised discourse of actual merchant adventure, Solanio's discussion of Antonio's afflictions as 'affections' locates the erotic in the economic, particularly as he makes

Antonio's fear of losing his ships sound much like the fear of losing a lover:[25]

> should I go to church
> And see the holy edifice of stone
> And not bethink me straight of dangerous rocks,
> Which touching my gentle vessel's side
> Would scatter all her spices on the stream,
> Enrobe the roaring waters with my silks. ...
>
> (I.i.29–34)

Solanio's displacement is all the more resonant in its religious overtones and its hints at a loss of Christian belief. Foreign adventure proves a dangerous distraction as the stones of the Christian church provoke reminders of the beguiling hazards of trade.

The potential dangers of Antonio's mercantile involvement with foreign Others, read as seductive sexual union, are offset by the rejection of difference in the golden world of Belmont. Bassanio's discussion of his intent to woo Portia suggests an interesting inversion of Antonio's economic adventures. The narrative of his romantic quest is filled with economic metaphors, and his description of Portia makes it obvious that there is an unfavourable balance of trade on the marriage market. Rather than bringing wealth into the country, suitors are coming to Belmont to win away Portia's wealth, as Bassanio notes:

> Nor is the wide world ignorant of her worth,
> For the four winds blow in from every coast
> Renowned suitors, and her sunny locks
> Hang on her temples like a golden fleece,
> Which makes her seat of Belmont Colchos' strond,
> And many Jasons come in quest of her.
>
> (I.i.167–72)

While Antonio participates in the expansion of Venice's economic influence, Bassanio insulates the sexual economy of Venice from foreign 'invasion'. In language closely approximating Bassanio's, his competitor, the prince of Morocco, 'a tawny moor' (and, we presume, a Muslim), frames his own courtship as colonial enterprise and religious pilgrimage when he chooses caskets:

> Why that's the lady, all the world desires her.
> From the four corners of the earth they come

> To kiss this shrine, this mortal breathing saint.
> The Hyrcanian deserts, and the vasty wilds
> Of wide Arabia are as throughfares now
> For princes to come view fair Portia.
> The watery kingdom, whose ambitious head
> Spets in the face of heaven, is no bar
> To stop the foreign spirits, but they come
> As o'er a brook to see fair Portia.
>   (II.vii.38–47)

Morocco reveals the peril of such international competition for wealth (and beauty). The test demanded by Portia's father expands the sex/gender system by opening up the romantic quest to foreign competition, as it were, inviting both the possibility of miscegenation and of another race absconding with the country's money and its native beauty. Morocco explicitly raises this idea and associates it with England:

>   They have in England
> A coin that bears the figure of an angel
> Stamp'd in gold, but that's insculp'd upon:
> But here an angel in a golden bed
> Lies all within.
>   (II.vii.55–9)

At the very moment in which he loses the game by making the wrong choice, Morocco raises the spectre of a monetary and sexual exchange in England with the image of Portia as an angel in a golden bed. Although the metaphor would seem to deny the comparison ('but that's insculp'd upon: / But here ...'), Portia is imaged here as the literalised coin of the realm. She, as object of an expanded sex/gender system, can like a coin be circulated among strangers.

The boundaries of Portia's island are hardly impregnable: the surrounding water 'is no bar' and no more than a 'brook' to outsiders; Portia herself is the open 'portal' to Venetian wealth. The sexual and the monetary anxieties of a Venetian state that is open to alien trade are displayed and dispelled in the casket plot, which allows Portia to avoid the threat of contact with others. The prince of Morocco is thus able to attempt to woo but ultimately to lose her. He also loses his right to reproduce his own bloodline, a right not explicitly denied the other suitors.[26] The momentary threat posed by the prince's wooing is dispelled, as is the larger cultural threat posed by the sexuality of the black male. The denial of his fertility should perhaps be looked at in juxtaposition with the fertility of Launcelot's Moor: the prince's sexuality denied, Launcelot then has licence to replace him as the Moor's 'cultural partner' and to appropriate her body.

The Morocco scene is only the most obvious example of the exclusionary values of Belmont. Portia derides all other suitors for their national shortcomings, reserving her praise for her countryman, Bassanio (a man who at first glance seems to have little to recommend him). Interestingly, the joking about the effects of intermarriage is preceded by the prince of Morocco's attempt to win Portia and Portia's deliverance as he chooses the wrong casket. Portia's response to her narrow escape, 'A gentle riddance, – draw the curtains, go, – / Let all of his complexion choose me so' (II.vii.78–9), is typical of the generally negative attitudes toward blacks prevalent at the time, but, in true Belmont fashion, in no way reveals the political and economic implications of her aversion.[27]

The economic issues which underlie the romantic world of Belmont rise to the surface in Venice, where there appears to be a real cash-flow problem. Most of the Christian men, it seems, are on the verge of bankruptcy. Bassanio reveals monetary woes in the opening of the play, ''Tis not unknown to you Antonio / How much I have disabled mine estate' (I.i.122–3). Despite Antonio's denial, his funds are stretched and the possibility of his financial ruin is evoked from the very beginning. Tellingly, Antonio has no hope for a legal remedy from his bargain because strangers in Venice have certain economic privileges:

> The duke cannot deny the course of law:
> For the commodity that strangers have
> With us in Venice, if it be denied,
> Will much impeach the justice of the state,
> Since that the trade and profit of the city
> Consisteth of all nations.
>   (III.iii.26–31)

In Antonio's case, the very openness of Venetian trade has negative effects for the city's males. The protection Venetian law should afford its 'own natural subjects' is weakened by the economic imperatives of mercantile trade.

In contrast to the males, the women are associated with an abundance of wealth. As we have seen, Portia comes with a large fortune

and Lorenzo 'steals' two thousand ducats along with a jewel-laden
Jessica. The comic resolution of the play is not merely the proper
pairing of male and female, but the redistribution of wealth from
women and other strangers to Venice's Christian males. Portia's
wealth goes to Bassanio, Antonio's is magically restored through her
agency, and, most importantly, Shylock's is given over to the state
through a law unearthed by Portia/Balthazar:

> It is enacted in the laws of Venice,
> If it be proved against an alien,
> That by direct, or indirect attempts
> He seek the life of any citizen,
> The party 'gainst the which he doth contrive,
> Shall seize one half his goods, the other half
> Comes to the privy coffer of the state.
> (IV.i.344–50)

The law that allegedly gave advantage to aliens is counteracted by a
law that repeals that advantage. More than providing an object
lesson for Shylock, 'hitting him where it hurts', as it were, the punishment makes sure that the uneven balance of wealth in the
economy is righted along racial and gender lines. Antonio's
modification of the sentence only highlights this impulse, as he
insists that his portion of Shylock's money be passed down 'unto
the gentleman / That lately stole his daughter' (IV.i.380–1).
Lorenzo's final expression of gratitude to Portia, 'Fair ladies, you
drop manna in the way / Of starved people' (V.i.294–5), typifies the
tonality of the play. Portia does indeed drop manna (which she re-
distributes from the city's aliens) upon the males of Venice: she is
the bearer of fortunes for Bassanio, Antonio, and Lorenzo.

Economic alliances in the play are made with expectations of one-
way exchange, which is often troped through conversion. Thus
Bassanio and Antonio stress Shylock's 'kindness' when making the
deal in order to give Shylock the illusion of a communal interest
and identity rooted in Christian values. Antonio takes his leave,
claiming, 'The Hebrew will turn Christian, he grows kind'
(I.iii.174), a phrase which only serves to remind Shylock and the
audience that his 'kindness' is still contingent. The pun on 'kind'
used throughout this scene reminds us that the courtesy and 'kindness' shown in the play's world is only extended to those who are
alike and judged of human 'kin' by Christians. Shakespeare also
demonstrates how selective such inclusion can be when the duke, in

an attempt to make Shylock forgo his bond, invites him into the community, not by imagining a shared humanity, but by creating a cultural hierarchy which stresses Shylock's difference: 'From stubborn Turks, and Tartars never train'd / To offices of tender courtesy' (IV.i.32–3). Such rhetorical moves only emphasise that the power of exclusion and inclusion rests with what Frank Whigham calls the 'elite circle of community strength' and that the outsider is powerless to determine his status within that group.[28]

The imagery associated with Shylock in the play reveals an ongoing link between perceptions of the racial difference of the black, the religious difference of the Jew, and the possible ramifications of sexual and economic contact with both. We can see clearly how the discourses of Otherness coalesce in the language of the play.[29] In claiming that Chus is one of his countrymen, Shylock gives himself a dual genealogy that associates him with blackness, forbidden sexuality, and the unlawful appropriation of property.[30] Obviously, Shylock's recounting of the Jacob parable has its own cultural overtones and serves to highlight his religious difference.[31] However, his incomplete genealogy is further complicated by the fact that Jacob, the progenitor of the Jews, robbed his brother, Esau, of his birthright as eldest brother.[32] Both Jews and blacks become signs for filial disobedience and disinheritance in Renaissance culture. In the two biblical accounts of blackness, Chus (or Cush), the son of Ham, is born black as a sign of the father's sin. A popular explanation of blackness recounted by George Best in his description of the Frobisher voyages shows the problem of disinheritance:

> and [Ham] being persuaded that the first childe borne after the flood (by right and Lawe of nature) should inherite and possesse all the dominions of the earth, hee contrary to his fathers commandement [to abstain from sex] while they were yet in the Arke, used company with his wife, and craftily went about thereby to dis-inherite the off-spring of his other two brethren: for the which wicked and detestable fact as an example for contempt of Almightie God, and disobedience of parents, God would a sonne should be borne whose name was Chus, who not onely it selfe, but all his posteritie after him should bee so blacke and lothsome, that it might remaine a spectacle of disobedience to all the world.[33]

Like Shylock's genealogy, Best's narrative gives disobedience and disinheritance a crucial role in the formation of difference. In reading Jews and blacks as signs for theft from rightful heirs, such genealogies may have supported the notion for the English reader that these 'aliens' usurp the rightful prerogatives of innocent (pre-Christian) victims. (In other words, forcible seizure of their property is excusable because their ownership is suspect.) The Ham story is a bit more problematic because Ham, the originator of the sin, was himself white. Only his offspring, Chus, bears the burden of the original sin, and the blackness thus becomes a reflection of the nether side of a white self. These biblical 'sub-texts' help support the play's central action: a circulation of wealth to an aristocratic, male elite that is predicated on the control of difference. Aliens must be either assimilated into the dominant culture (Shylock's and Jessica's conversions) and/or completely disempowered (Shylock's sentence). Their use as explanations for racial difference allows for the organisation of property, kinship, and religion within an emerging national – and imperial – identity.

III

Since the Venetian sex/gender system is constructed along the axis of foreign trade, it is not surprising that female characters play key (if little noted) roles in the circulation of wealth. The successful end of courtship (endogamous marriage) is achieved through the balancing of the problems of conversion, inheritance, and difference. The proper pairing of male and female thus comes to represent the re-alignment of wealth and the reassertion of control over difference. In their active desire, these outspoken women are often the more conservative agents of the play. Associated with conversion, they assure that wealth is redistributed into the hands of the male elite.

Merchant offers the Jessica–Lorenzo courtship as a successful type of cross-cultural interaction: one like our original model in Purchas, where cultural difference – and property – are controlled under the aegis of a Christian God. Unlike another disobedient daughter, *Othello*'s Desdemona, Jessica's filial disloyalty is lauded by the community largely because her actions constitute submission to the larger, racially motivated values of Belmont and Venice. Ironically, her very disobedience proves her 'faith' to her husband just as it shows her 'fairness'. Lorenzo declares, 'And fair she is, if that mine eyes be true, / And true she is, as she hath prov'd herself' (II.vi.54–5). In cutting herself off from her father, Jessica also divorces herself from her Jewish ancestry. When she leaves her father's house, Gratiano declaims, 'Now (by my hood) a gentle, and no Jew' (II.vi.51), punningly connecting her conversion with the race and the class privileges of Belmont.

In fact, the very desire to marry a Christian separates Jessica from her father's alienness. Shylock's claim of consanguinity is resolutely denied throughout the play. Salerio declares, 'There is more difference between thy flesh and hers, than between jet and ivory, more between your bloods, than there is between red wine and Rhenish' (III.i.34–6). The terms of Salerio's insistence on absolute difference go as far to exclude Shylock from the realm of humanity (so defined by Christian Venetians) as they do to include Jessica. Jessica herself, in a rehearsal of her own conversion, parodically stages herself as the bride of the Song of Songs, saying, 'I am glad 'tis night – you do not look on me' (II.vi.34), and covering herself with gold, 'I will make fast the doors and gild myself / With some moe ducats' (II.vi.49–50), as she begins the 'conversion' of money from Shylock to Lorenzo. Jessica's disobedience is acted out as a gender transgression: she escapes from her father's house dressed as a page and is playfully aware of her transgressive behaviour, 'For I am much asham'd of my exchange' (II.vi.35). Of the 'exchanges' Jessica makes (husband for father, male dress for female, Christian identity for Jewish), the change in dress is the one she marks as potentially subversive. However, Jessica's cross-dressing is seemingly less complicated than Portia's, since her transgression, taking place as it does during a carnival and facilitating her assimilation into the community of Belmont, is validated by the rest of the play.

Like Jessica's cross-dressing, which is not only excused but lauded in the play, Portia's actions work mainly to fulfil the larger economic needs of the commonwealth. Portia is the focal point of the Venetian economy and its marriage practices: it is through her that money is recirculated to the Christian males and difference is excluded or disempowered. She describes her betrothal as a conversion, 'Myself, and what is mine, to you and yours / Is now converted' (III.ii.166–7). Bassanio's 'pilgrimage' results in the 'conversion' of Portia and her possessions as she too fills the coffers of the male Christians. As Balthazar and as Portia she performs a valuable service to the state. Her disguise allows her to become the agent of conversion and, as Frank Whigham notes, compulsory conversion is associated historically with confiscation of goods by the state. It is she (as Balthazar) who silences the alien. She is the enabling factor that 'converts' cash to its 'rightful owners', not only hers to Bassanio, but Shylock's to the state and to his Christian heirs.

With their cross-dressing and their active pursuit of female desire, both Portia and Jessica break the constraints of gender; nevertheless, in a text dense with cultural, economic, and gender conflict, glorifying these women as the transgressive disrupters of social order may serve only to obscure the very complex nature of difference for a changing society in which racial categories developed along with changing organisations of gender.[34] To look solely at hierarchies of gender defines the issue too narrowly and valorises gender as the primary category of difference. Reading Portia as the heroic, subversive female proves particularly problematic when we place her actions in relation to other categories of difference. While her 'witty' remarks about her suitors display a verbal acumen and forwardness typical of the unruly woman, her subversiveness is severely limited, for her strongest verbal abilities are only bent toward supporting a status quo which mandates the repulsion of aliens and outsiders. To valorise such cross-dressed figures as liberating Others is to ignore the way their freedom functions to oppress the racial/cultural Others in the play. Portia's originally transgressive act is disarmed and validated by the play's resolution when these 'disorderly' women become pliable wives.

Although I have argued that these women serve in some ways as successful comic and economic agents, the play itself does not allow for the same neat elimination of difference offered by Purchas in the opening of this essay. Unlike other Shakespearean comedies, *The Merchant of Venice* ends not with a wedding or the blessing of the bridal bed, but with the exchange of rings and the evocation of adultery. The only immediately fertile couple presented in the play, Launcelot and the Moor, are excluded from the final scene. Her fecundity exists in threatening contrast to the other Venetians' seeming sterility, particularly as it is created with Launcelot Gobbo, the 'gobbling', prodigal servant whose appetites cannot be controlled. Like Shylock's absence, their exclusion qualifies the expected resolution of the text and reminds us of the ultimate failure to contain difference completely even as the play's aliens are silenced. The Moor, whose presence may be a visible sign for the conflation of economic and erotic union with the Other in the rhetoric of travel, provides a pregnant reminder of the problematic underpinnings of the Venetian economy.

In her *Literary Fat Ladies*, Patricia Parker charts the appearance of dilated female bodies in Renaissance texts. While they are specifically located within the rhetorical technique of dilation, these 'fat ladies' are figures for the delay and deferral that is a central topos of many important Renaissance subtexts such as the *Odyssey*, the *Aeneid*, and the Bible (texts that are also key in the troping of imperial desires). The chief purpose of dilation (amplification or the production of *copia*) is mired in an anxiety over uncontrolled excess; hence the texts become as preoccupied with mastery and control over expansion as with the expansion itself. Parker argues, 'Dilation, then, is always something to be kept within the horizon of ending, mastery, and control'.[35] Certainly the problem of controlled expansion reverberates within colonial discourses of the Renaissance as travel writers and editors struggle to produce texts which allow expansion but always within the confines of conversion and colonial mastery. In some ways, the figure of the fat lady serves the same purpose as Purchas's introduction: the promise of profitable conversion within the space allowed by deferral of the judgement of the Second Coming.

These fat ladies resonate within a varied field of meanings associated with the judicial, the temporal, the genealogical, and the erotic. Although Parker does not specifically name Launcelot's Moor in her catalogue of fat ladies, she too operates within a similar web of meaning. She appears in the dilated space of the play that postpones both the resolution of Antonio's dilemma and the consummation of Bassanio's and Portia's betrothal. Like Parker's first example (Nell from *The Comedy of Errors*), she is a large presence that is only described. Not permitted to speak, the Moor still encapsulates ideas of copious fertility and threatening female sexuality.[36] However, unlike the other Shakespearean fat ladies, Launcelot's Moor cannot be regarded as 'a dilative means to a patriarchal end',[37] that is, as a momentary disruption of the text or a deferral that contains the promise of an ordered conclusion. Her pregnancy is a reminder of the dangerous result of uncontrolled crossing of borders, of trade that holds the dual (and irreconcilable) promises of the production of new wealth and of an insupportable excess. The end she promises is a mixed child, whose blackness may not be 'converted' or absorbed within the endogamous, exclusionary values of Belmont.[38] This dusky dark lady is perhaps more like the women of the *Aeneid*, perpetrators 'of delay and even of obstructionism in relation to the master or imperial project of the completion of the text'.[39] She interferes with the 'master/imperial' project of *The Merchant of Venice* – the eradication or assimilation of difference. Unlike other fat ladies, her 'promised end' signals not resolution, but the potential disruption of Europe's imperial text, because in *Merchant*'s Venice – and Elizabeth's England – the possibility of wealth only exists within the dangers of cultural exchange.

From *Renaissance Drama*, 23 (1992), 87–111.

NOTES

[Kim Hall's essay comes at the play from an apparently insignificant detail – the ʼabsent figure of the Moor made pregnant by Launcelot. This leads Hall on to a discussion of the play's 'anxieties over miscegenation' through a discussion of its possible 'sub-texts', a term borrowed from the Marxist critic Fredric Jameson and implying a related text dealing with similar issues. Jameson's best known book is *The Political Unconscious*, and in a way that is also the topic of Hall's essay, how the play dramatises certain racial and political worries produced by imperial expansion and trade with other races. The general pattern of Hall's essay, however, might also be described as new historicist in so far as it is concerned with ideas of power and with bringing together texts from different genres (reports, travel narratives, the play). The method involves what is sometimes called a kind of 'thick description' which focuses on one specific cultural feature and explores it in great detail. What is important to note, though, is that the approach of the essay does not see the play as passive or a mere reflection of its culture but instead as a refashioning of existing ideas and values; all the time the stress is on the dynamics of the play and its larger symbolic history. Hall's essay might usefully be read in conjunction with a similar essay by Steven Mullaney, 'Brothers and Others, or the Art of Alienation', in *Cannibals, Witches, and Divorce: Estranging the Renaissance*, ed. Marjorie Garber (Baltimore and London, 1987). All quotations are from the Arden edition of *The Merchant of Venice*, ed. John Russell Brown (Cambridge, MA, 1959). Ed.]

1. Samuel Purchas, *Hakluytus Posthumus, or Purchas His Pilgrimes: Contayning a History of the World in Sea Voyages and Lande Travells by Englishmen and others* (London, 1625), 1:56. Richard Hakluyt (ed.), *The Principal Navigations, Voyages, Traffiques, & Discoveries of the English Nation* (London, 1598–1600), 3 vols.

2. Gayle Rubin, 'The Traffic in Women: Notes on the "Political Economy" of Sex', in *Toward an Anthropology of Women*, ed. Rayna Reiter (New York, 1975), pp. 157–210; p. 207.

3. Even though the word *intercourse* did not come to have its current sexual connotation until the eighteenth century, Purchas's use of 'commerce and intercourse of amity' resonates powerfully in this way for a modern reader, and I would like to retain this anachronistic sense for

the purposes of this paper. Indeed, this paper will read anachronistically throughout. *Miscegenation*, too, is an eighteenth-century term which has particular resonances for the modern American reader. Like 'race', the word *miscegenation* is particularly enabled by later scientific discourses; however, the concepts certainly predated the scientific sense. Although there certainly were Renaissance words, such as *mulatto*, for the offspring of certain interracial couples, I prefer to use the term *miscegenation*, just as I play on *intercourse*, to locate an emerging modern dynamic for which there was no adequate language.

4. William Shakespeare, *The Merchant of Venice*, ed. John Russell Brown, the Arden Shakespeare (Cambridge, 1959), III.v.35n (p. 99).

5. Anthony Gerard Barthelemy, *Black Face, Maligned Race: The Representation of Blacks in English Drama from Shakespeare to Southerne* (Baton Rouge, LA, 1987), p. 124. Eldred Jones sees this moment as the first glimmer of an emerging stereotype of black women (Eldred D. Jones, *Othello's Countrymen: The African in English Renaissance Drama* [London, 1965], p. 119). He also seems to agree with the Arden editor. He argues that the Launcelot/Moor liaison is an 'earthy basic relationship' which completes a structural pattern of romantic relationships in *Merchant*, yet he downplays the relationship's significance: 'This cold douche of earthy realism is not unlike the Jacques/Audrey contrast to the Orlando/Rosalind, Silvius/Phebe love types in *As You Like It*. The fact that Launcelot's partner is a Moor only lends emphasis to the contrast' (*Othello's Countrymen*, p. 71).

6. Fredric Jameson, *The Political Unconscious: Narrative as a Socially Symbolic Act* (Ithaca, NY, 1981), p. 81.

7. Quoted in Peter Fryer, *Staying Power: The History of Black People in Britain* (Sydney, 1984), p. 10.

8. Quoted in Eldred D. Jones, *The Elizabethan Image of Africa* (Charlottesville, VA, 1971), pp. 20–1. For a more complete discussion, see Peter Fryer's *Staying Power* (pp. 10–12). Fryer provocatively contends that the second order of expulsion was to make up the payment for the return of 89 English prisoners from Spain and Portugal.

9. Karen Newman, '"And wash the Ethiop white": Femininity and the Monstrous in *Othello*', in *Shakespeare Reproduced: The Text in History and Ideology*, ed. Jean E. Howard and Marion F. O'Connor (New York, 1987), pp. 143–62; p. 148.

10. The reprintings of this document indicate some confusion. I have used Eldred Jones's transcription of the 1602 draft proclamation in the Cecil papers, which reads 'are crept'. In contrast, James Walvin's version of this same proclamation reads 'are carried' (James Walvin, *The Black Presence: A Documentary History of the Negro in England, 1555–1860* [New York, 1971], p. 65), as does the version in Hughes

and Larkin (Paul F. Hughes and James F. Larkin [eds], *Tudor Royal Proclamations* [New Haven, CT, 1969], vol. 3, pp. 220–1). The fac-simile included in Jones (plate 5) appears to me to read 'are crept' and I have thus accepted his transcription.

11. English travel writers, not surprisingly, frequently compare their visions of colonial rule with the Spanish model. England saw itself as in part 'correcting' the vexed model of colonial rule in Spain. In his *View of the Present State of Ireland*, Spenser outlines one of the sources of this sense of Spain's mixed heritage, as he suggests that Spain's current riches are the inheritance of a long history of invasion, particularly by Africans: 'ffor the Spaniarde that now is, is come from as rude and salvage nacions, as theare beinge As it maye be gathered by Course of ages and view of theire owne historye (thoughe they thearein labour muche to ennoble themselues) scarse any dropp of the oulde Spannishe blodd lefte in them: ... And yeat after all these the mores and Barbarians breakinge over out of Africa did finallye possesse all spaine or the moste parte thereof And treade downe vnder theire foule hea-thenishe fete what euer litle they founde theare yeat standinge the which thoughe afterwardes they weare beaten out by *fferdinando* of *Arraggon* and Elizabeth his wiffe yeat they weare not so clensed but that thorogh the mariages which they had made and mixture with the people of the lande duringe theire longe Continvance theare they had lefte no pure dropp of Spanishe blodd no nor of Romayne nor Scithian So that of all nacions vnder heaven I suppose the Spaniarde is the most mingled moste vnertaine and most bastardlie ...' (Edmund Spenser, *A View of the Present State of Ireland*, ed. Rudolf Gottfried, in *The Complete Works of Edmund Spenser: A Variorum Edition*, ed. Edwin Greenlaw et al. [Baltimore, MD, 1949], vol. 9, pp. 90–1).

12. Andrew B. Appleby, *Famine in Tudor and Stuart England* (Stanford, CA, 1978), p. 137.

13. Hughes and Larkin, *Proclamations*, p. 172.

14. Kwame Anthony Appiah is the most recent purveyor of this view. In the entry 'Race', in *Critical Terms for Literary Study* (ed. Frank Lentricchia and Thomas McLaughlin [Chicago, 1990], pp. 274–87), he argues, '... in Shakespearean England both Jews and Moors were barely an empirical reality. And even though there were small numbers of Jews and black people in England in Shakespeare's day, attitudes to "the Moor" and "the Jew" do not seem to have been based on experi-ence of these people. Furthermore, despite the fact that there was an increasing amount of information available about dark-skinned foreign-ers in this, the first great period of modern Western exploration, actual reports of black or Jewish foreigners did not play an important part in forming these images. Rather, it seems that the stereotypes were based on an essentially theological conception of the status of both Moors and Jews as non-Christians; the former distinguished by their black

skin, whose colour was associated in Christian iconography with sin and the devil ...' (pp. 277–8). It seems apparent in Elizabeth's document that there was a black presence that had its own reality for Elizabeth and that religion appears as rationale after the fact.

15. Patricia Hill Collins lucidly outlines the connections between the welfare mother and mammy stereotypes, arguing 'Each image transmits clear messages about the proper limits among female sexuality, fertility and Black women's roles in the political economy' (*Black Feminist Thought: Knowledge, Consciousness, and the Politics of Empowerment* [Boston, 1990], p. 78). See also Angela Davis's description of specific political manipulations of the welfare mother image (*Women, Culture, and Politics* [New York, 1990], pp. 23–7).

16. Walter Cohen, *Drama of a Nation: Public Theater in Renaissance England and Spain* (Ithaca, NY, 1985), p. 210.

17. My brief description of cannibalism owes a great deal to Peter Hulme's materialist critique of the term 'cannibal' (*Colonial Encounters: Europe and the Native Caribbean, 1492–1797* [London, 1986], pp. 78–87) as well as to Maggie Kilgour's exploration of metaphors of incorporation. For an anthropologist's critique of the charge of cannibalism, see W. Arens, *The Man-eating Myth: Anthropology and Anthropophagy* (Oxford, 1979).

18. Eric Cheyfitz, *The Poetics of Imperialism: Translation and Colonization from 'The Tempest' to 'Tarzan'* (Oxford, 1991), p. 42; Hulme, *Colonial Encounters*, pp. 81–3; Maggie Kilgour, *From Communion to Cannibalism: An Anatomy of Metaphors of Incorporation* (Princeton, NJ, 1990), pp. 5–7.

19. Philip Massinger, *The Maid of Honour*, in *The Plays and Poems of Philip Massinger*, ed. Philip Edwards and Colin Gibson (Oxford, 1976), vol. 1, 117–97.

20. Hulme, *Colonial Encounters*, p. 83.

21. Richard Hakluyt, *Discourse of Western Planting. The Original Writings & Correspondence of the Two Richard Hakluyts*, Hakluyt Soc. no. 77 (London, 1935), vol. 2, pp. 211–326; p. 234.

22. On blood libel, see Leon Poliakov, *The History of Anti-Semitism*, trans. Richard Howard (New York, 1974–5), vol. 1, p. 58 and Kilgour, *From Communion to Cannibalism*, p. 5. Hulme also suggests a connection in his sense that the rise in accusations of anthropophagy involved the 'ritual purging of the body of European Christendom just prior to, and in the first steps of, the domination of the rest of the world: the forging of a European identity' (*Colonial Encounters*, pp. 85–6). Ben Jonson's *Every Man out of His Humour* contains similar links between economics, cannibalism, and anti-Semitism when Carlo Buffone exclaims, 'Marry, I say, nothing resembling man more than a swine, it follows

nothing can be more nourishing: for indeed, but that it abhors from our nice nature, if we fed upon one another, we should shoot up a great deal faster, and thrive much better: I refer me to your usurous cannibals, or such like: but since it is so contrary, pork, pork is your only feed' (*Every Man out of His Humour*, in *The Complete Plays of Ben Jonson*, ed. G. A. Wilkes [Oxford, 1981], vol. 1, V.v.61–6).

23. Kilgour, *From Communion to Cannibalism*, p. 23. Eric Cheyfitz briefly outlines the relationship of cannibalism to kinship structures in his discussion of Montaigne's 'Of Cannibals': 'Cannibalism expresses, or figures forth, a radical idea of kinship that cuts across the frontiers of hostile groups. To eat the other is to eat the self, for the other is quite literally composed of the selves of one's kin, who compose oneself, just as the self, it follows, is composed of the others one has eaten. Cannibalism, like kinship, expresses forthrightly the essentially equivocal relationship that obtains between self and other' (*The Poetics of Imperialism*, p. 149). As I have suggested, it is precisely this aspect of cannibalism that appears so upsetting to European notions of social order and control. In *A Report of the Kingdome of Congo* (1597), Abraham Hartwell expresses horror at the idea of cannibals who eat their own kin: 'True it is that many nations there are, that feede upon mans flesh as in the east *Indies*, and in *Bresill*, and in other places: but that is only the flesh of their adversaries and enemies, but to eat the flesh of their own friends and subjectes and kinefolkes, it is without all example in any place of the worlde, saving onely in this nation of the Anzichi' (Abraham Hartwell [trans.], *A Report of the Kingdome of Congo, a Region of Africa. And of the Countries that border rounde about the same* [1597], p. 36).

24. I borrow this multivalent use of 'chauvinist' from Susan Griffin, 'The Sacrificial Lamb', in *Racism and Sexism: An Integrated Study*, ed. Paula S. Rothenberg (New York, 1988), pp. 296–305.

25. For more on the gendering of the discourses of travel and trade, see Patricia Parker, *Literary Fat Ladies: Rhetoric, Gender, Property* (New York, 1987), p. 142.

26. Marc Shell, 'The Wether and the Ewe: Verbal Usury in *The Merchant of Venice*', *Kenyon Review*, ns 1:4 (Fall 1979), 65–92; p. 72.

27. In his liberally sympathetic discussion of Morocco's rejection, Frank Whigham ('Ideology and Class Conduct in *The Merchant of Venice*', *Renaissance Drama*, ns 10 [1979], 93–115) acknowledges the racism of courtly ideology by noting that '[t]hroughout the scenes with Morocco the element of complexion provides a measure of the exclusive implications of courtesy in Portia's society' (p. 98). However, Whigham then blames the Moroccan prince for his own loss because of 'his statement of defiant insecurity regarding his skin colour' (p. 98), which is rhetorically out of sync with courtesy theory. His reading remystifies the colour

problem by blaming it on the prince. Portia never mentions his 'imagery of martial exploit and confrontation' (p. 98), only his complexion; so too the tradition of failed suitors indicates to the audience that his unsuitability is not so much a question of rhetorical decorum as racial 'propriety'. In Morocco's case, 'defiant insecurity' may simply be a sensible response to the racism implicit in Portia's courtly ethic.

28. Whigham, 'Ideology and Class Conduct', 106–7.

29. Shakespeare draws upon a system of associations between the Jew and the black which is as old as Christianity itself. For a brief outline of the association of blackness with the Jew, see Sander L. Gilman, *Difference and Pathology: Stereotypes of Sexuality, Race, and Madness* (New York, 1985), pp. 30–5.

30. For an excellent discussion of racial and economic ramifications of the Jacob and Esau parable, see Shell, 'The Wether and the Ewe'.

31. In his *Pseudodoxia Epidemica*, Sir Thomas Browne uses this same parable to explain one theory of the causes of blackness, replacing the biblical injunctions against disobedience with a lesson about the powers of the imagination: '[I]t may be perpended whether it might not fall out the same way that Jacobs cattell became speckled, spotted and ringstraked, that is, by the power and efficacy of Imagination; which produceth effects in the conception correspondent unto the phancy of the Agents in generation' (Sir Thomas Browne, *Pseudodoxia Epidemica*, ed. Robin Robbins [Oxford, 1981], vol. 1, p. 513).

32. Lars Eagle argues that his story is purposely incomplete: 'It is this relation between Jacob and Laban, then, that Shylock is attempting to adduce as an explanation of his own place in the Venetian economy, and, more immediately, as a model for his relation to Antonio' (Lars Engle, '"Thrift is Blessing": Exchange and Explanation in *The Merchant of Venice*', *Shakespeare Quarterly*, 37 [1986], 20–37; 31).

33. Richard Hakluyt (ed.), *The Principal Navigations*, vol. 3, p. 52. It is in this same narrative that Best includes one of the earliest recorded instances of miscegenation in early modern England, which he uses to refute the climatic theory of the cause of blackness: 'I my selfe have seene an Ethiopian as blacke as a cole brought into England, who taking a faire Englishwoman to wife, begat a sonne in all respects as blacke as the father was, although England was his native countrey, and an English woman his mother: whereby it seemeth this blackness proceedeth rather of some natural infection of that man, which was so strong, that neither the nature of the Clime, neither the good complexion of the mother concurring, could any thing alter, and therefore wee cannot impute it to have the nature of the Clime' (*Principal Navigations*, vol. 3, pp. 50–1).

34. Among critics of *The Merchant of Venice*, particularly feminists, there is a great deal of debate over the possible feminist implications of Portia's

transvestite disguise. Is Portia truly the disorderly, unruly female preached against in tracts against cross-dressing or are such disguises diversions which ultimately serve to restore patriarchal order? Catherine Belsey finds the play less radical than its earlier counterparts: '*The Merchant of Venice* is none the less rather less radical in its treatment of women as subjects. ... [The play] ... reproduces some of the theoretical hesitation within which it is situated' (*The Subject of Tragedy: Identity and Difference in Renaissance Drama* [London, 1985], pp. 195–6). Lisa Jardine locates Portia within a tradition of 'confused cultural response[s] to the learned woman' ('Cultural Confusion and Shakespeare's Learned Heroines: "These Are Old Paradoxes"', *Shakespeare Quarterly*, 38 [1987], 1–18; 17) and notes that although Portia possesses many threatening advantages over the males in the play, the play still ends with the sexual subordination of women (p. 17). In contrast, Karen Newman finds in Portia a necessary threat to social order: 'Portia evokes the ideal of a proper Renaissance lady and then transgresses it; she becomes an unruly woman' ('Portia's Ring: Unruly Women and Structures of Exchange in *The Merchant of Venice*', *Shakespeare Quarterly*, 38 [1987], 18–33; 29). Lars Engle also notes a split between conservative and radical elements in the play; however, he sees Portia as part of the latter precisely because she is the agent of exchange: 'On the other hand, more than any other Shakespearean play, *The Merchant of Venice* shows a woman triumphing over men and male systems of exchange: the "male homosocial desire" of Antonio is almost as thoroughly thwarted in the play as is Shylock's vengefulness' ('"Thrift is Blessing"', 37). Nonetheless, male homosocial desire (which can be a conservative force) is also a force which threatens the sex/gender system. [For Newman, see essay 6 – Ed.]

35. Parker, *Literary Fat Ladies*, p. 14.

36. Parker draws on Jardine's connection of the figure of the pregnant woman and her 'grossesse' with fertility and threatening sexuality (Lisa Jardine, *Still Harping on Daughters: Women and Drama in the Age of Shakespeare* [New York, 1983], p. 131; Parker, *Literary Fat Ladies*, p. 18).

37. Parker, *Literary Fat Ladies*, p. 19.

38. Black Africans become in the Renaissance signs for the impossible, which often comes to include the impossibility of their being subdued to European order. The emblem for the impossible, 'washing the Ethiop white', suggests a sense of submission to a European order. Richard Crashaw's poem 'On the Baptized Ethiopian' specifically adapts this as a figure for conversion and the Second Coming. For more see Newman, 'And wash the Ethiop white', and ch. 2 of my dissertation, 'Acknowledging Things of Darkness: Race, Gender and Power in Early Modern England' (Diss. University of Pennsylvania [1990]).

39. Parker, *Literary Fat Ladies*, p. 13.

6

Portia's Ring: Unruly Women and Structures of Exchange in *The Merchant of Venice*

KAREN NEWMAN

The merchant of Shakespeare's title is ambiguous; it applies literally to Antonio, but also characterises Shylock, and indeed all the play's action, not only the 'bond' plot, but the love plot as well. The exchange of goods, whether they be 'rich lading wrack'd on the narrow seas' (III.i.3) or women, characterises the play's action. Readers have often remarked the language of commerce that characterises the Venetian world of the Rialto where even a church, 'the holy edifice of stone', would remind Christian merchants 'of dangerous rocks, / Which touching but my gentle vessel's side / Would scatter all her spices on the stream, / Enrobe the roaring waters with my skills' (I.i.30–4).[1] Here the feminine personification of merchant ship as woman wounded figures both the commodification of woman and her violation. Belmont seems at first to be presented quite differently – talk there is of love, sexuality, familial relationships seemingly free from Venetian economic motives and aims.[2] Portia's suitors are judged not on the basis of their wealth or goods, but in terms of personal and moral qualities, and it must be said, racial prejudice.[3]

But as many readers have noted, any simple binary opposition between Belmont and Venice is misleading, for the aristocratic

117

country life of Belmont shares much with commercial Venice: the matter and mottoes of the caskets suggest commercial values, and Portia's father's will rules her choice of husbands. Though venturing at Belmont is admittedly idealised – Bassanio's quest of Portia is likened to Jason's voyage, thus endowing it with a mythical dimension,[4] and Portia's father's will, through the mottoes, criticises rather than endorses commercial values – what is important is the *structure* of exchange itself which characterises both the economic transactions of Venice and the love relationships forged at Belmont. Venice and Belmont are throughout the play compared and contrasted, but the syntax of exchange itself functions in both locales; indeed, it seems universal.

Before considering structures of exchange in Shakespeare's play, I would like to look in some detail at the status of exchange in anthropology. In his *Essai sur le don*, Marcel Mauss describes and analyses one of the most remarkable features of primitive societies: the extent to which exchange – giving, receiving, and reciprocating gifts – dominates social intercourse.[5] Gift-giving is significant according to Mauss because it establishes and expresses social bonds between the partners of an exchange. In the cultures that Mauss describes, 'food, women, children, possessions, charms, land, labour, services, religious offices, rank' circulate in exchange.[6] By offering a gift, the giver solicits friendship, establishes a relationship, perhaps seeks a reward. Gift-giving can be competitive – its 'underlying motives are competition, rivalry, show and a desire for greatness and wealth'.[7] Acceptance of a gift creates a reciprocal relationship by implying a willingness to return a gift, so by giving a gift that cannot be reciprocated, either because of its kind or its excess, the giver can humiliate the receiver. Perhaps the most striking anthropological example of such gift-giving is the so-called Big Man of highland New Guinea who is assigned in adolescence a *buanyin* or exchange partner, and, apparently against indigenous norms of social behaviour, is trained to an entire system of exchange and gift-giving in excess of what can be reciprocated. Such behaviour results in prestige and power.

Claude Lévi-Strauss reworks Mauss's theory of the gift in his *Elementary Structures of Kinship* by proposing that marriage is the most fundamental form of gift exchange, and women the most basic of gifts. In studying the function and origins of exogamy, Lévi-Strauss argues that incest taboos and other rules prohibiting sexual relations and marriage between family members ensure alliances and relationships among men:

> The prohibition of incest is less a rule prohibiting marriage with the mother, sister, or daughter, than a rule obliging the mother, sister, or daughter to be given to others. It is the supreme rule of the gift. ...[8]

Gift-giving, then, for Mauss and Lévi-Strauss, establishes social bonds and is a strategy of power. For Lévi-Strauss, however, such bonds and strategies are gender specific: they are exercised by and forged between and among men by means of the exchange of women:

> The total relationship of exchange which constitutes marriage is not established between a man and a woman ... but between two groups of men, and the woman figures only as one of the objects in the exchange, not as one of the partners. ...
>
> (p. 115)

> Exchange – and consequently the rule of exogamy which expresses it – has in itself a social value. It provides the means of binding men together, and of superimposing upon the natural links of kinship the henceforth artificial links ... of alliance governed by rule. ... It provides the fundamental and immutable rule ensuring the existence of the group as a group.
>
> (pp. 480–1)

For Lévi-Strauss, the exchange of women is at the origin of social life. His androcentric analysis seeks to authorise the exchange of women and the male bonds it constitutes by claiming that culture depends upon such ties. Feminists have pointed out two related consequences of Lévi-Strauss's claims. On the one hand, the seeming centrality of the woman as desired object is a mystification: she is a pseudo-centre, a prize the winning of which, instead of forging a male/female relation, serves rather to secure male bonds.[9] Others have looked not so much at the woman in this system of exchange, but at the male bonds it establishes. The French psychoanalyst Luce Irigaray postulates that if, as Lévi-Strauss claims,

> the exchanges which organise patriarchal societies take place exclusively between men, ... [and if] women, signs, goods, money, pass from man to man or risk ... slipping into incestuous and endogamous relations which would paralyse all social and economic intercourse, ... [then] the very possibility of the socio-cultural order would entail homosexuality. Homosexuality would be the law that regulates the socio-cultural economy.[10]

Irigaray's use of the French conditional, *exigerait* and *serait*, translated here as 'would entail' and 'would be', and her stipulation that homosexual relations *per se* are prohibited because they risk short-circuiting the very systems of exchange that produce male bonds, suggest her polemical purpose in positing homosexuality as 'the law that regulates the socio-cultural economy'. Irigaray eroticises the ties between men Lévi-Strauss describes in order to suggest a continuum – which she expresses by her pun, 'hom(m)o-sexualité'[11] – that encompasses an entire range of male relations from the homoerotic to the competitive to the commercial. Recently Eve Sedgwick has made the perspectives first conceptualised by Kristeva and Irigaray available to the Anglo-American reader by appropriating the term 'homosocial' from the social sciences to describe 'the whole spectrum of bonds between men, including friendship, mentorship, rivalry, institutional subordination, homosexual genitality, and economic exchange – within which the various forms of the traffic in women take place'.[12]

The Merchant of Venice would seem to offer an exemplary case not only of Lévi-Strauss's exchange system but also of the French feminist critique of that system. The exchange of Portia from her father via the caskets to Bassanio is the *ur*-exchange upon which the 'main' bond plot is based: it produces Bassanio's request for money from Antonio and in turn the bond between Antonio and Shylock. Though the disposition of Portia by her father's will, and the financial arrangements between Bassanio and Antonio that permit Bassanio's courtship, lead to heterosexual marriage, the traffic in women paradoxically promotes and secures homosocial relations between men. Read from within such a system, Portia's seeming centrality is a mystification, a pseudo-centre, for woman in this series of transactions, to repeat Lévi-Strauss's phrase, 'figures only as one of the objects in the exchange, not as one of the partners'. The feminist rereading of Lévi-Strauss also provides another angle from which to read the *Merchant*'s much-debated male relationship. Commentators have often remarked Shakespeare's introduction of the theme of friendship, a shift from the paternal/filial relationship of *Il Pecorone* usually recognised as the *Merchant*'s primary source. But the relationship between Antonio and Bassanio has been interpreted not only as a version of idealised Renaissance friendship, but also as homoerotic.[13] Certainly textual evidence suggests the difficulty in distinguishing between the erotic and the platonic in Antonio's relations with Bassanio. Instead of choosing one interpretation over another, idealised male friendship or homosexuality, Irigaray's reading of Lévi-Strauss allows us to recognise in Antonio's relationship with Bassanio a homosocial bond, a continuum of male relations which the exchange of women entails.

Some anthropologists have challenged not the phallocentrism of Lévi-Strauss's claim that exogamous marriage and the exchange of women is a necessary condition for the formation of social groups and ultimately of culture, but his theory of kinship itself. Pierre Bourdieu, for example, adduces instances of parallel cousin marriage from nomadic and gatherer groups which refute the structuralist interpretation of kinship as a rule-governed *system*, arguing instead that kin relationships are social *practices* that produce and reproduce historically specific social relations. In the cultures Bourdieu examines, for example, women often take part in the choice of a spouse for their children: how marriages are made and what they do 'depend on the aims or collective strategies of the group involved' and are not constitutive *per se* of male bonds or of culture.[14] But Bourdieu's ungendered social science vocabulary ('the collective strategies of the group involved') glosses over the significant fact that these aims and strategies inevitably allot women secondary status, for it is always the bride, and never the groom, who is an object of exchange among family groups and the means whereby social relations are reproduced. However they may disagree about the reasons for and results of kinship 'rules' or 'practices', in both Lévi-Strauss's structural anthropology and Bourdieu's functionalist analysis, women figure as capital, as objects of exchange among men.

But the 'traffic in women' is neither a universal law on which culture depends, as Lévi-Strauss would have it, nor simply a means of producing and reproducing generalised 'social relations', as Bourdieu claims: Kristeva's and Irigaray's analysis of exchange exposes it as a strategy for ensuring hierarchical gender relations. The exchange of women produces and reproduces what Gayle Rubin has termed a 'sex/gender system' in which the traffic in women is only part of an entire system of

> Sexual access, genealogical statuses, lineage names and ancestors, rights and *people* – men, women and children – in concrete systems of social relationships. ... 'Exchange of women' is a shorthand for expressing that the social relations of a kinship system specify that men have certain rights in their female kin, and that women do not have the same rights either to themselves or to their male kin.
>
> (p. 177)

Such a sex/gender system functioned historically in early modern England where marriage, among the elite at least, was primarily a commercial transaction determined by questions of dowry, familial alliances, land ownership, and inheritance.[15] Daughters were pawns in the political and social manoeuvres of their families, particularly their male kin.[16] Marriage contracts and settlements, familiar letters and wills, conduct books and sermons alike recognise in marriage an economic transaction based on the exchange of gifts – women, cash, annuities, rents, land.[17] Divines preached sermons with such titles as 'A Good Wife Gods Gift'; women were explicitly commodified, as in John Wing's exemplary exhortation, in his treatise on marriage, that men seek wives not in the devil's place – playhouses, may games, dance matches – but in God's house, since

> [a]ll men love in merchandising for any commodity, to goe as neere the *welhead* as they can, to such as *make the commodities themselves*, and from whose hands they *doe originally* come.[18]

The commercial language to describe love relationships common in Elizabethan love poetry and in *The Merchant of Venice* displays not only the economic determinants of marriage in Elizabethan society, but England's economic climate more generally – its developing capitalist economy characterised by the growth and expansion of urban centres, particularly London; the rise of banking and overseas trade; and industrial growth with its concomitant need for credit and large amounts of capital.[19] Such changes, as Walter Cohen has demonstrated, inevitably generated anxiety that readers of *The Merchant of Venice* have recognised in the tension Shakespeare created between trade and usury, and in the ultimate triumph of Antonio and his incorporation into Belmont's world of aristocratic, landed values.[20]

The exchange of gifts dominated not only kinship relations, but power relations as well. Gift-giving was a significant aspect of Elizabethan and Jacobean social intercourse, as demonstrated by royal prestation and patronage, and by the New Year's gift roles, account books, and records of aristocratic families who vie with one another in their generosity to the monarch in quest of favour.[21] Not only the monarch and the aristocracy, but the gentry and the middling sort – all took part in these systems of exchange. Even the poorest families participated in such exchange systems: observers describe the custom in English villages of placing a basin in the church at weddings, into which guests placed gifts to help to establish the newly formed family in the community.[22] In the 1620s and

30s, gift-giving declined and signalled the alienation of the aristocracy, gentry, and urban elite from the court.[23]

In Act III, scene ii, of *The Merchant of Venice*, Portia offers her love to Bassanio in a speech that epitomises the Elizabethan sex/gender system:

> You see me Lord Bassanio where I stand,
> Such as I am; though for myself alone
> I would not be ambitious in my wish
> To wish myself much better, yet for you,
> I would be trebled twenty times myself,
> A thousand times more fair, ten thousand times more rich,
> That only to stand high in your account,
> I might in virtues, beauties, livings, friends
> Exceed account: but the full sum of me
> Is sum of something: which to term in gross,
> Is an unlesson'd girl, unschool'd, unpractised,
> Happy in this, she is not yet so old
> But she may learn: happier than this,
> She is not bred so dull but she can learn;
> Happiest of all, is that her gentle spirit
> Commits itself to yours to be directed,
> As from her lord, her governor, her king.
> Myself, and what is mine, to you and yours
> Is now converted. But now I was the lord
> Of this fair mansion, master of my servants,
> Queen o'er myself: and even now, but now,
> This house, these servants, and this same myself
> Are yours, – my lord's! – I give them with this ring.
>
> (III.ii.149–71)

This speech begins with what we might term an affective paradox. Portia presents herself to Bassanio using the first person in an engagingly personal, if highly rhetorical, manner: 'Such as I am.' But her account of herself, as my own dead metaphor suggests, illustrates the exchange between the erotic and the economic that characterises the play's representation of human relations. The rhetorical distance created by the mercantile metaphor shifts the speech from her personal commitment to a more formal bond marked by the giving of her ring, and that move is signalled by the shift to the third person ('an unlesson'd girl ... she'). Portia objectifies herself and thereby suppresses her own agency in bestowing herself on Bassanio. The passives are striking – she casts herself grammatically in the role of object 'to be directed'; she and all she owns 'is converted' to

Bassanio by an unstated agent. Perhaps the most marked stylistic feature of these lines is the repeated use of *now* which signals both temporal shifts and, more importantly, a moment of conversion. The rhetorical balance of line 166 is arrested by the caesura and the *now* of line 167 which insists on the present moment of commitment to Bassanio. The 'but now' that follows refers back in time, emphasising Portia's prior role as 'lord' of Belmont, a role that she yields to Bassanio with her vow 'I give them with this ring'; the moment of fealty is underscored by the repeated 'even now, but now' in line 169.

The governing analogy in Portia's speech is the Renaissance political commonplace that figures marriage and the family as a kingdom in small, a microcosm ruled over by the husband.[24] Portia's speech figures woman as microcosm to man's macrocosm and as subject to his sovereignty. Portia ratifies this prenuptial contract with Bassanio by pledging her ring, which here represents the codified, hierarchical relation of men and women in the Elizabethan sex/gender system in which a woman's husband is 'her lord, her governor, her king'.[25] The ring is a visual sign of her vow of love and submission to Bassanio; it is a representation of Portia's acceptance of Elizabethan marriage which was characterised by women's subjection, their loss of legal rights, and their status as goods or chattel. It signifies her place in a rigidly defined hierarchy of male power and privilege; and her declaration of love at first seems to exemplify her acquiescence to woman's place in such a system.

But Portia's declaration of love veers away in its final lines from the exchange system the preceding lines affirm. Having moved through past time to the present of Portia's pledge and gift of her ring, the speech ends in the future, with a projected loss and its aftermath, with Portia's 'vantage to exclaim on' Bassanio:

> I give them with this ring,
> Which when you part from, lose, or give away,
> Let it presage the ruin of your love,
> And be my vantage to exclaim on you.
>
> (ll.171–4)

Here Portia is the gift-giver, and it is worth remembering Mauss's description of gift-giving in the New Guinea highlands in which an aspiring 'Big Man' gives more than can be reciprocated and in so doing wins prestige and power. Portia gives more than Bassanio can ever reciprocate, first to him, then to Antonio, and finally to Venice itself in her actions in the trial which allow the city to preserve both its law and its precious Christian citizen. In giving more than can be reciprocated, Portia short-circuits the system of exchange and the male bonds it creates, winning her husband away from the arms of Antonio.[26]

Contemporary conduct books and advice about choosing a wife illustrate the dangers of marriage to a woman of higher social status or of greater wealth. Though by law such a marriage makes the husband master of his wife and her goods, in practice contemporary sources suggest unequal marriages often resulted in domination by the wife.[27] Some writers and Puritan divines even claimed that women purposely married younger men, men of lower rank or of less wealth, so as to rule them.[28] Marriage handbooks and sermons all exhort women to submit to their husbands, regardless of disparity in rank or fortune, as in this representative example from Daniel Tuvill's *St Pauls Threefold Cord*:

> Yea, though there were never so great a disproportion betwixt them in state and condition; as say the wife were a Princesse, the husband but a pesant, she must be yet in conjugall respects as a hand-mayd unto him; he must not be as a servant unto her. ... And this subjection is so necessary, that without it the world could not long subsist; yea nature herselfe would suddenly be dissolved. ...[29]

The vehemence and fear of chaos and disorder Tuvill betrays are characteristic and imply a growing need in the Stuart period to shore up eroding class and gender hierarchies.

Bassanio's answer to Portia's pledge of love implicitly recognises such a disparity and its effect by metaphorically making her the master:

> Madam, you have bereft me of all words,
> Only my blood speaks to you in my veins,
> And there is such confusion in my powers,
> As after some oration fairly spoke
> By a beloved prince, there doth appear
> Among the buzzing pleased multitude,
> Where every something being blent together,
> Turns to a wild of nothing, save of joy
> Express'd, and not express'd: but when this ring
> Parts from this finger, then parts life from hence, –
> O then be bold to say Bassanio's dead!
> (III.ii.175–85)

Bassanio's heavily marked epic simile is anomalous in Shakespearean comedy. It echoes the first and perhaps most famous Virgilian simile of the *Aeneid*, when Neptune's effect in quelling the storm inspired by Juno is compared to that of 'a man remarkable / for righteousness and service' for whom the people 'are silent and stand attentively; and he controls their passion by his words and cools their spirits'.[30] Shakespeare translates the Virgilian simile into his own romantic context in which the speaker's words, instead of having a quieting effect on heart and mind, create a Petrarchan paradox: blood that speaks, but a lover silenced. And in keeping with Petrarchan conventions, Bassanio's comparison figures Portia as dominating and distant – that is, as a prince. Renaissance rhetoricians such as Wilson and Puttenham define figurative language as *translation*, 'an inuersion of sence by transport'[31] – a kind of figurative exchange which disturbs normal communication and makes unexpected connections.[32] Poets use tropes so that 'the hearer is ledde by cogitation vppon rehearsall of a Metaphore, and thinketh more by remembraunce of a worde translated, then is there expressely spoken: or els because the whole matter seemeth by a similitude to be opened. ...'[33] Bassanio's political simile with its Virgilian intertextual exchange 'disguises' Portia as a man and prefigures her masculine role in the trial scene where she ensures the Venetian republic by reconciling the principle of equity with the rigour of the law.

We should also remember that Portia, whom Bassanio earlier describes as 'nothing undervalu'd / To Cato's daughter, Brutus' Portia' (I.i.165–6), is named after her classical ancestor who describes herself in *Julius Caesar* as 'A woman well-reputed, Cato's daughter. / Think you I am no stronger than my sex, / Being so fathered and so husbanded?' (II.i.295–7). *That* Portia was renowned in antiquity for sharing the political ideals of her father and husband, and Shakespeare represents her commitment to political action by her insistence, as Plutarch had recorded, on knowing of the plot to murder Caesar and by her taking part in the conference of Republicans at Antium. The *Merchant*'s Portia resembles her classical namesake and her figural persona ('beloved prince') by entering the male lists of law and politics. Far from simply exemplifying the Elizabethan sex/gender system of exchange, the *Merchant* short-circuits the exchange, mocking its authorised social structure and hierarchical gender relations.

For Portia's ring, we should remember, does not remain on Bassanio's finger, and *his* gift of the ring to Balthazar does indeed give Portia 'vantage to exclaim'. The gift of Portia's ring shifts the figurative ground of her speech from synecdoche to metonymy.[34] Her lines first figure the ring as a part of her which she gives as a sign of the whole to Bassanio; in the final lines, however, the prefigured loss of the ring signals not substitution, but contiguity, metonymic relations. By following the movements of her ring, we may discover something about how the play both enacts and interrogates Elizabethan structures of figural and sexual exchange. Objects, like words, change their meaning in different contexts; as things pass from hand to hand, they accumulate meanings from the process of exchange itself. Bassanio gives away his ring in payment for services rendered and in doing so transgresses his pledge to Portia. When it begins its metonymic travels from Bassanio to the young doctor, the ring picks up new meanings which contradict its status as a sign of male possession, fidelity, and values;[35] it moves from Bassanio to Balthazar to Portia to Antonio and back to Bassanio again and the very multiplicity of exchanges undermines its prior signification. The ring also makes a figural progress; in Renaissance rhetorical terms it is transmuted, 'which is, when a word hath a proper signification of the [sic] owne, and being referred to an other thing, hath an other meaning'.[36] Portia's ring becomes a sign of hierarchy subverted by establishing contiguities in which the constituent parts have shifting sexual and syntactic positions. By opening out the metonymic chain to include Balthazar, Bassanio opens his marriage to forces of disorder, to bisexuality, equality between the sexes, and linguistic equivalence in opposition to the decorous world of Renaissance marriage represented by the love pledges in Act III, scene ii. Bassanio gives his ring to an 'unruly woman', that is, to a woman who steps outside her role and function as subservient, a woman who dresses like a man, who embarks upon behaviour ill-suited to her 'weaker' intellect, a woman who argues the law.[37]

In her fine essay, 'Women on Top: Symbolic Sexual Inversion and Political Disorder in Early Modern Europe', Natalie Zemon Davis details the ways in which women's disorderliness manifested itself in England and Europe during this period. Davis observes that anthropologists generally agree that forms of sexual inversion – switches in sex roles, topsy turvy, and images of the world turned upside down, 'the topos of the woman on top' –

> like other rites and ceremonies of reversal, are ultimately sources of order and stability in hierarchical society. They can clarify the structure

by the process of reversing it. They can provide an expression of, and safety valve for, conflicts within the system. They can correct and relieve the system when it has become authoritarian. But, so it is argued, they do not question the basic order of the society itself. They can renew the system, but they cannot change it.[38]

Many feminist critics have agreed with such judgements in their readings of Shakespeare's comedies of sexual inversion. They argue that such play, usually in the service of courtship, is ultimately conservative, leading to conventional gender roles and patriarchal marriage.[39] Portia, we are told, in giving up her disguise and returning Bassanio's ring, returns to 'unthreatening "femininity"'.[40] But Davis herself disputes the interpretation of sexual inversion as simply a safety mechanism. She points out first that historians of early modern Europe are likely to find inversion and reversals less in prescribed rites than in popular festivities and carnival. Cultural play with the concept of the unruly woman, she argues, was a multivalent image which 'could undermine as well as reinforce' traditional hierarchical formations (p. 131). Davis adduces examples of comic and festive inversion that carried over into political action, that provided not only release, but also represented efforts or provided the means whereby the distribution of power in society was questioned and changed. And, I would add, inversion affects not only the distribution of power but also perhaps structures of exchange themselves that historically have ensured male hegemony and patriarchal power. Sexual inversion and play with the *topos* of the woman on top offered an alternative mode of conceiving family structure and gender behaviour within that structure.

When Bassanio leaves for Venice to aid his friend, Portia evokes the conventional ideal of a Renaissance lady: she promises 'My maid Nerissa, and myself meantime / Will live as maids and widows' (III.ii.308–9); to Lorenzo she claims they will live in a monastery to fulfil a vow 'to live in prayer and contemplation', behaviour which conforms to the Renaissance ideal of womanhood: chaste, silent, and obedient. Shakespeare evokes here the accepted codes of feminine behaviour in his culture, thereby distancing the action from the codes of dramatic comedy that permit masculine disguise, female dominance, and linguistic power. Portia evokes the ideal of a proper Renaissance lady and then transgresses it; she becomes an unruly woman.

The common remedies for the weaker sex's disorderliness were, even among the humanists such as Vives, Erasmus, and More, religious training to make her modest and humble, education of a restricted kind designed not to inflame her imagination but to acquaint her with her moral duty, and honest work of a sort appropriate to female capabilities. Transgression of the traditional expectations for women's behaviour brought down wrath such as John Knox's *The First Blast of the Trvmpet Against the Monstrvovs Regiment of Women*:

> ... the holie ghoste doth manifestlie expresse, saying: I suffer not that woman vsurpe authoritie aboue man: he sayth not, I will not, that woman vsurpe authoritie aboue her husband, but he nameth man in generall, taking frome her all power and authoritie, to speake, to reason, to interprete, or to teache, but principallie to rule or to iudge in the assemblie of men. ... [A] woman promoted to sit in the seate of God, that is, to teache, to iudge, or to reigne aboue man, is a monstre in nature, contumelie to God, and a thing most repugnāt to his will ād ordināce.[41]

It might be argued that the excess of Knox's attack, directed specifically against Mary Tudor, reflects his own rather than widely held views. But even humanist writers sympathetic to the cause of women's education assume the propriety of Knox's claims, if not his rhetoric. They exclude women from the public arena and assume the necessity of their silence.[42] Leonardo Bruni, for example, warns that 'rhetoric in all its forms – public discussion, forensic argument, logical fence, and the like – lies absolutely outside the province of women'.[43] When Portia takes off for Venice dressed as a man, she looses her tongue in public talk on subjects ill-suited to the ladylike conduct she posits as a model and does exactly those things Knox and others violently attacked. She engages, that is, in productive labour reserved for men, and not insignificantly, in linguistic labour, in a profession the successful practice of which depends on a knowledge of history and precedent, on logic and reasoning, and on rhetoric, all areas of education traditionally denied to women.

Portia's manner of winning her case, her 'integrative solution' as it has been called, deserves consideration. Her defence depends on a verbal quibble,[44] a characteristic linguistic strategy of Shakespearean clowns which allows them to express ideologically subversive or contradictory attitudes or ideas. Indeed, in the *Merchant*, Launcelot Gobbo uses the quibble for just such purposes. His wordplay around the command to come to dinner at Act III, scene v, line 43, and his earlier play with Jessica on damnation (III.v.4–7), give a double perspective to serious issues in the play, issues of social and Christian hierarchy and the like.[45] Portia and Launcelot Gobbo, woman and servant, are linked by this shared verbal strategy which allows them seemingly at least to reconcile irreconcilable perspectives and to challenge the play's overall mimetic design. They represent the 'other' in the play, those marginal groups that are oppressed under the Elizabethan class/gender system, but whose presence paradoxically is needed to ensure its existence. Their playful, quibbling misuse of language veils their subversive linguistic power. Portia's wise quibble saves the Venetian republic by enabling the Duke to follow the letter of the law *and* to save Antonio, to satisfy the opposing viewpoints represented by the Old and New law, by Shylock and Antonio. In another register, as Walter Cohen has pointed out, it unites the bourgeois values of self-interest with those of the traditional landed gentry, an imaginary literary solution to ideological conflicts manifest in late sixteenth-century England (pp. 776 ff.). But Portia's linguistic play here and in the final scene, like Launcelot Gobbo's, resists the social, sexual, and political system of which she is a part and provides a means for interrogating its distribution of power along gender lines.

The Merchant of Venice does not end with Portia's success in the courtroom; after her winning defence of Antonio, Portia asks Bassanio to return her ring, knowing, as her husband puts it, that 'There's more depends on this than the value.'[46] We know this ring symbolises the bargain of faith in patriarchal marriage Portia and Bassanio have made in Act III, scene ii. By obeying Antonio's exhortation and giving his ring to Balthazar, Bassanio affirms homosocial bonds – the exchange of women, here represented by Portia's ring, sustains relations between men. But Balthazar is, of course, Portia in disguise (and Portia, we should not forget, was played by a boy, so that literally all the love relations in the play are homosocial). When Portia laughs at the thought of 'old swearing / That they did give the rings away to men; / But we'll outface them and outswear them too' (IV.ii.15–17), she keeps her promise. In losing their rings and breaking their promises to Portia and Nerissa, Bassanio and Gratiano seem paradoxically to lose the male privileges the exchange of women and the rings ensured. When in the final act Portia returns her ring to her husband via Antonio, its multiple metonymic travels have changed it. The ring no longer represents the traditional relationship it figured in Act III, scene ii. On its figural as well as literal progress, it accumulates other meanings and associations: cuckoldry and thus female unruliness, female genitalia, woman's changeable nature and so-called animal temperament, her deceptiveness and potential subversion of the rules of possession and fidelity that ensure the male line.[47]

Natalie Zemon Davis observes that female disorderliness was grounded in nature rather than nurture, in cold and wet humours which 'meant a changeable, deceptive and tricky temperament' (p. 124). Physiology accounted for unruly women: shrews, scolds, transvestites, women who transgressed the rules of womanly decorum, were believed to suffer from hysteria, or a fit of what the Renaissance called the 'mother' or the 'wandering womb'. In the intervening time between their marriage and its putative consummation after the play's close, Portia has fallen victim to an imaginative fit of the 'mother' and become an unruly woman. Her so-called 'hysteria' leads her to act like a man, to bisexuality – she dresses up like a man and argues the law, imaginatively expressing her own sexuality by cuckolding her husband with Balthazar. As Portia says when she returns the ring, 'I had it of him: pardon me Bassanio, / For by this ring the doctor lay with me' (V.i.258–9).[48] Instead of the subservient woman of elaborate pledges at Act III, scene ii, Portia's speech at Act V, scene i, lines 266 ff. is filled with imperatives – 'Speak not so grossly ...· read it ... Unseal this letter. ...' Having expressly given over her house to Bassanio in Act III, scene ii, she says in Act V, scene i, 'I have not yet / Enter'd my house' (ll.272–3). She emphasises her power and secret knowledge by giving Antonio the mysterious letter, but refusing to reveal how she came by it: 'You shall not know by what strange accident / I chanced on this letter.'

It is often said that Act V of *The Merchant of Venice* is unusually harmonious even for Shakespearean comedy; certainly the world of usury, hatred, and aggression that characterises Venice has receded.[49] But Act V is far from presenting the harmonious view of love and marriage many have claimed, for even the idyllic opening dialogue between Jessica and Lorenzo is troubled by allusions to unhappy love and broken vows. Lorenzo mockingly calls Jessica a shrew and the play ends on an obscene pun on *ring* and a commonplace joke about female sexuality and cuckoldry, not on the idealised pledges of true love that characterise Act III, scene ii.[50] Portia's verbal skills, her quibbles and play with words, her duplicitous representation of herself as an unlessoned girl who vows 'to live in prayer and contemplation', even as she rules her household and prepares to argue the law, bring together contradictory attitudes and views toward women and their role and place both in drama and society.[51] Bassanio accepts the oppositions that her play with language enacts: 'Sweet doctor, you shall be my bedfellow', he says. But in an aside that scarcely requires a psychoanalytic gloss, Bassanio exclaims 'Why I were best to cut my left hand off, / And swear I lost the ring defending it' (V.i.177–8). Portia's unruliness of language and behaviour exposes the male homosocial bond the exchange of women ensures, but it also multiplies the terms of sexual trafficking so as to disrupt those structures of exchange that ensure hierarchical gender relations and the figural hegemony of the microcosm/macrocosm analogy in Elizabethan marriage. Instead of being 'directed, / As from her lord, her governor, her king', Portia resumes her role as lord of Belmont: 'Let us go in', she commands. As Davis suggests, in the 'little world of the family, with its conspicuous tension between intimacy and power, the larger matters of political and social order could find ready symbolisation' (p. 127). The sexual symbolism of transvestism, the transgression of traditional gender roles and the figural transgression of heterosexual relations, the multivalence of linguistic meanings in women's and clowns' speech, all interrogate and reveal contradictions in the Elizabethan sex/gender system in which women were commodities whose exchange both produced and reproduced hierarchical gender relations.

Portia's masterly speech and gift-giving in the play's final scene return us once more to anthropology and to the powerful Big Man of the New Guinea highlands that Mauss describes. To read Portia's transgression as subversive risks the theoretical accusation that her power finally depends on a reversal, on occupying the position of the Big Man, thereby preserving the oppositions that ground gender hierarchy. Even the term for such a gift-giver – Big <u>Man</u> – is problematic and suggests the reinscription of binary notions of sexual difference, of male and female, binarisms that inevitably allot to one pole, usually the masculine, a positive value, to the other a negative.[52] From such a perspective, all resistance is always already contained, dissipated, recuperated finally to the *status quo*. But *Derrida's* deconstruction of such inversion, unlike many of its ahistorical and ultimately conservative applications, recognises that particular strategies, languages, rhetorics, even behaviours, receive meaning only in sequences of differences,[53] and that those sequences of differences are produced within a particular discourse – philosophy or linguistics, for example – or within a particular historical instance. Behaviours and rhetorics signify within particular discourses, histories, and economies. I have therefore argued that the *Merchant* interrogates the Elizabethan sex/gender system and resists the 'traffic in women', because in early modern England a woman occupying the position of a Big Man, or a lawyer in a Renaissance Venetian courtroom, or the lord of Belmont, is not the same as a man doing so. For a woman, such behaviour is a form of simulation,[54] a confusion that elides the conventional poles of sexual difference by denaturalising gender-coded behaviours; such simulation perverts authorised systems of gender and power. It is inversion with a difference.

From *Shakespeare Quarterly*, 38 (1987), 19–33.

NOTES

[Karen Newman's essay examines the complex social obligations that were at work in Elizabethan marriage exchanges. It is an essay that seeks to challenge much of the implicit ideology in these rituals in which women were constructed as a passive 'Other' affirming male control and rule. What is striking about the essay is the range of theoretical material it employs and challenges, beginning with the anthropology of Lévi-Strauss with its narrow and constricting view of women's role in the social nexus, then moving on to feminist theory, using the French theorists Irigaray and Kristeva to posit a more disruptive – and positive – role of Portia. But what is equally important about Newman's essay is how it returns time and again to the text, to specific words, specific problems. The result is that theory constantly finds itself checked, modified by text as the essay seeks to achieve a different reading of the play, one where woman is not controlled, one where there is always a contestation of the *status quo*. A further and modified version of the essay appears in *The Merchant of Venice*, ed. Nigel Wood (Bristol, 1996), part of the interesting Theory in Practice series published by the Open University. Ed.]

1. *The Merchant of Venice*, The Arden Shakespeare, ed. John Russell Brown (London, 1955: rpt. 1977). All future references are to the Arden edition.

2. Lawrence Danson and other readers have noted 'the play's unusually prominent series of binary relationships', *The Harmonies of 'The Merchant of Venice'* (New Haven, CT, 1989), p. 10.

3. I have chosen deliberately to leave Shylock out of my reading of *The Merchant of Venice* in order to disturb readings of the play that centre their interpretive gestures on the Jew. I recognise the suggestive possibilities, however, of readings such as Marianne Novy's which link Shylock and Portia as outsiders by virtue respectively of their race and

sex, *Love's Argument: Gender Relations in Shakespeare* (Chapel Hill, NC, 1984), pp. 64 ff.

4. See Elizabeth Sklar's interesting comparison of Bassanio and Jason in 'Bassanio's Golden Fleece', *Texas Studies in Literature and Language*, 18 (1976), 500–9.

5. I am indebted to Gayle Rubin's discussion of Mauss in 'The Traffic in Women: Notes on the "Political Economy" of Sex', *Toward an Anthropology of Won en*, ed. Rayna Reiter (New York, 1975). I also thank Lynda Boose whose careful reading of this paper and its anthropological frame steered me to the specific analogy between Portia and the Big Man which I develop here.

6. *Essai sur le don*, trans. Ian Cunnison (New York, rpt. 1967), pp. 11–12.

7. Mauss, 'Traffic in Women', p. 26.

8. *The Elementary Structures of Kinship*, ed. Rodney Needham (Boston, 1969), p. 481.

9. See Julia Kristeva, *Texte du roman* (The Hague, 1970), pp. 160, 60.

10. *Ce sexe qui n'en est pas un* (Paris, 1977), p. 189, my translation. Also available in English translation, *This Sex Which Is Not One*, trans. Catherine Porter with Carolyn Burke (Ithaca, NY, 1985).

11. Irigaray, *Ce sexe*, p. 168. I am grateful to Jonathan Goldberg for reminding me of this orthographic play.

12. 'Sexualism and the Citizen of the World: Wycherley, Sterne and Male Homosocial Desire', *Critical Inquiry*, 11 (1984), 227. For a more extended discussion, including a fine chapter on the sonnets, see her *Between Men: English Literature and Male Homosocial Desire* (New York, 1985). See also Lars Engle, '"Thrift is Blessing": Exchange and Explanation in *The Merchant of Venice*', *Shakespeare Quarterly*, 37 (1986), 20–37, for a discussion of Sedgwick's work in relation to the *Merchant*.

13. Recent critics who explain Antonio's melancholy as a loss of friendship include Leonard Tennenhouse, 'The Counterfeit Order of *The Merchant of Venice*', in *Representing Shakespeare: New Psychoanalytic Essays*, ed. Murray M. Schwartz and Coppélia Kahn (Baltimore, MD, 1980), pp. 57–66, and Keith Geary, 'The Nature of Portia's Victory: Turning to Men in *The Merchant of Venice*', *Shakespeare Survey*, 37 (1984), 55–68. Graham Midgley, '*The Merchant of Venice*: A Reconsideration', *Essays in Criticism*, 10 (1960), 119–33; W. H. Auden, 'Brothers and Others', in *The Dyer's Hand and Other Essays* (New York, 1962); Lawrence W. Hyman, 'The Rival Lovers in *The Merchant of Venice*', *SQ*, 21 (1970), 109–16; and W. Thomas MacCary, *Friends and Lovers: The Phenomenology of Desire in Shakespearean Comedy* (New York, 1985), claim a homoerotic impulse in Antonio's attachment.

14. *Outline of a Theory of Practice*, trans. Richard Nice, Studies in Social Anthropology, No. 16 (Cambridge, 1977), p. 58.

15. Lawrence Stone, *The Family, Sex and Marriage in England 1500–1800* (New York, 1977).

16. See Lisa Jardine, *Still Harping on Daughters: Women and Drama in the Age of Shakespeare* (Brighton, 1983), ch. 3.

17. See E.T., *The Lawes Resolution of Women's Rights: or The Lawes Provision for Women* (London, 1632), also known as *The Women's Lawyer*, which gathers together in one volume contemporary laws about women, property, and marriage. In Bk II, ch. xxxii, there is an extended discussion specifically of the 'condiments of love', that is, the gifts given at marriage. In his recent essay on exchange in the *Merchant*, Lars Engle (see note 12 above) claims Portia's name suggests the marriage portion, a common means of relieving debt in early modern England. Though it is conceivable that an audience might hear 'Portia' as an aural pun on 'portion', the name is not etymologically related to the Latin *portio, -onis*, a share, part, proportion, but Latin *porcus*, pig, and the Roman clan, the Porcii, breeders of pigs.

18. *The Crowne Conjugall or the Spouse Royal* (London, 1632), sig. K2^r.

19. See R. H. Tawney, *Religion and the Rise of Capitalism* (New York, 1947); Christopher Hill, *The Century of Revolution: 1603–1714* (New York, 1982); Lawrence Stone, *The Crisis of the Aristocracy, 1558–1641* (Oxford, 1965), and Keith Wrightson, *English Society 1580–1680* (New Brunswick, NJ, 1982), pp. 122–48.

20. See Walter Cohen's admirable 'The Merchant of Venice and the Possibilities of Historical Criticism', *ELH*, 49 (1983), 765–89, which appears in part in his book, *Drama of a Nation: Public Theater in Renaissance England and Spain* (Ithaca and London, 1985).

21. See particularly Wallace T. MacCaffrey, 'Place and Patronage in Elizabethan Politics', *Elizabethan Government and Society*, ed. S. T. Bindoff, J. Hurstfield, and C. H. Williams (London, 1961), pp. 97–125. For a discussion of prestation and literary fictions in Elizabethan culture, see Louis Adrian Montrose, 'Gifts and Reasons: The Contexts of Peel's *Araygnement of Paris*', *ELH*, 47 (1980), 433–61.

22. See William Vaughn, *The Golden Grove* (London, 1600), sig. M8^r.

23. For a more detailed account of Jacobean gift-giving, see Coppélia Kahn's '"Magic of bounty": *Timon of Athens*, Jacobean Patronage, and Maternal Power', *Shakespeare Quarterly*, 38 (1978), 34–57, especially pp. 41 ff.

24. Kenneth Burke calls this figure the '"noblest synecdoche", the perfect paradigm or prototype for all lesser usages, [which] is found in metaphysical doctrines proclaiming the identity of "microcosm" and 'macrocosm". In

such doctrines, where the individual is treated as a replica of the universe, and vice versa, we have the ideal synecdoche ...' *A Grammar of Motives and A Rhetoric of Motives* (Cleveland, OH, 1962), p. 508.

25. For a contemporary discussion of the giving of rings, see Henry Swinburne, *Treatise of Spousals or Matrimonial Contracts* (London, 1686), but written and published much earlier; see also Anne Parten, 'Re-establishing Sexual Order: The Ring Episode in *The Merchant of Venice*', *Selected Papers of the West Virginia Shakespeare and Renaissance Association*, 6 (1976), 27–34. Parten also remarks this link between Portia's ring and her submission. Engle, cited note 12 above, claims that Portia's actions in the final acts represent 'her triumphant manipulation of homosocial exchange' and her 'absolute mastery' (p. 37). Not only the historical and cultural position of women in early modern England, but also the generic boundaries of comedy seem to me to pre-clude such optimism. We can, however, claim resistance, a dislocation of the structures of exchange.

26. For a discussion of 'negative usury' or 'giving more than you get', see Harry Berger, Jr, 'Marriage and Mercifixion in *The Merchant of Venice*', *SQ* (1981), 155–62. Some readers have argued that Portia must redeem Antonio who 'may make impossible the marriage union Portia seeks', Marc Shell, 'The Wether and the Ewe: Verbal Usury in *The Merchant of Venice*', *Kenyon Review*, 1 (1979), 65–92; see also Engle, cited in note 12 above.

27. Cf. Bartholomew Battus, *The Christian Mans Closet*, trans. William Lowth (London, 1581), Bk 11.

28. William Gouge, *Of Domesticall Duties* (London, 1634), sig. T2^r.

29. (London, 1635), sigs. B4^v–B5^v.

30. Virgil knew the simile from the end of Hesiod's prologue to the *Theogony*, but Shakespeare would only have known it, of course, through Virgil.

31. Puttenham, *The Arte of English Poesie* (1589), in *English Literary Criticism: The Renaissance*, ed. O. B. Hardison, Jr (London, 1967), p. 177.

32. Compare Lévi-Strauss's discussion of language and the emergence of sym-bolic thought in the final pages of *Elementary Structures*: 'But woman could never become just a sign and nothing more, since even in a man's world she is still a person, and since in so far as she is defined as a sign she must be recognised as a generator of signs. In the matrimonial dialogue of men, woman is never purely what is spoken about; for if women in general represent a certain category of signs, destined to a certain kind of communication, each woman preserves a particular value. ... In contrast to words, which have wholly become signs, a woman has remained at once a sign and a value' (p. 496).

33. Thomas Wilson, *The Arte of Rhetorique* (1560), in Hardison, *Renaissance*, p. 42.

34. See Burke's account of metonymy, the basic strategy of which is to convey an 'incorporeal or intangible state in terms of the corporeal or tangible' (p. 506; see note 24 above).

35. This is also the case with the play's other lost ring given as a pre-nuptial pledge, from Leah to Shylock, which Jessica gives to one of Antonio's creditors for a monkey.

36. Wilson, *Arte of Rhetorique*, in Hardison, p. 45.

37. Lisa Jardine discusses the significance of Portia's 'arguing the law', in 'Cultural Confusion and Shakespeare's Learned Heroines: "These are old paradoxes"', *Shakespeare Quarterly*, 38 (1978), 1–18, pp. 12 ff.

38. *Society and Culture in Early Modern France* (Stanford, CA, 1965, rpt. 1975), p. 130. [Further references are given in the text – Ed.] Davis refers to the work of several anthropologists including Gluckman, Turner, Bateson, Flügel, Delcourt, and Meslin.

39. See, for example, Clara Clairborne Park, 'As We Like It: How a Girl Can Be Smart and Still Popular', in *The Woman's Part: Feminist Criticism of Shakespeare*, ed. Carolyn Ruth Swift Lenz, Gayle Green, and Carol Thomas Neely (Urbana, IL, 1980), pp. 100–16; Irene Dash, *Wooing, Wedding and Power: Women in Shakespeare's Plays* (New York, 1981), and more recently, Peter Erickson's *Patriarchal Structures in Shakespeare's Drama* (Berkeley and London, 1985). Compare Richard Horwich who claims that the ring trick is 'a device by which she may exercise her free will'; it restores 'what from the start she complained of lacking – the power of choice', 'Riddle and Dilemma in *The Merchant of Venice*', *Studies in English Literature*, 18 (1977), 199.

40. Parten, 'Re-establishing Sexual Order', p. 32.

41. (London, 1558), sigs. 16^v–17^r.

42. On the position of the learned lady in the Renaissance, see Lisa Jardine, '"O decus Italiae virgo", or the Myth of the Learned Lady in the Renaissance', *Historical Journal*, 28 (1985), 799–819, as well as the opening pages of her essay in *Shakespeare Quarterly*, 38 (1978).

43. *De Studiis et litteris*, trans. William H. Woodward in *Vittorino de Feltre and Other Humanist Educators* (Cambridge, 1897), pp. 124, 126, quoted in Constance Jordan, 'Feminism and the Humanists: The Case of Sir Thomas Elyot's *Defence of Good Women*', *Renaissance Quarterly*, 36 (1983), 181–201. See also Vives's discussion of women and eloquence in Foster Watson (ed.), *Vives and the Renascence Education of Women* (New York, 1912), pp. 48–56 and More's letters, quoted in Watson, esp. pp. 179 ff. Similar exhortations can be found in Protestant tracts.

44. O. Hood Phillips observes that Portia's solution would never have succeeded in court in *Shakespeare and The Lawyers* (London, 1972), pp. 91–118. Bullough claims on the basis of Mosaic Law that 'the separation of flesh and blood is less of a quibble than critics have thought', *Narrative and Dramatic Sources of Shakespeare* (London and New York, 1957), I, 448.

45. See Cohen, cited in note 20 above, pp. 779–81, and Robert Weimann's discussion of inversion and wordplay in *Shakespeare and the Popular Tradition in the Theatre*, ed. Robert Schwartz (Baltimore, MD, 1978), esp. pp. 39–48, 120–50. [Further references to Cohen are given in the text – Ed.]

46. See Murray Biggs's 'A Neurotic Portia', *Shakespeare Survey*, 25 (1972), 153–9, which recognises from an opposite perspective the meaning of Portia's request: 'she, perversely, asks for Bassanio's wedding ring. It is her one fall from heavenly grace.' For a heavily psychoanalytic reading of Portia's behaviour and her quest for mastery, see Vera Jiji, 'Portia Revisited: The Influence of Unconscious Factors Upon Theme and Characterisation in *The Merchant of Venice*', *Literature and Psychology*, 26 (1975), 5–15.

47. Norman Holland presents a number of psychoanalytic accounts of the link between rings and female sexuality in *Psychoanalysis and Shakespeare* (New York, 1966); for folktale sources, see, for example, the Tudor jest book *Tales and Quick Answers* (1530) cited in Parten (see note 25 above).

48. E. A. M. Colman argues in his *The Dramatic Use of Bawdy Shakespeare* (London, 1976) that Shakespeare's bawdy is associated with anarchic and dissident impulses.

49. C. L. Barber claims 'No other comedy ... ends with so full an expression of harmony ... And no final scene is so completely without irony about the joys it celebrates', *Shakespeare's Festive Comedy* (Princeton, NJ, 1957; rpt. 1972), p. 187.

50. In *Love's Argument* Novy claims 'the threats of possessiveness and promiscuity are both dispelled', but does not explain how this should be so (p. 79).

51. Lisa Jardine analyses the link between learning in women and sexual 'forwardness' in her essay in *Shakespeare Quarterly*, 38 (1978), 1–18.

52. See Jacques Derrida, *Of Grammatology*, trans. Gayatri C. Spivak (Baltimore, MD, 1977), and *Writing and Difference*, trans. Alan Bass (Chicago, 1978).

53. Derrida, *Of Grammatology*, pp. 19, 33 ff.

54. See Irigaray's discussion of 'mimetisme' as self-conscious or reflexive imitation in *Ce sexe qui n'en est pas un*, pp. 134 ff.

7

Love in Venice

CATHERINE BELSEY

I

Love in Venice generally has a poor record. For Othello and Desdemona, as three centuries later for Merton Densher and Kate Croy, things work out badly. Love in Venice withholds happiness from Henri and Villanelle, the protagonists of Jeanette Winterson's novel, *The Passion*. It is fatal, of course, to Thomas Mann's Gustav Aschenbach. And Jessica, the twentieth-century heroine of Erica Jong's *Serenissima*, goes to Venice to play her namesake, and has the misfortune to fall in love with Shakespeare.[1] Though the nature of their tragedies changes with cultural history, Venice is generally no place for lovers.

In the circumstances, this essay, which is about *The Merchant of Venice*, should perhaps have been called 'Love in Belmont'. Belmont, after all, is so evidently the location in the play of happy love. Belmont is a fairytale castle, where three suitors come for the hand of the princess, and undergo a test arranged by her father in order to distinguish between true love on the one hand and self-love and greed on the other. It is a refuge for eloping lovers, who flee the precarious world of capital and interest and trade, to find a haven of hospitality, music, poetry, old love stories retold in the night – and the infinite wealth (without origins) which makes all this possible. Belmont is the conventional critical *other* of Venice, its defining romantic opposite. Belmont, it is widely agreed, is feminine, lyrical, aristocratic – and vanishing – while Venice represents the new world of men, market forces and racial tensions.

And yet it is the relationship between Venice and Belmont which generates the romantic plot of the play. Portia's princely suitors are in the event an irrelevance: true love turns out to rely on credit. And when Portia takes an active hand in the affairs of capital, true love undergoes, I want to argue, a radical transformation which has continuing repercussions for us now.

It is surely perverse in a volume on politics and Shakespeare to talk about *The Merchant of Venice* without discussing Shylock, who has quite properly come for twentieth-century criticism, particularly since the Second World War, to represent the crucial issue of this puzzling and in many ways disturbing play. The history of anti-Semitism in our own epoch demands that this question be accorded full attention. If I say nothing about it, that is not because I regard it as less than central, but only because I have nothing of value to add to the existing debate.[2] And meanwhile, the play also presents a sexual politics which is beginning to be the focus of feminist criticism and the cultural history of gender.[3] This essay is offered as a contribution to that discussion.

A reading of the sexual politics of the play might begin where interest in Shylock ends, in Act V. The action of the play seems to have been completed already: the conflict, for better or worse, is over. Act V constitutes a coda to the main plot, a festival, set in Belmont, of love and concord and sexuality, combining elements of poetry and comedy, just as weddings do. Although it has no part in the main events of the play, Act V is conventionally held to complete its 'harmonies', to dissipate tension and reconcile differences.[4] The classic analysis is surely C. L. Barber's:

> No other comedy, until the late romances, ends with so full an expression of harmony as that which we get in the opening of the final scene of *The Merchant of Venice*. And no other final scene is so completely without irony about the joys it celebrates.[5]

It is true that Act V *alludes to* harmony in Lorenzo's account of the music of the spheres. But it also reminds us that we cannot hear the celestial concord 'whilst this muddy vesture of decay / Doth grossly close it in' (V.i.64–5), and this way of talking about the body might seem, if not ironic, at least incongruous in an unqualified celebration of the joy of love. So too, perhaps, is the choice of love stories the newly married Lorenzo and Jessica invoke so lyrically: Troilus and Cressida, Pyramus and Thisbe, Dido, Medea (V.i.1–14).

Nor does the text select from their tragic narratives moments of reciprocal happiness. On the contrary, Troilus is represented on the walls of Troy, sighing his soul towards the Greek camp and the absent Cressida. Thisbe is fearful and dismayed, Dido already deserted. Medea, gathering enchanted herbs, has not yet murdered her children in revenge for Jason's infidelity, but the text hints at her demonic powers and begins her characterisation as a witch.[6]

The stories of Troilus and Cressida, Dido and Aeneas, and Pyramus and Thisbe are also represented on the walls of the temple of Venus in Chaucer's *Parliament of Fowls* (lines 289–91).[7] The temple, with its near-naked goddess lying on a bed of gold in the scented half-light, is surely a perfect allegory of desire. But desire is predicated on deprivation: love's acolytes in the temple include pale-faced Patience and bitter Jealousy; two young people kneel to the goddess crying for help; the altar-candles flicker, fanned by lovers' sighs. The stories painted on the walls tell more of sorrow than of joy. Happy love, as Denis de Rougemont repeatedly reminds us, so that the phrase becomes a kind of refrain running through *Love in the Western World*, happy love has no history.[8] In Chaucer's poem the parliament of the birds, to which the account of the temple of Venus is no more than a prelude, would have no story at all if Nature simply prevailed, and the fowls unproblematically chose their mates and flew away. But the narrative is sustained by the courtly eagles, all three in love with the same mistress, so that two at least are doomed to despair, and all three compelled to wait in hope and fear and longing.

'The moon shines bright. In such a night as this ...' The rhythms and the internal rhymes, in conjunction with the climatic conditions, 'When the sweet wind did gently kiss the trees' (*The Merchant of Venice*, V.i.1–2), all serve to contain and dissipate what is most distressing in Shakespeare's classical and Italian narratives transmuted into medieval romance. The effect is thrilling to the degree that pleasure is infused with danger. It is also profoundly nostalgic in that it looks back to a world, fast disappearing in the late sixteenth century, where love was seen as anarchic, destructive, and dangerous. In the play this world is no longer dominant. Love in *The Merchant of Venice* means marriage, concord, consent, and partnership. It means mutual compatibility and sympathy and support. But the older understanding of love leaves traces in the text, with the effect that desire is only imperfectly domesticated, and in consequence the extent to which Venice is superimposed on Belmont becomes visible to the audience.

II

Desire, as characterised in Western culture, is dangerous. It depends on lack: you desire what you don't have; desire fulfilled is desire suspended. Psychoanalytically, desire can be satisfied only at the level of the imaginary, in that it insists upon absolute recognition from the other.[9] Lacan distinguishes desire from demand, the appeal for love which can be formulated – and met. Desire is the residue of demand, the unutterable within or beyond it. Lacan calls it the 'want-to-be' ('manque-à-être') that demand 'hollows within itself'. Because love cannot be fully present in the signifier, desire is brought to light precisely by the signifying chain itself, the otherness of language, in which it can never be met, since language too lacks being.[10]

Western literature presents desire as immoderate, disproportionate, unstable, thrilling precisely because it is hazardous. Villanelle, Jeanette Winterson's web-footed, cross-dressed Venetian croupier heroine, consistently associates desire with gambling, gambling with passion. Both are compulsive and urgent; both risk the possibility of loss. 'Somewhere between fear and sex passion is.'[11] Gustav Aschenbach is paradoxically elated by the discovery of disease in Venice because he senses a correspondence between the concealed, physical threat to the population and the dangerous secret of his own emotional condition.

Desire is perilous because it annihilates the speaking, knowing, mastering subject, the choosing, commanding self so precious to the Free West. Lovers are conventionally speechless (what can they say that would do justice to desire?). They are uncertain, irrational, out of control; transformed, transported, other than they are. Gustav Aschenbach, the rational, disciplined writer, knows that he ought to warn the Polish family about the pestilence and then leave Venice, but he also knows that passion will prevent him from doing either. 'It would restore him, would give him back himself once more; but he who is beside himself revolts at the idea of self-possession.'[12] For these reasons, desire also undermines the *idea* of the self, calling in question the dualism on which it is founded, deconstructing the opposition between mind and body, as each manifests itself in the province of the other.

We know from endless accounts of burning, freezing Petrarchan lovers, still pursuing, still disdained, wrecked and racked by love neglected, that the Renaissance took full account of the element of danger in desire.[13] And we know it too from the efforts of Astrophil to resist his own destruction, from the ambivalence of Antony towards his strong Egyptian fetters, and from countless tragedies of love in the period, most particularly, perhaps, the work of Middleton. Passion turns women to whores; it renders men effeminate, incapable of manly pursuits; it threatens identity, arousing fears that subjectivity itself is unstable.[14]

Bassanio is able to solve the riddle of the caskets not only because he sees through outward show, but also because he alone among the suitors recognises the appropriate emblem of desire: 'thou meagre lead / Which rather threaten'st than dost promise aught, / Thy paleness moves me more than eloquence ...' (III.ii.104–6).[15] The Prince of Arragon thinks of his own desert, and the silver casket acts as a mirror for his narcissism, revealing the portrait of a blinking idiot (II.ix.30–2, 50, 53). Morocco resolves to take his own desert for granted (II.vii.31–4) and thinks of Portia's value: 'never so rich a gem / Was set in worse than gold' (II.vii.54–5). The golden casket contains death, the destiny of those who serve mammon. Only Bassanio is motivated by desire and knows that lovers give and hazard all they have. His choice vindicates Portia's conviction: 'If you do love me, you will find me out' (III.ii.41).

Even in his triumph Bassanio displays all the symptoms of passion: he is bereft of words; only his blood speaks in his veins, reducing subjectivity to sensation. Turmoil within the subject confounds the familiar system of differences: 'Where every something being blent together / Turns to a wild of nothing save of joy / Expressed and not expressed.' And in case it should all be too easy from now on, he willingly accepts the new hazard that Portia has set him: 'when this ring / Parts from this finger, then parts life from hence' (III.ii.175–84). Even Portia's picture, which is no more than her 'shadow', is full of metaphorical dangers. Her parted lips are sweet friends *sundered*; her hair is a spider's web, 'A golden mesh t'entrap the hearts of men / Faster than gnats in cobwebs.' And in a strange, baroque conceit, Bassanio argues that the rendering of her eyes should surely have blinded the painter: 'having made one, / Methinks it should have power to steal both his / And leave itself unfurnished' (III.ii.118–29).

III

Riddles too are traditionally dangerous because they exploit the duplicity of the signifier, the secret alterity that subsists in meaning.

They prevaricate, explicitly deferring and obscuring the truth. Riddles demonstrate that meaning is neither single nor transparent, that words can be used to conceal it. They show that language itself seduces and betrays those who believe themselves to be in command of it, who imagine it to be an instrument for their use, at their disposal. Riddles equivocate: Portia is what many men desire; but so is death. His own portrait is what Arragon deserves precisely because he supposes that he deserves Portia.

'What has one voice, and goes on four legs in the morning, two legs in the afternoon, and three legs in the evening?' The sphinx posed her riddle to the Thebans, and each time they got it wrong, she devoured one of them. In the play suitors who fail to solve the riddle of the caskets undertake never to marry. Penalties of this kind are common. Riddles are posed by the wise to isolate the foolish. Solomon delighted in them. They feature prominently in the book of Proverbs. The riddle for Portia's hand has the sacred character of a trial by ordeal. As Nerissa explains:

> Your father was ever virtuous, and holy men at their death have good inspirations; therefore the lottery that he hath devised in these three chests of gold, silver, and lead, whereof who chooses his meaning chooses you, will no doubt never be chosen by any rightly but one who you shall rightly love.
>
> (I.ii.27–32)

Traditionally riddles are no joke. It is only the Enlightenment regulation of language, with its insistence on the plain style, affirming the transparency of the signifier, that relegates riddles to the nursery,[16] along with ogres and fairies and all the remaining apparatus of the uncanny.

In folk-tales riddles are a common way of exalting the humble and meek. The youngest of three brothers or the poorest of three candidates has only ingenuity or virtue to draw on. Success depends on quick wits or the help of a grateful friend. One of the commonest situations in folk-tales is a contest for the hand of the princess, and the motif of winning a bride by solving a riddle goes back to the Greek romances, and reappears in the middle ages.[17] Bruno Bettelheim proposes a broadly Freudian interpretation of this recurrent phenomenon:

> Solving the riddle posed by a particular woman stands for the riddle of woman in general, and since marriage usually follows the right

solution, it does not seem farfetched that the riddle to be solved is a sexual one: whoever understands the secret which the other sex presents has gained his maturity.[18]

In a broadly Lacanian reformulation of this proposition it could be argued that the riddle for the hand of the princess is a riddle about the nature of desire, and that the text of *The Merchant of Venice* comes close to making this explicit. In the presumed source in the *Gesta Romanorum*, where the protagonist, interestingly, is a woman, the inscription on the lead vessel is providential: 'Who so chooseth mee, shall finde that God hath disposed for him.'[19] Shakespeare's change locates the meaning of the lead casket firmly in the realm of the secular and the sexual.

Moreover, riddles could be said to enact at the level of the signifier something of the character of desire. Both entail uncertainty, enigma. Both are dangerous. Riddles tease, torment, elude, challenge, and frustrate. Once the answer is known the riddle ceases to fascinate, just as desire evaporates once the *otherness* of the other is mastered. Both riddles and desire depend on a sense of the unpresentable within the process of representation, though desire imagines a metaphysical presence, a real existence elsewhere, while riddles refer to the unpresented, the meaning which is not there but which can be found, and found nowhere else but there.[20] In this sense the wooing of Portia displays a perfect appropriateness, a ceremonial decorum which endows it with all the traditional impersonality of the Anglican marriage service itself (this man ... this woman, making a formal undertaking).[21]

IV

The riddle for Portia's hand is posed, appropriately enough, by a dead father, and solved by the romantic hero. Portia, who also has immoderate desires, cannot act on them but waits, a sacrificial virgin, for the happy outcome of the ordeal (III.ii.111–14, 57). The news from Venice, however, changes everything. Antonio's predicament also poses a riddle: how can he fulfil his contract without losing his life? This time, Bassanio stands helplessly by while Portia and Nerissa turn to men, and Portia-as-Balthazar finds the equivocation which releases her husband's friend: flesh is not blood. An apparently archetypal and yet vanishing order is radically challenged by cross-dressed women who travel from Belmont to Venice and, uniquely in Shakespearian comedy, intervene not only in the public world of history, but specifically in the supremely masculine and political world of law, with the effect of challenging the economic arrangements of the commercial capital of the world.

And then in the final episode of the play it is the women who produce a series of equivocations which constitute yet another riddle, this time concerning the meaning of gender difference within a new kind of marriage, where a wife is a partner and a companion. The exchanges in Act V between Lorenzo and Jessica about old tales of love and death and the unheard music of the spheres are interrupted by the voice of Portia (V.i.110, 113), and her first words to them constitute a riddle to which, of course, the audience knows the answer: 'We have been praying for our husbands' welfare, / Which speed (we hope) the better for our words' (V.i.114–15). The remainder of the play (almost 180 lines of it) consists largely of a series of increasingly bawdy puns and doubles entendres about rings, and this festival of plurality at the level of the signifier poses a riddle about sexual identity which presumably pleases the audience, but entirely baffles Bassanio.

George Puttenham discusses riddles in his handbook of vernacular writers, *The Arte of English Poesie*, printed in 1589. For Puttenham, with his clear humanist and Renaissance commitments, riddles are already becoming childish, though it is possible to see more in them than children might.

> My mother had an old woman in her nurserie, who in the winter nights would put us forth many pretty riddles, whereof this is one:
>
> > *I have a thing and rough it is*
> > *And in the midst a hole Iwis:*
> > *There came a yong man with his ginne,*
> > *And he put it a handfull in.*
>
> The good old Gentlewoman would tell us that were children how it was meant by a furd glove. Some other naughtie body would peradventure have construed it not half so mannerly.[22]

Evidently for Puttenham riddles are engaging, harmless equivocations or ambiguities (unless they're unduly lewd), and the answer can be deduced from the terms of the puzzle itself, though it is not necessarily the first solution a grown-up might think of.[23]

But Puttenham also identifies another category of equivocation, this time profoundly disturbing, to which Steven Mullaney has drawn attention. This is the kind that seduces and betrays Macbeth, because it lies like truth, making it impossible to tell where truth resides. Puttenham calls this figure *amphibology*, and he condemns it roundly as a threat to order. Amphibologies are frequently without evident human or social origin: they emanate from oracles, pagan prophets –or witches, of course. And they particularly constitute the figure of insurrection, misleading the people in times of rebellion,

> as that of Iacke Straw, & Iacke Cade in Richard the seconds time, and in our time by a seditious fellow in Norffolke calling himself Captaine Ket and others in other places of the Realme lead altogether by certaine propheticall rymes, which might be constred two or three wayes as well as that one whereunto the rebelles applied it.[24]

Amphibologies depend on an indeterminacy of meaning which only events can resolve. Puttenham has no patience with them because they have unexpected consequences, and because he associates them with challenges to the social order.

It is difficult to identify with any confidence a clear formal distinction between Puttenham's amphibologies and his riddles. Both depend on ambiguity; both prevaricate and equivocate. Both use words to conceal what is meant, paradoxically bringing out into the open the hidden alterity of meaning. The difference seems to lie in the question of mastery. Riddles promise closure: the old woman in the nursery has the answer, and the children can expect to be told if they have guessed correctly. Like Macbeth, however, Captain Ket has to wait until experience reveals the truth. The proof of the pudding is deferred until it is too late to be any use. Amphibologies mislead. Riddles instal the knowing subject: amphibologies undermine the subject's power to know and consequently to control events.

The riddles posed by Portia and Nerissa in the rings episode of *The Merchant of Venice* mostly concern the sex of the lawyer. 'In faith, I gave it to the judge's clerk. / Would he were gelt that had it for my part', Graziano stoutly affirms (V.i.143–4). The clerk *is* 'gelt', of course, to the extent that in the Renaissance, as in a different way for Freud, women are incomplete men,[25] and the pleasure for the audience lies in identifying a meaning which is not available to the speaker.

> **Nerissa**   The clerk will ne'er wear hair on's face that had it.
> **Graziano**   He will an if he live to be a man.
> **Nerissa**   Ay, if a woman live to be a man.
> **Graziano**   Now by this hand, I gave it to a youth …
>   (V.i.158–61)

All these utterances are true. By a radical transgression of the differences that hold meaning in place, the youth and the woman are the same person, though Nerissa and the woman she speaks of are not the same. The speed of the exchanges requires some agility on the part of the audience, though not, perhaps, the degree of mobility needed to follow the dizzying series of shifts in the meanings Portia attributes to the 'doctor':

> Since he hath got the jewel that I loved,
> And that which you did swear to keep for me,
> I will become as liberal as you.
> I'll not deny him anything I have,
> No, not my body nor my husband's bed:
> Know him I shall, I am well sure of it.
> Lie not a night from home. Watch me like Argus.
> If you do not, if I be left alone,
> Now by mine honour, which is yet mine own,
> I'll have that doctor for my bedfellow.
>   (V.i.224–33)

Here Bassanio once again confronts three apparently exclusive options. First, the doctor is a woman (but not Portia, whose honour is still her own), and the woman has taken the 'jewel' that Bassanio promised, by marrying her, to keep for Portia herself. Second, the doctor is a man, and Portia is willing to share her bed with him. And finally the doctor is Portia, her bedfellow when she is alone. Each of the options contains part of the answer. No wonder Bassanio is baffled, and Portia has to spell out the truth for him (V.i.269–70).

The full answer to the riddle of the rings is that Portia has more than one identity. There is a sense in which the multiple meanings here recapitulate the action of the play. Portia has always been other than she is. The fairytale princess, a sacrificial virgin, as she characterised herself, was not only 'an unlessoned girl' but also (and in the same speech) 'the lord / Of this fair mansion, master of my servants, / Queen o'er myself' (III.ii.159, 167–9). Evidently to be an heiress is already to disrupt the rules of gender. But her marriage in conjunction with her Venetian journey (and the deferred consummation confirms them as inextricable) invests her with a new kind of polysemy. The equivocations and doubles entendres of Act V celebrate a sexual indeterminacy, which is not in-difference but multiplicity.

In this sense the episode of the rings surely resembles Puttenham's category of amphibology rather than his concept of the riddle. The answer cannot be deduced from the terms of the puzzle itself. At one level, of course, the solution to the ambiguities and equivocations of the scene is readily available: the doctor and his clerk are also women. That knowledge sustains all the puns and resolves all the contradictions, and thus ensures for the audience the pleasure of mastering a succession of rapidly shifting meanings. This pleasure may help to account for the feeling of harmony which so many critics derive from Act V. But there is another sense in which the implications of the episode are more elusive. The double act between Portia and Nerissa takes their performance beyond the realm of the individual, endowing it with a representative quality, and the reference back through the text which the episode invites, suggests a more metaphysical question: what, in a world where Belmont encounters the values of Venice, does it mean to be a wife?

Portia claims the ring in return for rescuing Bassanio's friend and thus, indirectly, Bassanio himself. Like Britomart, the lady becomes a warrior, and the equal of her man. 'If you had known,' she says to Bassanio, 'half her worthiness that gave the ring ...' (V.i.199–200). The role of desire is fully acknowledged in the casket scene, and the importance of sexual difference is repeatedly affirmed in the bawdy double meanings of Act V. This is evident in the final pun, delivered, appropriately, by Graziano: 'Well, while I live I'll fear no other thing / So sore, as keeping safe Nerissa's ring' (V.i.306–7), though Stephen Orgel points out that an element of indeterminacy remains even here. Anatomical rings may be masculine as well as feminine, and the preceding lines are: 'But were the day come, I should wish it dark / Till I were couching with the doctor's clerk.' But the other non-sexual, non-differential 'half' of Portia's worthiness as a wife is made apparent in her performance as Bassanio's fellow-warrior, partner and friend. The solution to the riddle of the rings is thus a utopian vision of the new possibilities of marriage. The riddle does not originate with Portia and Nerissa, nor even entirely with their author, for all his familiar human wisdom. On the contrary, it is the effect of a specific cultural moment when the meaning of marriage is unstable, contested, and open to radical reconstruction.[26] The riddle is also deeply socially disruptive in its fundamental challenge to the patriarchal order.

In the episode of the rings happy love acquires a history by super-imposing a similitude on the existing difference. The otherness which is the condition of desire is brought into conjunction with a comradeship which assumes a parallel, a likeness of values and dispositions. The gap that lies between these two 'halves' of what constitutes conjugal worth is dramatised both in the disjunction between the two parts of Act V and in the multiple identity that is required of Portia.

V

If the term 'wife' absorbs the meaning of 'friend', what place in the signifying chain, what specific difference is left for the meaning of friendship? We can, of course, reduce the metaphysical burden of Antonio's apparently unmotivated melancholy to disappointed homoerotic desire. This is a possible reading and not one that I wish to discredit.[27] Certainly the play constructs a symmetry between Antonio and Portia. It is Antonio who assures Bassanio, 'My purse, my person, my extremest means / Lie all unlocked to your occasions' (I.i.138–9), but it might equally have been Portia who said it (see III.ii.304–5). And certainly in Acts IV and V this symmetry turns into the contest between two kinds of obligation which is evident in the episode of the rings. But my view is that the play here presents to the audience the implications of a contest for meaning, including the meaning of sexuality, which throws into relief something of the distance between the culture of Renaissance England and our own.

In court in Act IV Bassanio declares:

> Antonio, I am married to a wife
> Which is as dear to me as life itself,
> But life itself, my wife, and all the world
> Are not with me esteemed above thy life.
> I would lose all, ay, sacrifice them all
> Here to this devil, to deliver you.
> (IV.i.279–84)

Bassanio's priorities are surely shocking to a modern audience. Men are not supposed to prefer their friends to their wives. On the contrary, in our normative society, while adolescent sexuality is allowed to include homosocial or even homoerotic desire, this phase is

supposed to be left behind by adults, who 'naturally' privilege heterosexual marriage. (At least one recent reading of *The Merchant of
Venice* takes this pattern of 'normal' development for granted.[28])

But Bassanio's position is not without a Renaissance pedigree. In
Sir Thomas Elyot's *The Governour* (1531) Titus and Gysippus grow
up together and are inseparable until Gysippus falls in love and
decides to marry. But when Titus meets his friend's proposed bride,
to his own horror, he instantly falls in love with her too. Overcome
by the double anguish of desire and disloyalty, Titus takes to his
bed. At last Gysippus prises the secret out of him, and once he
knows the truth he is easily able to resolve the problem. The friends
agree to substitute Titus for Gysippus on the wedding day. Thus
friendship is preserved. Gysippus is publicly embarrassed, and has to
leave town for a time, but otherwise all is well, and Elyot tri-
umphantly cites the story as an 'example in the affectes of frend-
shippe'.[29] The values here resemble those of Chaucer's *Knight's
Tale*, where love tragically destroys chivalric friendship. The relationship between Palamon and Arcite is heroic; love, on the other
hand, is high folly, according to Theseus, and the text does nothing
to counteract this view (lines 1798–9). According to Geron's
aphoristic assessment of the priorities in Lyly's *Endimion*,

> Love is but an eye-worme, which onely tickleth the heade with hopes,
> and wishes: friendshippe the image of eternitie, in which there is
> nothing moveable, nothing mischeevous … Time draweth wrinckles
> in a fayre face, but addeth fresh colours to a faste friende, which
> neither heate, nor cold, nor miserie, nor place, nor destiny, can alter
> or diminish.
>
> (3.4.123–36)[30]

Eumenides accepts this evaluation, chooses friendship, and is re-
warded with love too.

When Damon is falsely accused of spying in the play by Richard
Edwards, his friend Pithias volunteers to take his place in prison and
to be executed if Damon fails to return in time. The hangman finds
this remarkable:

> Here is a made man I tell thee, I have a wyfe
>   whom I love well,
> And if iche would die for her, chould iche
>   weare in Hell:
> Wylt thou doo more for a man, then I woulde
>   for a woman(?)

And Pithias replies firmly, 'Yea, that I wyll' (lines 1076–80).[31] It is not clear how seriously we are invited to take the values of the hangman, but it is evident that Pithias is right about the supreme obligations of friendship in this most pedagogic of plays, written in the 1560s by the Master of the Chapel Royal for the Children to perform. Even as late as *The Two Noble Kinsmen* in 1613 the conflicting claims of marriage and friendship are matter for debate this time between women. Hippolyta reflects without rancour on the affections of Theseus, divided between herself and his friend Pirithous:

> Their knot of love,
> Tied, weaved, entangled, with so true, so long,
> And with a finger of so deep a cunning,
> May be outworn, never undone. I think
> Theseus cannot be umpire to himself,
> Cleaving his conscience into twain and doing
> Each side like justice, which he loves best.
> (I.iii.41–7)

Hippolyta finally concludes that Theseus prefers her (I.iii.95–7), but not before Emilia has put the case for friendship between members of the same sex as the stronger force: 'the true love 'tween maid and maid may be / More than in sex dividual' (I.iii.81–2). In the end Hippolyta and Emilia agree to differ.

Both *The Governor* and *Endimion* are cited by Bullough as possible sources of *The Two Gentlemen of Verona*, where Valentine offers his beloved Silvia to his friend Proteus.[32] Bullough finds Valentine's gesture 'Quixotic', as presumably most twentieth-century commentators would.[33] And indeed the play has so enlisted our sympathy for Julia that we cannot want Proteus to accept his friend's generosity. Elsewhere too Shakespeare's texts tend to opt, however uneasily, for the nuclear couple. Othello, who should prefer his wife, tragically listens to his friend. More specifically, in *Much Ado About Nothing*, which is chronologically closer to *The Merchant of Venice*, Beatrice's imperative to Benedick on behalf of her cousin also foregrounds the conflicting obligations of lovers and friends. The loyalty of Beatrice to Hero is absolute, and at the moment when Benedick declares his love for Beatrice, her immediate concern is Hero's honour. Beatrice's challenge necessarily threatens the loyalty of Benedick to Claudio.

Benedick   Come, bid me do anything for thee.
Beatrice   Kill Claudio.
Benedick   Ha! Not for the wide world.

(IV.i.289–91)

Whether or not Benedick's moment of recoil is played as comedy, the play goes on in the event to realign him explicitly as Beatrice's 'friend' (IV.i.319) and thus as Claudio's enemy. Later the text reverts to this issue when, in the course of a series of teasing exchanges, an instance of the verbal friction characteristic of desire,[34] Beatrice sets up an opposition between Benedick's friendship and his 'heart'. But this time she opts for friendship with Benedick even at the price of love:

Benedick   ... I love thee against my will.
Beatrice   In spite of your heart, I think. Alas, poor heart. If you spite it for my sake I will spite it for yours, for I will never love that which my friend hates.

(V.ii.61–4)[35]

This *is* comedy. The play's treatment of the issue is more complex: Beatrice's challenge to Benedick to fight for her evokes classical myth and medieval romance, rather than the new model of marriage. At the same time, we are invited to understand that Benedick qualifies as a husband to the degree that he is prepared to sacrifice his friend. It is no surprise, therefore, that in *The Merchant of Venice* Bassanio's declaration that his friend comes first does not go unchallenged. At once Balthazar, uniquely in the court scene, draws the attention of the audience to his/her other identity: 'Your wife would give you little thanks for that / If she were by to hear you make the offer' (IV.i.285–6). When Bassanio surrenders the ring to Balthazar it is in response to Antonio's persuasion, and the conflict of obligations is made explicit:

My Lord Bassanio, let him have the ring.
Let his deservings and my love withal
Be valued 'gainst your wife's commandement.

(IV.i.446–8)

Bassanio subsequently excuses himself to Portia in the vocabulary of chivalry:

Even he that had held up the very life
Of my dear friend. What should I say, sweet lady?
I was enforced to send it after him.
I was beset with shame and courtesy.
My honour would not let ingratitude
So much besmear it.

(V.i.214–19)

And here, perhaps, is a pointer to the residual meaning of friendship in the period. Georges Duby gives a graphic account of the life of chivalry among the 'youth' of twelfth-century France. These men constituted a substantial proportion of the audience, and therefore, no doubt, much of the motive, for the new romantic love stories and troubadour poems of the period. A version of their image survives in ideal form in the nostalgic culture of late sixteenth-century England, most obviously in texts like *The Faerie Queene*, in response to the Queen's enthusiastic cultivation of the heroic and courtly ideal.

Duby's 'youths' were fully grown knights who were not yet fathers. This stage of life might last, it appears, for upwards of twenty years. During this period the 'youth', often accompanied by a slightly more experienced 'youth', or as one of a group of fast friends who loved each other like brothers, roamed in pursuit of adventure and, more specifically, in quest of a wife. The eldest son could expect in due course to inherit his father's property. But in a world where the patrimony was expected to provide a living for the couple as well as a marriage settlement for the wife, younger sons had usually little to hope for outside a career in the church, unless they could locate an heiress, secure her father's approval and marry her.

Since the life the 'youth' was violent and dangerous, whole male lineages were in practice eliminated, and rich women were not as rare as might be expected, though only a tiny minority of the 'youth' could hope to secure one. In the meantime, groups of men, officially celibate, lived and fought together. We may assume that in such circumstances the virtue of loyalty was paramount: at least in their idealised, literary form, the knights were conventionally bosom friends and inseparable companions. Once married, and a father, the knight gave priority to his own establishment, though he might well retain some of his former comrades in his household, and indeed help them to find suitable brides.[36]

Duby's account gives no indication of a conflict between love and friendship. In a chivalric culture love endangers friendship when it becomes rivalry, as *The Knight's Tale* shows, but wives do not supplant friends: their role is quite different. The new model of marriage in the sixteenth century, however, identified wives precisely as friends, and the texts of the period bring to light some of the uncertainties and anxieties which attend the process of redefinition. Antonio is sad because he is in mourning for friendship. Of course, Portia does it nicely. She gives the ring to Antonio to give back to Bassanio, so that Antonio feels included. But he knows from the beginning of the play that things will never be the same again.

And what about the place of homoerotic desire? Perhaps we shall never know. Eve Kosofsky Sedgwick is surely right to urge that 'the sexual context of that period is too far irrecoverable for us to be able to disentangle boasts, confessions, undertones, overtones, jokes, the unthinkable, the taken-for-granted, the unmentionable-but-often-done-anyway, etc.'[37] It seems unlikely that medieval knights were as chaste as the chivalric code required. On the other hand, while sodomy was consistently identified as an abominable crime, homosexual acts were very rarely prosecuted in England in the middle ages or the Renaissance.[38] In practice the whole issue seems to have generated relatively little anxiety. Stephen Orgel in a brilliant contribution to the cultural history of the sixteenth century argues that homosexual acts were perceived as less dangerous to men than heterosexual love, because it was association with women which was effeminating.[39]

A single example may indicate the difficulty we have in construing the meanings of a vanished culture. In *The Two Noble Kinsmen* the relationship between Palamon and Arcite is treated in remarkable detail. They love each other; they lighten each other's imprisonment. Arcite declares, apparently without embarrassment, that since imprisonment will prevent them from marrying, 'We are one another's wife, ever begetting / New births of love' (II.ii.80–1). At the same time, it is clear that their explicit sexual preferences are heterosexual. The whole plot depends on this. And besides, the text makes clear that they admire each other greatly for their former heterosexual conquests (III.iii.30–42).

Possibly our difficulty resides in the plurality of the word 'love'? Palamon loves Arcite; Arcite loves Palamon; but both Palamon and Arcite love Emilia. Perhaps it is not only our difficulty: Palamon explicitly distinguishes between love and desire, in order to be sure that his cousin is really his rival. 'You love her then?' 'Who would not?' 'And desire her?' (II.ii.159–61). It could be argued, then, that the play sets up its own system of differences: that while love might or might not be sexual, desire is erotic in this text. It could be argued, were it not for Palamon's final words to the dying Arcite, which surely deconstruct any such opposition:

> O cousin,
> That we should things desire which do cost us
> The loss of our desire! That nought could buy
> Dear love, but loss of dear love.
> (V.vi.109–12)

Here heterosexual passion and homosocial friendship are defined in exactly the same terms: both are dear love; both are desire. It remains for the audience to determine whether Palamon's words are best understood as conflating difference (one love, one desire, at the price of its similitude) or as turning to account the difference within the signifier (one love, one desire, at the cost of its distinguishing, differentiating other).

VI

A tentative history of our own cultural moment emerges from all this. Our more carefully regulated meanings impose narrow limits on the range of possibilities available to us. Since Freud we have learned that all intense emotion is 'really' sexual; since the Enlightenment we have known how to classify and evaluate deviance; and since *The Merchant of Venice* we have known that marriage, which includes every imaginable adult relationship, ought to be enough for anyone.

I wonder ...

From *Shakespeare Survey*, 44 (1991), 41–53.

NOTES

[Catherine Belsey describes her essay as a contribution to a discussion of the play's sexual politics, a topic of interest both to feminist criticism and also to cultural historians. The essay focuses attention on the festivity of Act V. As Belsey notes, the move in the final Act is from Venice and its 'new world of men, market forces and racial tensions' to 'its romantic opposite Belmont ... feminine, lyrical, aristocratic'. But the last Act, Belsey contends, is marked not by harmony but instead is troubled by stories of deceit and trickery, by allusions to a world where 'love was seen anarchic, destructive, and dangerous' rather than the equivalent of 'marriage, concord, consent, and partnership'. It is these two understandings of love the essay is concerned with thematically, but its real concern is with a Lacanian reading of the text, using Lacan's notion of desire – that which cannot be met or fulfilled – to discuss the play's riddling language. At the same time the essay sets the play in a broader framework of comedy and romance, exploring the conflict between love and friendship to question and throw into doubt what we can know about a vanished culture, or indeed, our own culture. All quotations are from the Arden edition of *The Merchant of Venice*, ed. John Russell Brown (London, 1959). Ed.]

1. I owe this reference to Kristina Engler.

2. For an account of the debate (and selective bibliography), see Walter Cohen, *Drama of a Nation: Public Theater in Renaissance England and Spain* (Ithaca, NY, 1985), pp. 196–7. See also Cohen's own analysis, pp. 195–211; Thomas Moisan, '"Which is the Merchant here? and Which the Jew"?: Subversion and Recuperation in *The Merchant of Venice*', *Shakespeare Reproduced: The Text in History and Idelogy*, ed. Jean E. Howard and Marion F. O'Connor (New York, 1987), pp. 188–206; Kiernan Ryan, *Shakespeare* (London, 1989), pp. 14–24; and John Drakakis, '*The Merchant of Venice*, or Christian Patriarchy and its Discontents', *In Mortal Shakespeare: Radical Readings*, ed. Manuel Barbeito (Santiago de Compostela, 1989), pp. 69–93. [For Cohen, see essay 3; for Ryan, see essay 2; for Drakakis, see essay 9 – Ed.]

3. See for example Linda Bamber, *Comic Women, Tragic Men: A Study of Gender and Genre in Shakespeare* (Stanford, CA, 1982), pp. 109–33; Keith Geary, 'The Nature of Portia's Victory: Turning Men in *The Merchant of Venice*', *Shakespeare Survey*, 37 (1984), 55–68: Lars Engle, '"Thrift and Blessing": Exchange and Explanation in *The Merchant of Venice*', *Shakespeare Quarterly*, 37 (1986), 20–37, Karen Newman, 'Portia's Ring: Unruly Women and Structure of Exchange in *The Merchant of Venice*', *Shakespeare Quarterly*, 38 (1987), 19–33 [see essay 6 – Ed.]; Jean Howard, 'Crossdressing, the Theatre, and Gender Struggle in Early Modern England', *Shakespeare Quarterly*, 39 (1988), 418–40.

4. See for example Lawrence Danson, *The Harmonies of 'The Merchant of Venice'* (New Haven, CT, 1978), pp. 170–95.

5. C. L. Barber, *Shakespeare's Festive Comedy: A Study of Dramatic Form and its Relation to Social Custom* (Princeton, NJ, 1959), p. 187.

6. The specific reference is to Ovid, *Metamorphoses* vii, 162 ff. Medea treats Aeson with rejuvenating herbs. When the daughters of Pelias subsequently ask for her help, she deliberately offers them inefficacious herbs and thus causes them to being about his death. I owe this point

to Michael Comber. See also Jonathan Bate, 'Ovid and the Mature Tragedies: Metamorphosis in *Othello* and *King Lear*', *Shakespeare Survey*, 41 (1989), 133–44, pp. 134–5.

7. Geoffrey Chaucer, *Works*, ed. F. N. Robinson (London, 1957).

8. Denis de Rougemont, *Love in the Western World*, trans. Montgomery Belgion (Princeton, NJ, 1983), pp. 15 and *passim*.

9. Jean Laplanche and J.-B. Pontalis, 'Wish (Desire)', in *The Language of Psychoanalysis*, trans. Donald Nicholson-Smith (London, 1973), pp. 481–3. Cf. Jacques Lacan, *Ecrits: A Selection*, trans. Alan Sheridan (London, 1977), p. 58.

10. Lacan, *Ecrits*, pp. 263, 265.

11. Jeanette Winterson, *The Passion* (London, 1988), p. 62. Cf. pp. 55, 66.

12. Thomas Mann, *Death in Venice, Tristan, Tonio Kröger* (London, 1955), p. 74.

13. See Scott Wilson, 'Racked on the Tyrant's Bed: The Politics of Pleasure and Pain and the Elizabethan Sonnet Sequences', *Textual Practice*, 3 (1989), 234–49.

14. Laura Levine, 'Men in Women's Clothing: Antitheatricality and Effeminization from 1579–1642', *Criticism*, 28 (1986), 121–43; Stephen Orgel, 'Nobody's Perfect: Or Why Did the English Stage Take Boys for Women?', *South Atlantic Quarterly*, 88 (1989), 7–29.

15. Freud argues that Bassanio's choice (which is really a choice between three women) betrays an acknowledgement of ineluctable death, masked as the choice of a desirable woman (Sigmund Freud, 'The Theme of the Three Caskets', *Complete Psychological Works*, SE 12, ed. James Strachey [London, 1958], pp. 291–301). Sarah Kofman, developing Freud's argument, sees the episode as a representation of the 'ambivalence' (or duplicity) of love: the wish for love is superimposed on the awareness of death, but the imagery prevents the complete success of the process, so that the audience is satisfied at the level of fantasy but also at the level of the intellect (Sarah Kofman, 'Conversions: *The Merchant of Venice* Under the Sign of Saturn', in *Literary Theory Today*, ed. Peter Collier and Helga Geyer-Ryan [Cambridge, 1990], pp. 142–66).

16. Mark Bryant, *Dictionary of Riddles* (London, 1990), p. 51.

17. Stith Thompson, *The Folktale* (Berkeley, CA, 1977), pp. 153–8.

18. Bruno Bettelheim, *The Uses of Enchantment: The Meaning and Importance of Fairy Tales* (London 1978), p. 128.

19. John Russell Brown (ed.), *The Merchant of Venice* (London, 1959), p. 173.

20. Wyatt exploits the parallel in his riddles of forbidden desire. See for example 'A ladye gave ne a gyfte she had not ...' and 'What wourde is that that chaungeth not?', *The Collected Poems of Sir Thomas Wyatt*, ed. Kenneth Muir and Patricia Thomson (Liverpool, 1969), pp. 238, 36.

21. The view that Bassanio is no more than a fortune-hunter who desires Portia only, or primarily, for her money seems to me anachronistic, probably filtered by Victorian fiction, where love and money are commonly opposed.

22. George Puttenham, *The Arte of English Poesie*, ed. G. D. Willcock and A. Walker (Cambridge, 1936), p. 188.

23. William Dodd identifies a structural analogy between riddle and comedy, which also sets a puzzle and finally solves it, though not in the most obvious way. See *Misura per misura: la transparenza della commedia* (Milano, 1979), pp. 203 ff.

24. Puttenham, *Arte*, pp. 260–1. Steven Mullaney, 'Lying Like Truth: Riddle, Representation and Treason in Renaissance England', *ELH*, 47 (1980), 32–47.

25. Stephen Greenblatt, 'Fiction and Friction', *Shakespearean Negotiations: The Circulation of Social Energy in Renaissance England* (Oxford, 1988), pp. 66–93.

26. See Catherine Belsey, 'Disrupting Sexual Difference: Meaning and Gender in the Comedies', in *Alternative Shakespeares*, ed. John Drakakis (London, 1985), pp. 166–90; *The Subject of Tragedy: Identity and Difference in Renaissance Drama* (London, 1985), pp. 129–221. Eighty years later it would be possible for a good woman to propose that it would be 'nobler' to be her husband's friend than his wife (John Dryden, *Troilus and Cressida*, II.i.143–5, *Works*, vol. 13, ed. Maximillian E. Novak [Berkeley, CA, 1984]). I owe this point to M. C. Bradbrook.

27. This has been a recurrent interpretation of the play at least since Tillyard toyed with the idea in 1966. See Danson, *Harmonies*, pp. 34–40.

28. W. Thomas MacCary, *Friends and Lovers: The Phenomenology of Desire in Shakespearean Comedy* (New York, 1985), especially pp. 167–8.

29. Sir Thomas Elyot, *The Governour* (London, 1907), p. 183.

30. John Lyly, *Endimion, The Complete Works*, ed. R. Warwick Bond (Oxford, 1902), 3 vols, vol. 3. Cf. Elyot, *The Governour*, 11.xi, and Montaigne, 'Of Friendship', cited in Eugene Waith (ed.), *The Noble Kinsman* (Oxford, 1989), p. 50.

31. Richard Edwards, *Damon and Pythias* (Oxford, 1957).

32. Geoffrey Bullough, *Narrative and Dramatic Sources of Shakespeare*, vol. 1 (London, 1957), pp. 203–17.

33. Bullough, *Sources*, vol. 1, p. 203.

34. Greenblatt, 'Fiction and Friction', pp. 88–91.

35. I owe this point to A. D. Nuttall.

36. Georges Duby, 'Youth in Aristocratic Society', *The Chivalrous Society*, trans. Cynthia Postan (London, 1977), pp. 112–22. I owe this connection to Mary Beth Rose, *The Expense of Spirit: Love and Sexuality in English Renaissance Drama* (Ithaca, NY, 1988), pp. 178–235, though she reads the texts with a rather different emphasis.

37. Eve Kosofsky Sedgwick, *Between Men: English Literature and Male Homosocial Desire* (New York, 1985), p. 35.

38. For a discussion of the available evidence see David F. Greenberg, *The Construction of Homosexuality* (Chicago, 1988).

39. Orgel, 'Nobody's Perfect'.

8

How to Read *The Merchant of Venice* without being Heterosexist

ALAN SINFIELD

It has been recognised for a long time that *The Merchant of Venice* is experienced as insulting by Jewish people, who constitute a minority in Western Europe and North America. So powerful, though, is the reputation of Shakespeare's all-embracing 'humanity' that this scandal has often been set aside. Nevertheless, in 1994 a newspaper article entitled 'Shylock, Unacceptable Face of Shakespeare?' described how directors were acknowledging that the text requires radical alterations before it can be produced in good faith.[1] David Thacker at the Royal Shakespeare Company was changing some of Shylock's most famous lines and moving scenes around. And Jude Kelly at the West Yorkshire Playhouse was presenting a Portia ready to embrace racist attitudes in her determination to be worthy of her father and a Jessica weeping inconsolably at the end as she laments her loss of her Jewish heritage.

For some commentators, it is a sign of the deterioration of our cultures that minority out-groups should feel entitled to challenge the authority of Shakespeare. Christopher Booker, writing in the *Daily Telegraph* in 1992, complained bitterly about an English Shakespeare Company production of *The Merchant* set in 1930s Italy, with Shylock as a suave, sophisticated modern Jewish businessman confronted by fascists. 'In other words,' Booker writes, 'the producer had given up on any distasteful (but Shakespearean) idea of presenting Shylock as an archetypal cringing old miser. He really had to be more sympathetic than the "Christians".' To Booker this was 'bleatings about racism', whereas 'Shakespeare so wonderfully evokes something infinitely more real and profound ... a cosmic view of human nature which is just as true now as it was in his own day'.[2]

The problem is not limited to Jewish people. The Prince of Morocco is made to begin by apologising for his colour – 'Mislike me not for my complexion,' he pleads (II.i.1), taking it for granted that Portia will be prejudiced. And he is right, for already she has declared her distaste: 'if he have the condition of a saint, and the complexion of a devil, I had rather he should shrive me than wive me' (I.ii.123–5); and after Morocco has bet on the wrong casket she concludes: 'Let all of his complexion choose me so' (II.vii.79). And how might gay men regard the handling of Antonio's love for Bassanio, or the traffic in boys that involves Launcelot, the disguised Jessica, the disguised Nerissa and the disguised Portia?

The question of principle is how readers not situated squarely in the mainstream of Western culture today may relate to such a powerful cultural icon as Shakespeare. In a notable formulation, Kathleen McLuskie points out that the pattern of 'good' and 'bad' daughters in *King Lear* offers no point of entry to the ideas about women that a feminist criticism might want to develop; such criticism 'is restricted to exposing its own exclusion from the text'.[3] This challenge has caused some discomfort: must exclusion from Shakespeare be added to the other disadvantages that women experience in our societies? But it has not, I think, been successfully answered. In this essay I pursue the question as it strikes a gay man.

I ANTONIO vs PORTIA

As W. H. Auden suggested in an essay in *The Dyer's Hand* in 1962, *The Merchant of Venice* makes best sense if we regard Antonio as in love with Bassanio.[4] In the opening scene their friends hint broadly at it. Then, as soon as Bassanio arrives, the others know they should leave the two men together – 'We leave you now with better company. ... My Lord Bassanio, since you have found Antonio / We two will leave you' (I.i.59, 69–70). Only Gratiano is slow to go, being too foolish to realise that he is intruding (I.i.73–118). As soon as he departs, the tone and direction of the dialogue switch from formal banter to intimacy, and the cause of Antonio's sadness emerges:

> Well, tell me now what lady is the same
> To whom you swore a secret pilgrimage –
> That you to-day promis'd to tell me of?
> (I.i.119–21)

Bassanio moves quickly to reassure his friend and to ask his help: 'to you Antonio / I owe the most in money and in love' (I.i.130–1). The mercenary nature of Bassanio's courtship, which troubles mainstream commentators who are looking for a 'good' heterosexual relationship, is Antonio's reassurance. It allows him to believe that Bassanio will continue to value their love, and gives him a crucial role as banker of the enterprise.

Whether Antonio's love is what we call sexual is a question which, this essay will show, is hard to frame, let alone answer. But certainly his feelings are intense. When Bassanio leaves for Belmont, as Salerio describes it, he offers to 'make some speed / Of his return'. 'Do not so,' Antonio replies:

> And even there (his eye being big with tears),
> Turning his face, he put his hand behind him,
> And with affection wondrous sensible
> He wrung Bassanio's hand, and so they parted.
> (II.viii.37–8, 46–9)

The intensity, it seems, is not altogether equal. As Auden observes in his poem 'The More Loving One', the language of love celebrates mutuality but it is unusual for two people's loves to match precisely:

> If equal affection cannot be,
> Let the more loving one be me.[5]

Antonio the merchant, like Antonio in *Twelfth Night* and the Shakespeare of the sonnets, devotes himself to a relatively casual, pampered younger man of a higher social class.

In fact, Antonio in the *Merchant* seems to welcome the chance to sacrifice himself: 'pray God Bassanio come / To see me pay his debt, and then I care not' (III.iii.35–6). *Then* Bassanio would have to devote himself to Antonio:

> You cannot better be employ'd Bassanio,
> Than to live still and write mine epitaph.
>   (IV.i.117–18)

As Keith Geary observes, Antonio's desperate bond with Shylock is his way of holding on to Bassanio;[6] when Portia saves Antonio's life, Lawrence W. Hyman remarks, she is preventing what would have been a spectacular case of the 'greater love' referred to in the Bible (John 15:13), when a man lays down his life for his friend.[7]

That theme of amatory sacrifice contributes to an air of homoerotic excess, especially in the idea of being bound and inviting physical violation. When Bassanio introduces Antonio to Portia as the man 'To whom I am so infinitely bound', she responds:

> You should in all sense be much bound to him,
> For (as I hear) he was much bound for you.
>   (V.i.135–7)

At the start, Antonio lays open his entire self to Bassanio:

>   be assur'd
> My purse, my person, my extremest means
> Lie all unlock'd to your occasions.
>   (I.i.137–9)

Transferring this credit – 'person' included – to Shylock's bond makes it more physical, more dangerous and more erotic:

>   let the forfeit
> Be nominated for an equal pound
> Of your fair flesh, to be cut off and taken
> In what part of your body pleaseth me.
>   (I.iii.144–7)

In the court, eventually, it is his breast that Antonio is required to bare to the knife, but in a context where apparent boys may be disguised girls and Portia's suitors have to renounce marriage altogether if they choose the wrong casket, Shylock's penalty sounds like castration. Indeed, Antonio offers himself to the knife as 'a tainted wether of the flock'; that is, a castrated ram (IV.i.114).

The seriousness of the love between Antonio and Bassanio is manifest, above all, in Portia's determination to contest it. Simply, she is at a disadvantage because of her father's casket device, and wants to ensure that her husband really is committed to her. The key critical move, which Hyman and Geary make, is to reject the sentimental notion of Portia as an innocent, virtuous, 'Victorian' heroine. Harry Berger regards her 'noble' speeches as manipulations: 'Against Antonio's failure to get himself crucified, we can place Portia's divine power of mercifixion; she never rains but she pours.' Finally, she mercifies Antonio by giving him back his ships.[8]

Antonio's peril moves Bassanio to declare a preference for him over Portia:

> Antonio, I am married to a wife
> Which is as dear to me as life itself,
> But life itself, my wife, and all the world,
> I would lose all, ay sacrifice them all
> Here to this devil, to deliver you.

Portia, standing by as a young doctor, is not best pleased:

> Your wife would give you little thanks for that
> If she were by to hear you make the offer.
> (IV.i.278–85)

It is to contest Antonio's status as lover that Portia, in her role of young doctor, demands of Bassanio the ring which she had given him in her role of wife. Antonio, unaware that he is falling for a device, takes the opportunity to claim a priority in Bassanio's love:

> My Lord Bassanio, let him have the ring,
> Let his deservings and my love withal
> Be valued 'gainst your wife's commandement.
> (IV.ii.445–7)

The last act of the play is Portia's assertion of her right to Bassanio. Her strategy is purposefully heterosexist: in disallowing Antonio's sacrifice as a plausible reason for parting with the ring, she disallows the entire seriousness of male love. She is as offhand with Antonio as she can be with a guest:

> Sir, you are very welcome to our house:
> It must appear in other ways than words,
> Therefore I scant this breathing courtesy.
> (V.i.139–41)

She will not even admit Antonio's relevance: 'I am th'unhappy subject of these quarrels', he observes; 'Sir, grieve not you, – you are welcome not withstanding', she abruptly replies (V.i.238–9). Once more, self-sacrifice seems to be Antonio's best chance of staying in the game, so he binds himself in a different project: *not* to commit his body again to Bassanio in a way that will claim a status that challenges Portia:

> I once did lend my body for his wealth,
> Which but for him that had your husband's ring
> Had quite miscarried. I dare be bound again,
> My soul upon the forfeit, that your lord
> Will never more break faith advisedly.
>   (V.i.249–53)

Portia seizes brutally on the reminiscence of the earlier bond: 'Then you shall be his surety' (V.i.254). Antonio's submission is what she has been waiting for. Now she restores Bassanio's status as husband by revealing that she has the ring after all, and Antonio's viability as merchant – and his ability to return to his trade in Venice – by giving him letters that she has been withholding.

A gay reader might think: well, never mind; Bassanio wasn't worth it, and with his wealth restored, Antonio will easily find another impecunious upper-class friend to sacrifice himself to. But, for most audiences and readers, the air of 'happy ending' suggests that Bassanio's movement towards heterosexual relations is in the necessary, the right direction (like Shylock's punishment, perhaps). As Coppélia Kahn reads the play, 'In Shakespeare's psychology, men first seek to mirror themselves in a homoerotic attachment … then to confirm themselves through difference, in a bond with the opposite sex – the marital bond'.[9] And Janet Adelman, in a substantial analysis of male bonding in Shakespeare's comedies, finds that 'We do not move directly from family bonds to marriage without an intervening period in which our friendships with same-sex friends help us to establish our identities'.[10] To heterosexually identified readers this might not seem an exceptional thought, but for the gay man it is a slap in the face of very familiar kind. 'You can have these passions,' it says, 'but they are not sufficient, they should be a stage on the way to something else. So don't push it.'

To be sure, Kahn points out that 'it takes a strong, shrewd woman like Portia to combat the continuing appeal of such ties between men'.[11] And Adelman remarks the tendency towards casuistical 'magical restitutions' and the persistence of 'tensions that comedy cannot resolve'.[12] So hetero-patriarchy is not secured without difficulty or loss. None the less, when Adelman writes 'We do not move directly ... to marriage', the gay man may ask, 'Who are "We"?' And when Kahn says 'men first seek to mirror themselves in a homoerotic attachment', the gay man may wonder whether he is being positioned as not-man, or just forgotten altogether. If Antonio is excluded from the good life at the end of the *Merchant*, so the gay man is excluded from the play's address. The fault does not lie with Kahn and Adelman (though in the light of recent work in lesbian and gay studies they might want to formulate their thoughts rather differently). They have picked up well enough the mood and tendency of the play, as most readers and audiences would agree. It is the Shakespearean text that is reconfirming the marginalisation of an already marginalised group.

II   PROPERTY AND SODOMY

The reader may be forgiven for thinking that, for a commentator who has claimed to be excluded from the *Merchant*, this gay man has already found quite a lot to say. Perhaps the love that dared not speak its name is becoming the love that won't shut up. In practice, there are (at least) two routes through the *Merchant* for out-groups. One involves pointing out the mechanisms of exclusion in our cultures – how the circulation of Shakespearean texts may reinforce the privilege of some groups and the subordination of others. I have just been trying to do this. Another involves exploring the ideological structures in the playtexts – of class, race, ethnicity, gender and sexuality – that facilitate these exclusions. These structures will not be the same as the ones we experience today, but they may throw light upon our circumstances and stimulate critical awareness of how our life-possibilities are constructed.[13]

In *The Merchant*, the emphasis on the idea of being bound displays quite openly the way ideological structures work. Through an intricate network of enticements, obligations and interdictions – in terms of wealth, family, gender, patronage and law – this culture sorts out who is to control property and other human relations. Portia, Jessica and Launcelot are bound as daughters and sons; Morocco and Arragon as suitors; Antonio and Bassanio as friends, Gratiano as friend or dependant, Nerissa as dependant or servant, and Launcelot as servant; Antonio, Shylock and even the Duke are bound by the law; and the Venetians, Shylock rather effectively remarks, have no intention of freeing their slaves (IV.i.90–8).

Within limits, these bonds may be negotiable: the Duke may commission a doctor to devise a way round the law, friendships may be redefined, servants may get new masters, women and men may contract marriages. Jessica can even get away from her father, though only because he is very unpopular and Lorenzo has very powerful friends; they 'seal love's bonds newmade' (II.vi.6). Otherwise, trying to move very far out of your place is severely punished, as Shylock finds. It is so obvious that this framework of ideology and coercion is operating to the advantage of the rich over the poor, the established over the impotent, men over women and insiders over outsiders, that directors have been able to slant productions of the *Merchant* against the dominant reading, making Bassanio cynical, Portia manipulative and the Venetians arrogant and racist.

The roles of same-sex passion in this framework should not be taken for granted (I use the terms 'same-sex' and 'cross-sex' to evade anachronistic modern concepts). For us today, Eve Sedgwick shows this in her book *Between Men*, homosexuality polices the entire boundaries of gender and social organisation. Above all, it exerts 'leverage over the channels of bonding between all pairs of men'. Male–male relations, and hence male–female relations, are held in place by fear of homosexuality – by fear of crossing that 'invisible, carefully blurred, always-already-crossed line' between being 'a man's man' and being 'interested in men'.[14] We do not know what the limits of our sexual potential are, but we do believe that they are likely to be disturbing and disruptive; that is how our cultures position sexuality. Fear even of thinking homosexually serves to hold it all in place. So one thing footballers must *not* be when they embrace is sexually excited; the other thing they mustn't be is in love. But you can never be quite sure; hence the virulence of homophobia.

If this analysis makes sense in Western societies today, and I believe it does, we should not assume it for other times and places. As Sedgwick observes, ancient Greek cultures were different.[15] In our societies whether you are gay or not has become crucial – the more so since lesbians and gay men have been asserting themselves. An intriguing thought, therefore, is that in early modern England same-sex relations *were not terribly important*. In *As You Like It* and *Twelfth Night*, homoeroticism is part of the fun of the wooing ('Ganymede', the name taken by Rosalind, was standard for a male same-sex love-object); but it wouldn't be fun if such scenarios were freighted with the anxieties that people experience today. In Ben Jonson's play *Poetaster*, Ovid Senior expostulates: 'What! Shall I have my son a stager now? An engle for players? A gull, a rook, a shot-clog to make suppers, and be laughed at?'.[16] It is taken for granted that boys are sexual partners (engles) for players; it is only one of the demeaning futures that await young Ovid if he takes to the stage. Moralists who complained about theatre and sexual licence took it for granted that boys are sexually attractive.

'Sodomy' was the term which most nearly approaches what is now in England called 'gross indecency'; it was condemned almost universally in legal and religious discourses, and the penalty upon conviction was death. Perhaps because of this extreme situation, very few cases are recorded. Today, staking out a gay cruising space is a sure-fire way for a police force to improve its rate of convictions. But in the Home Counties through the reigns of Elizabeth I and James I – sixty-eight years – only six men are recorded as having been indicted for sodomy. Only one was convicted, and that was for an offence involving a five-year-old boy.[13]

In his book *Homosexual Desire in Shakespeare's England*, Bruce R. Smith shows that while legal and religious edicts against sodomy were plain, paintings and fictive texts sometimes indicate a more positive attitude. This derived mainly from the huge prestige, in artistic and intellectual discourses, of ancient Greek and Roman culture where same-sex passion is taken for granted.[18] Smith locates six 'cultural scenarios': heroic friendship, men and boys (mainly in pastoral and educational contexts), playful androgyny (mainly in romances and festivals), transvestism (mainly in satirical contexts), master–servant relations, and an emergent homosexual subjectivity (in Shakespeare's sonnets). Within those scenarios, it seems, men did not necessarily connect their practices with the monstrous crime of sodomy – partly, perhaps, because that was so unthinkable. As Jonathan Goldberg emphasises, the goal of analysis is 'to see what the category [sodomy] enabled and disenabled, and to negotiate the complex terrains, the mutual implications of prohibition and production'.[19] The point is hardly who did what with whom, but the contexts in which anxieties about sodomy might be activated. So whether the friendships of men such as Antonio and Bassanio should be regarded as involving a homoerotic element is not just a matter of what people did in private hundreds of years ago; it is a matter of definition within a sex-gender system that we only partly comprehend.

Stephen Orgel asks: 'why were women more upsetting than boys to the English?' That is, given the complaints that boy-actors incite lascivious thoughts in men and women spectators, why were not women performers employed – as they were in Spain and Italy? Orgel's answer is that boys were used because they were less dangerous; they were erotic, but that was less threatening than the eroticism of women. So this culture 'did not display a morbid fear of homosexuality. Anxiety about the fidelity of women, on the other hand, does seem to have been strikingly prevalent'.[20] Leontes and Polixenes lived guiltlessly together, we are told in *The Winter's Tale*, until they met the women who were to be their wives (I.ii.69–74). The main faultlines ran through cross-sex relations.

Because women may bear children, relations between women and men affected the regulation of lineage, alliance and property, and hence offered profound potential disruptions to the social order and the male psyche. Same-sex passion was dangerous if, as in the instance of Christopher Marlowe's *Edward II*, it was allowed to interfere with other responsibilities. Otherwise, it was thought compatible with marriage and perhaps preferable to cross-sex infidelity. The preoccupation, in writing of this period, is with women disturbing the system – resisting arranged marriages, running off with the wrong man, not bearing (male) children, committing adultery, producing illegitimate offspring, becoming widows and exercising the power of that position. In comedies things turn out happily, in tragedies sadly. But, one way or the other, Shakespearean plays, as much as the rest of the culture, are obsessively concerned with dangers that derive from women.

'We'll play with them the first boy for a thousand ducats', Gratiano exclaims, betting on whether Nerissa or Portia will bear the first boy-child (III.ii.213–14). As Orgel remarks, patriarchy does not oppress only women; a patriarch is not just a man, he is the head of a family or tribe who rules by paternal right.[21] To be sure, women are exchanged in the interest of property relations in Shakespearean plays, as in the society that produced them. But the lives of young, lower-class and outsider men are determined as well. In *The Merchant*, as everywhere in the period, we see a traffic in boys who, because they are less significant, are moved around the employment-patronage system more fluently than women. Class exploitation was almost unchallenged; everyone – men as much as women – had someone to defer to, usually in the household where they had to live. The most likely supposition is that, just as cross-sex relations took place all the time – Launcelot is accused, in passing, of getting a woman with child (III.v.35–6) – same-sex passion also was widely indulged.[22]

Traffic in boys occurs quite casually in *The Merchant*. Launcelot is a likely lad. He manages to square it with his conscience to leave his master, Shylock, but it is unclear where he will go (II.ii.1–30). He runs into his father, who indentured Launcelot to Shylock and is bringing a present for the master to strengthen the bond. Launcelot persuades him to divert the gift to Bassanio, who is providing 'rare new liveries', for the expedition to Belmont (II.ii.104–5). The father attempts to interest Bassanio in the boy, but it transpires that Shylock has already traded him: 'Shylock thy master spoke with me this day, / And hath preferr'd thee' (II.ii.138–9). Nor is Launcelot the only young man Bassanio picks up in this scene: Gratiano presents his own suit and gets a ticket to Belmont conditional upon good behaviour. And when Jessica assumes the guise of a boy, the appearance is of another privileged young man, Lorenzo, taking a boy into his service and giving him new livery: 'Descend, for you must be my torch-bearer. ... Even in the lovely garnish of a boy' (II.vi.40, 45). When the young doctor claims Portia's ring from Bassanio for services rendered, therefore, a pattern is confirmed.

My point is not that the dreadful truth of the *Merchant* is here uncovered: it is really about traffic in boys. Rather, that such traffic is casual, ubiquitous and hardly remarkable. It becomes significant in its resonances for the relationship between Antonio and Bassanio because Portia, subject to her father's will, has reason to feel insecure about the affections of her stranger-husband.

III   FRIENDLY RELATIONS

Heroic friendship is one of Smith's six 'cultural scenarios' for same-sex relations.[23] In Shakespeare, besides the sonnets, it is represented most vividly in the bond between Coriolanus and Aufidius in *Coriolanus*:

> Know thou first,
> I lov'd the maid I married; never man
> Sigh'd truer breath; but that I see thee here,
> Thou noble thing, more dances my rapt heart
> Than when I first my wedded mistress saw
> Bestride my threshold.
>   (IV.v.114–19)[24]

Unlike Portia, Aufidius's wife is not there to resent him finding his warrior-comrade more exciting than she.

In his essay 'Homosexuality and the Signs of Male Friendship in Elizabethan England', Alan Bray explores the scope of the 'friend'.[25] Even as marriage was involved in alliances of property and influence, male friendship informed, through complex obligations, networks of extended family, companions, clients, suitors and those influential in high places. Claudio in *Measure for Measure* explains why he and Juliet have not made public their marriage vows:

> This we came not to
> Only for propagation of a dower
> Remaining in the coffer of her friends,
> From whom we thought it meet to hide our love
> Till time had made them for us.
> (I.ii.138–42)

On the one hand, it is from friends that one anticipates a dowry; on the other hand, they must be handled sensitively. Compare the combination of love and instrumentality in the relationship between Bassanio and Antonio: the early modern sense of 'friend' covered a broad spectrum.

While the entirely respectable concept of the friend was supposed to have nothing to do with the officially abhorred concept of the sodomite, in practice they tended to overlap.[26] Friends shared beds, they embraced and kissed; such intimacies reinforced the network of obligations and their public performance would often be part of the effect. So the proper signs of friendship could be the same as those of same-sex passion. In instances where accusations of sodomy were aroused, very likely it was because of some hostility towards one or both parties, rather than because their behaviour was altogether different from that of others who were not so accused.

The fact that the text of the *Merchant* gives no plain indication that the love between Antonio and Bassanio is informed by erotic passion does not mean that such passion was inconceivable, then; it may well mean that it didn't require particular presentation as a significant category. What is notable, though, is that Portia has no hesitation in envisaging a sexual relationship between Bassanio and the young doctor: 'I'll have that doctor for my bedfellow', she declares, recognising an equivalence (V.i.33). She develops the idea:

> Let not that doctor e'er come near my house –
> Since he hath got the jewel that I loved,
> And that which you did swear to keep for me.
>   (V.i.223–5)

The marriage of Bassanio and Portia is unconsummated and 'jewel' is often genital in Shakespearean writing: the young doctor has had the sexual attentions which were promised to Portia. 'Ring', of course, has a similar range, as when Gratiano says he will 'fear no other thing / So sore, as keeping safe Nerissa's ring' (V.i. 306–7).[27] Portia's response to Bassanio (allegedly) sleeping with the young doctor is that she will do the same:

> I will become as liberal as you,
> I'll not deny him anything I have,
> No, not my body nor my husband's bed.
>   (V.i.226–8)

Notice also that Portia does not express disgust, or even surprise, that her husband might have shared his bed with a young doctor. Her point is that Bassanio has given to another something that he had pledged to her. Nor does she disparage Antonio (as she does Morocco). Shylock, for the social cohesion of Venice, has to be killed, beggared, expelled, converted or any combination of those penalties. Same-sex passion doesn't matter nearly so much; Antonio has only to be relegated to a subordinate position.

Bray attributes the instability in friendly relations to a decline in the open-handed 'housekeeping' of the great house. Maintaining retinues such as those Bassanio recruits – young men who look promising and relatives who have a claim – was becoming anachronistic. So the social and economic form of service and friendship decayed, but it remained as a cultural form, as a way of speaking. The consequent unevenness, Bray suggests, allowed the line between the intimacies of friendship and sodomy to become blurred.[28] Don Wayne, in his study of Ben Jonson's poem 'To Penshurst' and the country-house genre, relates the decline of the great house to the emergence of a more purposeful aristocracy of 'new men' who 'constituted an agrarian capitalist class with strong links to the trading community'; and to the emergence, also, of 'an ideology in which the nuclear, conjugal family is represented as the institutional foundation of morality and social order'. We associate that development with the later consolidation of 'bourgeois ideology', but 'images and values we tend to identify as middle class had already begun to appear in the transformation of the aristocracy's own self-image'.[29]

The Merchant of Venice makes excellent sense within such a framework. Portia's lavish estate at Belmont is presented as a fairy-tale place; in Venetian reality Bassanio, an aristocrat who already cultivates friends among the merchant class, has to raise money in the market in order to put up a decent show. At the same time, Portia's centring of the matrimonial couple and concomitant hostility towards male friendship manifests an attitude that was to be located as 'bourgeois'. This faultline was not to be resolved rapidly; Portia is ahead of her time. Through the second half of the seventeenth century, Alan Bray and Randolph Trumbach show, the aggressively manly, aristocratic rake, though reproved by the churches and emergent middle-class morality and in violation of the law, would feel able to indulge himself with a woman, a young man or both.[30]

If I have begun to map the ideological field in which same-sex passion occurred in early modern England and some of its points of intersection in *The Merchant*, I am not trying to 'reduce' Shakespeare to an effect of history and structure. I do not suppose that he thought the same as everyone else – or, indeed, that *anyone* thought the same as everyone else. First, diverse paths may be discerned in the period through the relations between sexual and 'platonic', and same-sex and cross-sex passions. These matters were uncertain, unresolved, contested – that is why they made good topics for plays, satires, sermons and so on. Second, playtexts do not have to be clear-cut. As I have argued elsewhere, we should envisage them as working across an ideological terrain, opening out unresolved faultlines, inviting spectators to explore imaginatively the different possibilities. Anyway, readers and audiences do not have to respect closures; they are at liberty to credit and dwell upon the adventurous middle part of a text, as against a tidy conclusion.[31] As Valerie Traub remarks, whether these early comedies are found to instantiate dissidence or containment is a matter of 'crediting *either* the expense of dramatic energy *or* comedic closure'.[32]

Generally, though, there is a pattern: the erotic potential of same-sex love is allowed a certain scope, but has to be set aside. The young men in *Love's Labour's Lost* try to maintain a fraternity but the women draw them away. In *Romeo and Juliet* Mercutio has to die to clear the ground for Romeo and Juliet's grand passion. In

Much Ado About Nothing Benedick has to agree to kill Claudio at his fiancée's demand. *As You Like It* fantasises a harmonious male community in the forest and intensifies it in the wooing of Orlando and Ganymede, but finally Rosalind takes everyone but Jacques back into the old system. Yet there are ambiguities as well. In the epilogue to *As You Like It* the Rosalind/Ganymede boy-actor reopens the flirting: 'If I were a woman, I would kiss as many of you as had beards that pleased me, complexions that liked me, and breaths that I defied not' (V.iv.214–17).[33] And Orsino in *Twelfth Night* leaves the stage with Viola still dressed as Cesario because, he says, her female attire has not yet been located. Even Bassanio can fantasise: 'Sweet doctor', he says to Portia when she has revealed all, 'you shall be my bedfellow, – / When I am absent then lie with my wife' (V.i.284–5).

And why not? Was it necessary to choose? Although the old, open-handed housekeeping was in decline, the upper-class household was not focused on the marital couple in the manner of today. Portia welcomes diverse people to Belmont; Gratiano and Nerissa for instance, whose mimic-marriage reflects the power of the household. *The Two Gentlemen of Verona* starts with the disruption of friendship by love for a woman, but ends with a magical reunion in which they will all live together: 'our day of marriage shall be yours, / One feast, one house, one mutual happiness' (V.iv.170–1). In a discussion of *Twelfth Night* elsewhere, I have suggested that Sebastian's marriage to a stranger heiress need not significantly affect Antonio's relationship with him.[34] They might all live together in Olivia's house (as Sir Toby does); she may well prefer to spend her time with Maria and Viola (who will surely tire of Orsino) rather than with the naïve, swashbuckling husband whom she has mistakenly married. So Antonio need not appear at the end of *Twelfth Night* as the defeated and melancholy outsider that critics have supposed; a director might show him delighted with his boyfriend's lucky break.

This kind of ending might be made to work in the *Merchant*. R. F. Hill suggests it, and Auden reports a 1905 production which had Antonio and Bassanio enter the house together.[35] However, Portia plays a harder game than Rosalind and Viola. She doesn't disguise herself, as they do, to evade hetero-patriarchal pressures, but to test and limit her husband. When disguised as a boy she does not, Geary observes, play androgynous games with other characters or the audience.[36] Antonio is invited into the house only on her terms.

Overall in these plays, Traub concludes, the fear 'is not of homo-eroticism *per se*; homoerotic pleasure is explored and sustained *until* it collapses into fear of erotic exclusivity and its corollary: non-re-productive sexuality' – a theme, of course, of the sonnets.[37] The role of marriage and child-(son-)bearing in the transmission of property and authority is made to take priority. If (like me) you are inclined to regard this as a failure of nerve, it is interesting that the *Merchant*, itself, offers a comment on boldness and timidity. 'Who chooseth me, must give and hazard all he hath' – that is the motto on the lead casket (II.ix.21). Bassanio picks the right casket and Portia endorses the choice but, as Auden points out, it is Shylock and Antonio who commit themselves entirely and risk everything; and in the world of this play there are penalties for doing that.[38]

IV   SUBCULTURES AND SHAKESPEARE

Traub notes a reading of *Twelfth Night* that assumes Olivia to be punished 'comically but unmistakably' for her same-sex passion for Viola. But 'to whom is desire between women funny?' Traub asks.[39] This was my initial topic: must Shakespeare, for out-groups such as Jews, feminists, lesbians, gays and Blacks, be a way of re-experienc-ing their marginalisation? I have been trying to exemplify elements in a critical practice for dissident readers. Mainstream commenta-tors on the *Merchant* (whether they intend to or not) tend to confirm the marginalisation of same-sex passion. Lesbian and gay men may use the play (1) to think about alternative economies of sex-gender; (2) to think about problematic aspects of our own sub-cultures. But (the question is always put): Is it Shakespeare? Well, he is said to speak to all sorts and conditions, so if gay men say 'OK, this is how he speaks to us' – that, surely, is our business.

With regard to the first of these uses, the *Merchant* allows us to explore a social arrangement in which the place of same-sex passion was different from that we are used to. Despite and because of the formal legal situation, I have shown, it appears not to have attracted very much attention; it was partly compatible with marriage, and was partly supported by legitimate institutions of friendship, patron-age and service. It is not that Shakespeare was a sexual radical, therefore. Rather, the early modern organisation of sex and gender boundaries was different from ours, and the ordinary currency of that culture is replete with erotic interactions that strike strange chords today. Shakespeare may speak with distinct force to gay men and lesbians, simply because he didn't think he had to sort out sexuality in modern terms. For approximately the same reasons, these plays may stimulate radical ideas about race, nation, gender and class.

As for using *The Merchant* as a way of addressing problems in gay subculture, the bonds of class, age, gender and race exhibited in the play have distinct resonances for us. The traffic in boys may help us to think about power structures in our class and generational interactions. And while an obvious perspective on the play is resentment at Portia's manipulation of Antonio and Bassanio, we may bear in mind that Portia too is oppressed in hetero-patriarchy, and try to work towards a sex-gender regime in which women and men would not be bound to compete.[40] Above all, plainly, Antonio is the character most hostile to Shylock. It is he who has spat on him, spurned him and called him dog, and he means to do it again (I.iii.121–6). At the trial it is he who imposes the most offensive requirement – that Shylock convert to Christianity (V.i.382–3). Seymour Kleinberg connects Antonio's racism to his sexuality:

> Antonio hates Shylock not because he is a more fervent Christian than others, but because he recognises his own alter ego in this despised Jew who, because he is a heretic, can never belong to the state. ... He hates himself in Shylock: the homosexual self that Antonio has come to identify symbolically as the Jew.[41]

Gay people today are no more immune to racism than other people, and transferring our stigma onto others is one of the modes of self-oppression that tempts any subordinated group. And what if one were Jewish, and/or Black, as well as gay? One text through which these issues circulate in our culture is *The Merchant of Venice*, and it is one place where we may address them.

From *Alternative Shakespeares: Volume 2*, ed. Terence Hawkes (London, 1996), pp. 122–39.

NOTES

[*Alternative Shakespeares: Volume 2* is a sequence to the first *Alternative Shakespeares* volume (ed. John Drakakis [London, 1985]), a collection of radical essays designed to challenge the prevailing critical climate that, paradoxically, did much to cement the new critical approaches to Shakespeare. As Terence Hawkes notes in his introduction to *Volume 2*, Alan Sinfield's essay focuses on 'sexuality, sexual behaviour and the presuppositions of a society committed to a heterosexual and firmly gendered viewpoint' (p. 11). In terms of Shakespeare this also means a society committed to a view of the plays as similarly heterosexual, so that they seem to exclude from critical engagement with them '"minority out-groups"', including gay men. This is all the more bizarre, Hawkes notes, in the case of *The Merchant of Venice* given its apparent theme of the love of two men for each other. But as Sinfield himself observes in the essay, he has plenty to say about the text, so that we might conclude that the text itself already contains an alternative viewpoint that finds an echo in Sinfield's reading. The issue Sinfield's essay raises is thus also one of how recent theory resites the text both in its own culture and in ours. All quotations are from the Arden edition of *The Merchant of Venice*, ed. John Russell Brown (London, 1959). Ed.]

1. David Lister, 'Shylock: Unacceptable Face of Shakespeare', *Independent on Sunday*, 17 April 1994, p. 3. See Alan Sinfield, *Cultural Politics – Queer Reading* (Philadelphia, 1994), pp. 1–8, 19–20.

2. Christopher Booker, 'A Modern Tragedy of Errors', *Daily Telegraph*, 23 April 1992.

3. Kathleen McLuskie, 'The Patriarchal Bard: Feminist Criticism and Shakespeare', in Jonathan Dollimore and Alan Sinfield (eds), *Political Shakespeare: New Essays in Cultural Materialism* (Manchester, 1985), p. 97. For a reply to her critics by McLuskie, see her *Renaissance Dramatists* (Hemel Hempstead, 1989), pp. 224–9, and for further comment see Jonathan Dollimore, 'Shakespeare, Cultural Materialism, Feminism and Marxist Humanism', *New Literary History*, 21 (1990), 471–93.

4. W. H. Auden, 'Brothers and Others', in *The Dyer's Hand* (London, 1963); see also Graham Midgley, '*The Merchant of Venice*: A Reconsideration', *Essays in Criticism*, 10 (1960), 119–33.

5. W. H. Auden, *Collected Shorter Poems 1927–1957* (London, 1969), p. 282.

6. Keith Geary, 'The Nature of Portia's Victory: Turning to Men in *The Merchant of Venice*', *Shakespeare Survey*, 37 (1984), 63–4.

7. Lawrence W. Hyman, 'The Rival Loves in *The Merchant of Venice*', *Shakespeare Quarterly*, 21 (1970), 112.

8. Harry Berger, 'Marriage and Mercifixion in *The Merchant of Venice*: The Casket Scene Revisited', *Shakespeare Quarterly*, 32 (1981), 161–2; see also Hyman. 'Rival Lovers' and Geary, 'Portia's Victory'.

9. Coppélia Kahn, 'The Cuckoo's Note: Male Friendship and Cuckoldery in *The Merchant of Venice*', in Peter Erickson and Coppélia Kahn (eds), *Shakespeare's 'Rough Magic'* (Newark, DE, 1985), p. 106.

10. Janet Adelman, 'Male Bonding in Shakespeare's Comedies', in Erickson and Kahn, *Shakespeare's 'Rough Magic'*, p. 75.

11. Coppélia Kahn, 'The Cuckoo's Note', p. 107.

12. Janet Adelman, 'Male Bonding', p. 80.

13. Another way is blatantly reworking the authoritative text so that it is forced to yield, against the grain, explicitly oppositional kinds of understanding; see Alan Sinfield, *Faultlines* (Berkeley and Oxford, 1992), pp. 16–24, 290–302.

14. Eve Kosofsky Sedgwick, *Between Men* (Columbia, OH, 1985), pp. 88–9; see also Jonathan Dollimore, *Sexual Dissidence: Augustine to Wilde, Freud to Foucault* (Oxford, 1992), chs 17–18.

15. Eve Kosofsky Sedgwick, *Between Men*, p. 4.

16. Ben Jonson, *Poetaster*, ed. Tom Cain (Manchester, 1995), I.ii.15–17; see also III.iv.277–8, V.iii.580–1. On boys in theatre, see Lisa Jardine, *Still Harping on Daughters: Women and Drama in the Age of Shakespeare* (Brighton, 1983), ch. 1.

17. See Alan Bray, *Homosexuality in Renaissance England* (London, 1982), pp. 38–42, 70–80; Bruce R. Smith, *Homosexual Desire in Shakespeare's England: A Cultural Poetics* (Chicago, 1991), pp. 47–52.

18. Cf. Smith, ibid., pp. 13–14, 74–6 *et passim*.

19. Jonathan Goldberg, *Sodometries: Renaissance Texts, Modern Sexualities* (Stanford, CA, 1992), p. 20; see also Alan Bray, *Homosexuality*, p. 79.

20. Stephen Orgel, 'Nobody's Perfect: Or Why Did the English Stage Take Boys for Women?' *South Atlantic Quarterly*, 88 (1989), 8, 18.

21. Ibid., p. 10.

22. See Lisa Jardine, 'Twins and Travesties: Gender, Dependency and Sexual Availability in *Twelfth Night*'; and Susan Zimmerman, 'Disruptive Desire: Artifice and Indeterminacy in Jacobean Comedy', both in Susan Zimmerman (ed.), *Erotic Politics: Desire on the Renaissance Stage* (New York and London, 1992).

23. Smith, *Homosexual Desire*, pp. 35–41, 67–72, 96–9, 139–43.

24. See Alan Sinfield, *The Wilde Century* (London and New York, 1994), pp. 25–37; and Sinfield, *Faultlines*, pp. 127–42 (this is an extension of the discussion of *Henry V* published first in John Drakakis [ed.],

Alternative Shakespeares [London, 1985]), and pp. 237–8 (on *Tamburlaine*).

25. Alan Bray, 'Homosexuality and the Signs of Male Friendship in Elizabethan England', *History Workshop*, 29 (1990), 1–19.

26. See Bray, ibid.

27. See Eric Partridge, *Shakespeare's Bawdy* (London, 1955), pp. 135, 179.

28. Bray, 'Homosexuality', 12–13.

29. Don E. Wayne, *Penshurst: The Semiotics of Place and the Poetics of History* (London, 1984), pp. 23–5.

30. See Bray, *Homosexuality*; Ralph Trumbach, 'Sodomitical Subcultures, Sodomitical Roles, and the Gender Revolution of the Eighteenth Century: The Recent Historiography', in Robert Purks Maccubin (ed.), *'Tis Nature's Fault* (Cambridge, 1987); Ralph Trumbach, 'Gender and the Homosexual Role in Modern Western Culture: The 18th and 19th Centuries Compared', in Dennis Altman, Carole Vance, Martha Vicinus and Jeffrey Weeks (eds), *Homosexuality, Which Homosexuality?* (London, 1989); Sinfield, *The Wilde Century*, pp. 33–42.

31. Cf. Sinfield, *Faultlines*, pp. 47–51, 99–106.

32. Valerie Traub, *Desire and Anxiety: Circulations of Sexuality in Shakespearean Drama* (London and New York, 1992), p. 120; see also Bruce R. Smith, 'Making a Difference: Male/Male "Desire" in Tragedy, Comedy and Tragic-Comedy', in Zimmerman (ed.), *Erotic Politics*.

33. See Valerie Traub, *Desire and Anxiety*, p. 128.

34. Cf. Sinfield, *Faultlines*, p. 73.

35. R. F. Hill, '*The Merchant of Venice* and the Patterns of Romantic Comedy', *Shakespeare Survey*, 28 (1975), 86; W. H. Auden, 'Brothers and Others', p. 233.

36. Geary, 'Portia's Victory', p. 58.

37. Traub, *Desire and Anxiety*, pp. 123, 138–41.

38. W. H. Auden, 'Brothers and Others', p. 235.

39. Traub, *Desire and Anxiety*, p. 93.

40. See the suggestive remarks in Goldberg, *Sodometries*, pp. 142, 273–4.

41. Seymour Kleinberg, '*The Merchant of Venice*: The Homosexual as Anti-Semite in Nascent Capitalism', in Stuart Kellog (ed.), *Literary Visions of Homosexuality* (New York, 1985), p. 120. Anti-Semitism and homophobia are linked by Leslie Fielder, *The Stranger in Shakespeare* (St Albans, 1974), ch. 2, and by Hans Mayer, *Outsiders*, trans. Denis M. Sweet (Cambridge, MA, 1982), pp. 278–85.

9

Historical Difference and Venetian Patriarchy

JOHN DRAKAKIS

I

In his 'Introduction' to the Penguin edition of *The Merchant of Venice*, Moelwyn Merchant rejects Harley Granville-Barker's dismissive account of the play as a 'fairy-tale' on the grounds that

> It is usually unsafe to mistake Shakespeare's lightness of touch for levity, or assume that an illogical fantasy, as early as *The Merchant of Venice* or as late as *The Tempest*, is a mere tale, a moment of relaxation.[1]

But he goes on to assert that although the play 'is much preoccupied with two matters of Elizabethan concern: Jewry and usury', there are dangers in the assumption that 'the play is "about" race and greed'.[2] Throughout, Merchant is aware of a Shakespearean evenhandedness in his opposing of the different economic practices of Antonio and Shylock in the play, the dramatist allegedly refusing, and by implication, choosing not, to take sides, and as a result evincing a moral tone which is neither indignant of usury, nor expedient.[3] Clearly, Merchant is troubled by the play, but his unease – which extends to a comprehensive critique of the ways in which the play manipulates the niceties of the Elizabethan judicial system – is compromised by an overwhelming concern to find an order which vindicates Shakespeare's superior artistry, while at the same time asserting that the play ends unequivocally in concord: 'The "concord"

181

has been hard-won in *The Merchant of Venice* but it is achieved with a gracious dignity and with wit'.[4]

What plays across Merchant's very sensitive essay is a simultaneous awareness of the *difference* which a text such as *The Merchant of Venice* generates between its own historically specific concerns and those of the modern world, and of its *sameness* in so far as those historical differences can be collapsed into a timeless presence. It is to this notion of a 'timeless presence' that a materialist account of a text such as *The Merchant of Venice* addresses itself. Moreover, this location of 'sameness' is part of a general process to which Bertold Brecht objected in his *A Short Organum for the Theatre*, where he advocated a redefinition of theatrical practice in 'historically relative terms'. His argument is of direct relevance to a play such as this in which complex and problematical historical factors are often filtered out through the cognate processes of reading and theatrical representation;[5] indeed, what he demanded of the analysis and representation of social structures in general is *a fortiori* true of the critical mediations of literary productions of the past. Brecht insists that:

> we must drop our habit of taking the different social structures of past periods, then stripping them of everything that makes them different; so that they all look more or less like our own, which then acquire from this process a certain air of having been there all along, in other words of permanence pure and simple. Instead we must leave them their distinguishing marks and keep their impermanence always before our eyes, that our own period can be seen to be impermanent too.[6]

This emphasis upon historical 'process', and 'change', this regarding 'of nothing as existing except insofar as it changes, in other words is in disharmony with itself',[7] directs our attention away from questions of aesthetic coherence, and of the finished work as the proper object of an allegedly disinterested critical contemplation, and towards the historically specific conditions of its production and subsequent reception. These conditions are necessarily inscribed within a dialectic of *difference* which only a politically involved and theoretically aware reading can properly recover. To locate 'change' in the past is to affirm the possibility of change in the present, and to detect the process working imaginatively through the tensions, structural discontinuities, and contradictions negotiated through any text, is to observe the manner in which such change might be articulated, perceived and possibly secured. It should also be emphasised that this fundamentally political trajectory is simultaneously a product of *reading* as much as it is the property of any text. In other words, it is the reception of a text by subsequent generations of readers (and in the case of a theatrical text, spectators) that will determine the cultural use that is made of it. Texts themselves do not usually or systematically *resist*, although there are exceptions such as Laurence Sterne's novel *Tristram Shandy* (1759–67), Trevor Griffiths's play *Comedians* (1976), or, indeed, many of the plays of Brecht, whereas reading always identifies interests in a particular text which it frequently ascribes to an authorial intention. To resist the dynamics of this process is no less political in its determination to establish 'sameness', continuity, or the primacy of 'ideas' over material cultural practice, though its politics, unselfconscious and divested of a theoretical rigour, are displaced into the sphere of aesthetics and invariably ascribed to the text itself. Merchant's account of the variability of the play's language presupposes an existing formal 'pattern':

> When Shakespeare, then, came to write *The Merchant of Venice* he had at his command a range of dramatic verse and prose to express every modulation which the play's pattern demanded. In the transitions from the trial scene of the fourth Act to the closing tones of Belmont this range was tested to its furthest point in Shakespeare's early maturity.[8]

But we may juxtapose against this Theodor Adorno's insistence that 'I have no wish to soften the saying that to write lyric poetry after Auschwitz is barbaric; it expresses in negative form the impulse which inspires committed literature',[9] except that, perhaps, the truly barbaric activity might consist in the self-apologetic emotional response to lyric poetry which in certain circumstances the text of *The Merchant of Venice* might elicit from a modern reader.[10] The question, therefore, for us, is not whether as modern readers we should refrain from reading a text such as *The Merchant of Venice*, a form of readerly cynicism which might parallel the negative valuation of writing and accept Adorno's verdict; rather it is a question of *how* we might read it, given the inescapable modern conditions of the text's reception. It also raises fundamental questions about the role and function of 'art' both in Elizabethan society, and in our own.

II

In his book *The Stranger in Shakespeare* (1973), Leslie Fiedler argues that Shakespeare's *The Merchant of Venice* is 'undeniably, among other things, a play about a Jew'. Following a number of commentators, he suggests that the occasion of the play may have been the scandal of Elizabeth I's Portuguese Jewish physician, Roderigo Lopez, who was executed for treason, and that this incident was still in the minds of theatre audiences who 'having scarcely any other Jews on whom to vent their wrath, demanded on stage symbolic scapegoats'.[11] In addition, Fiedler locates a further tension in the play arising out of the conflict between Judaism and Christianity, a conflict deeply implicated in the structures of patriarchy, whereby figures such as Antonio represent those 'Christian sons, who, in seeking to destroy Judaism, have turned against the father of Jews and Christians alike, the patriarch Abraham'.[12] Fiedler's argument proceeds from there to the proposition that the play embodies a range of 'myths' and 'archetypes' within whose framework the fate of a figure such as Shylock represents

> an attempt to translate into mythological form the dogmatic compromise by which Christianity managed to make the New Testament its Scripture without surrendering the Old, and in the course of doing so, worked out ways of regarding the Jews simultaneously as the ultimate enemy, the killers of Christ, and the chosen people, with whom God made the covenant, the bond (this is the meaning of 'testament'), under which all who believe in Jesus the Christ are saved.[13]

A little later, in a provocative comment in his chapter on *Othello*, Fiedler goes on to argue, in relation to the maid Emilia's defence of female infidelity as 'woman's sole weapon in what she takes to be the endless battle of the sexes', that 'Exploited outsiders tend to resemble each other strangely, so that women and Jews fall together not only in Shakespeare but in the imagination of the Western world as a whole'.[14]

Fiedler's general approach, which moves swiftly from the demands of 'history' to those of 'myth', finally falls prey to precisely that 'operational movement' whereby, as Barthes observed, concrete social relations emerge through the process of mythologising as 'a harmonious display of essences'.[15] Thus Fielder's displacement of the historically specific concerns of a play such as *The Merchant of Venice* to the level of 'myth' enacts a process of essentialising, analogous to that of the text itself, which, Barthes argues, 'embodies a defaulting' upon the representation of 'the whole of human relations in their real, social structure, in their power of making the world'.[16]

A critical raising of the text to the level of 'myth' is, however, a slightly different proposition from the process of mythologising that might be detected at work in the text itself, as a material practice. Here we come up against questions of historical context which extend beyond the kind of stimulus to which I have already referred, to encompass the role and status of theatrical art in Elizabethan society, and the extent to which it may or may not be complicit with cultural myths. If, as Adorno has observed, 'Art is the negative knowledge of the actual world',[17] then the historical question that we need to ask of this problematical text is, to what extent does it succeed in achieving an internal distance from the cultural material with which it deals? The answer to that question is closely tied up with the actual social positioning of the Elizabethan theatre as institution, not one based on a model of capitalist consumption, but one based on a tense opposition between 'work' and 'pleasure', as opposed to the development of a leisure industry, and an exchange involving the simultaneous representation *and* critical mediation of communal values and assumptions. Or, to put it another way, the Elizabethan theatre stood in a relation of *difference* to the values and norms of Elizabethan culture, and as such could not but be sensitive to the differentially constructed relationships which constituted that culture. Being in a position of 'otherness' itself, that is to say, existing *outwith* the boundaries of official ideology, but at the same time being symbolically central to its definition, it could recuperate for its practices those images of the dominant order, at times simply representing them, at others inverting them, but always rendering them 'open': at times reinforcing their ideological power, while at others exposing the inadequacies of ideology to contain contradiction. It would be wrong to regard the theatre as existing wholly in an ironic relationship to culture, but it had available to it a variety of different positions, all of which could be represented within a single text. This is not to restate the proposition that Shakespearean texts were characterised by their stylistic and linguistic plenitude, rather that the variety of modes of articulation could produce discordant effects within the text itself, and thus render the demand for generic conformity inoperable. I want to argue that *The Merchant of Venice* is just such a text.

III

In her recent book, *Strangers to Ourselves*, Kristeva observes:

> Strangely, the foreigner lives within us: he is the hidden face of our identity, the space that wrecks our abode, the time in which

understanding and affinity founder. By recognising him within ourselves, we are spared detesting him in himself.[18]

Later she goes on to suggest that 'The foreigner who imagines himself to be free of borders, by the same token challenges any sexual limit', and she further suggests that the foreigner 'can only be defined in negative fashion'; he is 'the other of the family, the clan, the tribe'.[19] If we apply this to the figure of Shylock in *The Merchant of Venice*, then it will be clear that he stands in a negative relation of 'otherness' to Venetian society. But, as a number of commentators on the play have observed, Venetian society is not presented uncritically. So there is a sense in which Shylock represents an externalisation, and a demonisation of a force that Venice finds necessary in order for it to conduct its daily commercial activity, but which it cannot acknowledge as such. Indeed, we may say, provisionally, along with Greenblatt, that in this play 'the Jew seems to embody the abstract principle of *difference* itself'[20] which, in the trial scene in Act IV, resolves itself into the negative pole of the opposition between 'reason' and 'madness'. If this were simply the case, then the difference between the two radically opposed mercantile activities in Venice would achieve a sinister clarity in its reinforcement of that anti-Semitism which was known to have been rife in Elizabethan society. Shylock is certainly the victim of judicial violence in the play, and Venice certainly depicts him negatively. But unless we are to think along certain oversimplified new historicist lines that Shylock is merely an effect of Venetian power which requires to be contained, then we are forced to recognise that there is much more at stake in this conflict. In this more complex version, Shylock is not primarily a realistic representation, not a 'Jew' in the strictly ethnological sense of the term, but both a subject position *and* a rhetorical means of prising open a dominant Christian ideology no longer able to smooth over its own internal contradictions, and therefore a challenge and a threat. But the nature of this threat is rendered in a combination of theatrical and sociological terms in the play. We know that the figure of the 'Jew' was a theatrical type, and as such identified with the theatre itself, but in the play Shylock is depicted as a repressive puritan who presents a challenge to the orthodoxies of restraint and pleasure to which the theatre itself would claim allegiance. Shylock's own pronouncement on Venetian masques issues an implicit challenge to the play-world as he instructs Jessica:

> Clamber not you up to the casements then,
> Nor thrust your head into the public street
> To gaze on Christian fools with varnished faces;
> But stop my house's ears – I mean my casements:
> Let not the sound of shallow fopp'ry enter
> My sober house.
>
> (II.v.31–6)

Later, when his daughter has eloped with Lorenzo, he confronts Salerio and Solanio, the latter identifying him as 'the devil' (III.i.19) and proceeding to play bawdily upon the alleged sexual effects of puritanical repression; to Shylock's expostulation: 'My own flesh and blood to rebel!', Solanio retorts: 'Out upon it, old carrion, rebels it at these years'? (III.i.132–4). Here the challenge to Shylock's patriarchy, which, as we shall see later, the play takes very seriously, is turned back upon him as an allegation of sexual deviation, aligning corrupt venality with the faint suggestion of incest. Sexual rebellion is posited as the transgressive 'other' of those romantic rituals and property relations which, elsewhere in the play, are venerated as necessary for the sustenance of Venetian society. Interestingly, Shylock's patriarchal law has no force in relation to Jessica, unlike that 'will of a dead father' (I.ii.24) which restrains the 'blood' and living will of Portia.

But let us return for a moment to the question of 'realism' in relation to the figure of Shylock, and particularly to Stephen Greenblatt's brief remarks on *The Merchant of Venice* as a prologue to his reading of Marlowe's *The Jew of Malta* through Marx's early essay 'On the Jewish Question'. It is Greenblatt's contention that Marx's essay 'represents the nineteenth-century development of a late sixteenth-century idea or, more accurately, a late sixteenth-century trope'. He continues:

> Marlowe and Marx seize upon the Jew as a kind of powerful rhetorical device, a way of marshalling deep popular hatred and clarifying its object. The Jew is charged not with racial deviance or religious impiety but with economic and social crime, crime that is not only committed *against* the dominant Christian society but, in less 'pure' form, by that society. Both writers hope to focus attention upon activity that is seen as at once alien and yet central to the life of the community and to direct against the activity the anti-Semitic feeling of the audience. The Jews themselves in their real historical situation are finally incidental in these works, Marx's as well as Marlowe's, except insofar as they excite the fear and loathing of the great mass of Christians.[21]

Greenblatt concludes that the difference between Marx and Marlowe is that where 'Marx can finally envisage the liberation of mankind from what he inexcusably calls "Judaism" Marlowe cannot'. For Marlowe's Barabas, a radical commitment to 'the anarchic, playful discharge of his energy' functions to divest him of 'hope' and leads to his ultimate self-destruction, whereas for Marx 'there is the principle of hope without the will to play'.[22] By contrast, in the more evenly dialectical world of *The Merchant of Venice*, Shylock both is and is not the alienated essence of Christian society; indeed, his appeal to what Greenblatt calls 'moments of sameness' which run 'like a dark current through the play, intimating secret bonds that no one, not even the audience, can fully acknowledge', can often compel them to transform 'into a reassuring perception of difference'.[23] Greenblatt insists that Shylock represents the point of convergence of a series of constitutive structural oppositions in the text, but what traditional criticism has come to regard as a fullness of characterisation, here becomes a substantive *subject position* which the phrase 'rhetorical device' only partly encompasses. This is not so much the construction of the figure of Shylock as an *effect* of linguistic difference, rather it represents that convergence of a multiplicity of identities in the figure of Shylock *against* which Venetian identity defines itself. This does not so much rule out 'history' as an effect of discourse; on the contrary, it marks that complex point of entry of a range of discrete 'histories' as 'absent causes', into discourse, showing how textual forms make accessible to audiences and readers that which resists reduction to the status of 'text'.[24] What Shylock represents in *The Merchant of Venice* is what Barthes would describe as a transformation of history 'into nature', at the same time as the 'myth' which he embodies 'is a type of speech chosen by history'.[25]

The process that we see operating through the text of *The Merchant of Venice* is one which, with the benefit of hindsight, can be shown to constitute a systematic 'forgetting', effected through the conversion of Shylock, and the formal shift into the genre of comedy as a means of effecting closure. Whereas in tragedy what we experience is the *isolation* of the protagonist, in comedy the closure is usually one which incorporates participants into an inclusive definition of 'society'. But the play also, uncomfortable with its own formal means of resolution, testifies to a history which Lyotard outlines in his statement that

'The jews', never at home where they are, cannot be integrated, converted, or expelled. They are also always away from home when they are at home, in their so-called own tradition, because it includes exodus as its beginning, excision, impropriety, and respect for the forgotten.[26]

As we shall see, the language of 'forgetting' paradoxically carries its own intractable history with it, which the formal mechanisms of comedy cannot successfully bring to full closure.

From a purely historical perspective *The Merchant of Venice* is a play which, as has often been recognised, appears to confront economic questions directly. Some fifty years ago (1945), E. C. Pettet observed that it 'contains one of Shakespeare's rare considerations of a major socio-economic problem of his time', that of usury;[27] although, in what is arguably the best materialist account of the play to date, Cohen has pointed out that the bond between Antonio and Shylock is not usurious in the strict sense of the term at all.[28] Indeed, Cohen goes on to suggest that the play's conflict is 'a special instance of the struggle, widespread in Europe, between Jewish quasi-feudal fiscalism and native bourgeois mercantilism, in which the indigenous forces usually prevailed', and in this context Shylock is conceived as 'an old man with obsolete values trying to arrest the course of history'.[29] Cohen's argument, quite different from Pettet's or indeed from R. H. Tawney's which inscribes the response to a generalised conception of usury within the framework of medieval ideology, 'as part of a hierarchy of values, embracing all interests and activities, of which the apex was religion',[30] derives its emphasis directly from Marx's chapter on 'Precapitalist Relations' in *Capital* Volume 3. Here it is argued that 'usury centralises monetary wealth. It does not change the mode of production, but clings to it like a parasite and impoverishes it'; thus, Marx continues, 'In place of the old exploiter, whose exploitation was more or less patriarchal, since it was largely a means of political power, we have a hard money-grubbing upstart. But the mode of production remains unaltered.'[31] Indeed, we may deduce from this that although the position of the usurer was clearly, in moral and ethical terms, on the margins of the social order, the political effect of his activity was symbolically central to its operation and to its self-definition. In other words, the usurer stood in a relation of *difference* to the dominant order, he was its 'other', having no independent existence or self-definition. But at another level usurious capital fulfilled a potentially revolutionary function, since, aligned with 'mercantile wealth', it helped to 'bring about the formation of a monetary wealth independent of landed property'.[32] In the play this notion of the landless usurer is given an added historical piquancy in its emphasis upon the inverted and 'devilish' household attributed to Shylock, compared with the fully integrated and legitimised household of Belmont. For Marx usury is conservative in that it reinforces an already extant mode of production, but makes it 'more wretched',[33] at the same time, as we saw earlier in relation to Leslie Fiedler, that is, it is associated with a particular form of patriarchal control; but it is also potentially subversive in that it accelerates the erosion of the very means through which patriarchal power and authority realise themselves fully: landed property.

If we bear this in mind, then the proliferation of treatises on the subject of usury, from the time of Martin Luther onwards, takes on a slightly different complexion from its usual designation as 'background' material. Indeed, they may be said to constitute a web of discourses into which the text of *The Merchant of Venice* intervenes. For Luther, usury 'lays burdens upon all lands, cities, lords, and people, sucks them dry, and brings them to ruin', and eliminates the influence of God in human affairs.[34] Sir Thomas Wilson, in his *A Discourse Upon Usurye* (1572) argues that the practice is 'against nature',[35] and destructive of the entire social fabric of society. Perhaps one of the most interesting alignments of usurious practice with femininity occurs in Philip Caesar's *A General Discourse Against The Damnable Sect of Usurie* (1578), where it is conceived as a form of self-deception analogous to an unruliness associated with the figure of the biblical Eve: 'For thei whiche painte their couetousnesse vnder this colour, beeyng deceiued by their domesticall *Eve*, their corrupt Nature whiche was misreablie seduced by Sathan, wilfully destroy them selues, and by their owne sophistrie are deceiued.'[36] This strategic feminising of usury is also augmented with images which abound in tracts, and later plays, concerned with rapaciousness and sterility. The tracing through of these images as part of a series of discursive strategies lays down a radical challenge to traditional hierarchical methods of delineating 'source' material for a play such as *The Merchant of Venice*, and functions to suggest a recontextualisation of its concerns way beyond those of a formal textual nature.

IV

In a provocative essay on *The Merchant of Venice*, W. H. Auden detected a series of disharmonies in the play. Like other commentators, he characterised Shylock as a marginalised figure, and a threat to the order of Venice: 'a professional usurer who, like a prostitute, has a social function but is an outcast from the community'.[37] He saw this fundamental division echoed first in the character of Antonio, excluded from the pattern of marriage relationships at the end of the play because, 'though his conduct may be chaste [it] is concentrated upon a member of his own sex',[38] and finally in the opposition between Venice and Belmont – although they are related spheres of activity, 'their existences are not really compatible with each other'.[39]

At a deep structural level there is less opposition between Venice and Belmont than at first seems to be the case, but the division that Auden identifies operates both at an external level in the opposition between 'Christian' and 'Jew', and at an internal level in the self-division of individual characters torn between romance and money, although the hidden motivation may be more complex than Auden himself believed.

To take the external division between 'Christian' and 'Jew' first: ostensibly, this would appear to be a straightforward conflict between two mutually hostile cultures, expressed in terms of religious and economic difference. To this extent Shylock may be said to represent both a challenge to the ethos of Venice, while at the same time providing the differential means through which that ethos achieves its own ideologically inflected self-definition. But it is worth recalling that although formulated as an external conflict between 'Christian' and 'Jew' – the position which in one sense Marx accedes to, as we have seen – many of the objections to usury levelled by English commentators at the time were expressly against *Christians* who practised it: 'I do not knowe', lamented Sir Thomas Wilson, 'anye place in Christendome, so much subiect to thys foule synne of usurie, as the whole realme of Englande ys at thys present, and hathe bene of late yeares.'[40] To this extent the Venetians in the play project onto Shylock a hatred which stems from their recognition of the need of his money to sustain their own society, but they refuse to acknowledge that his means of acquisition, which are in effect a practical necessity, can have either a religious or an ethical validation. In this sense, Shylock is the object upon whom Venetian society vents its own hatred of itself, and in this respect his own dramatic characterisation is made to incorporate those negative social forces, such as puritanism, which challenge the norms of Venetian/Elizabethan society. It is within this complex web of significations, both as an *effect* of Venetian self-hatred, and as the representative of a historically ostracised ethnic group, that Shylock is forced to eke out a precarious existence, marginal, yet symbolically central to Venice's own perception of itself, tolerated, yet repressed.

Dollimore has recently reminded us that in Marlowe's *Doctor Faustus*, 'Faustus violates Christianity in the name and image of Christ', and in so doing demonstrates how repressed energies return, 'via the very images, structures, and mechanisms of repression itself'.[41] At one level, of course, it would appear that the dominant order *produces* its 'other' and prescribes, in order to limit, the resistance to which the latter has access. If we push this argument a little further we might say that Faustus's resistance is, therefore, *contained*. But, as Dollimore goes on to argue, this imitation of 'the dominant from below' results in a 'transgressive mimesis' whereby the repressed, 'even as it imitates, reproducing itself in terms of its exclusion, also demystifies, producing a knowledge of the dominant which excludes it, this being a knowledge which the dominant has to suppress in order to dominate'.[42] Michel Pêcheux articulates this problem in terms of an opposition between the 'good subject', who adopts a position in which his/her subjection is 'freely consented to', and the 'bad subject' who takes up a position of 'separation (distantiation, doubt, interrogation, challenge, revolt ...)' in relation to the reality to which he/she is expected to give consent; the result is 'a struggle against ideological evidentness on the terrain of that evidentness with a negative sign, reversed in its own terrain'.[43] Thus, the 'bad subject' is involved in what Pêcheux calls a counter-identification with the dominant discourse through which resistance to its ideological imperatives is made possible. In *The Merchant of Venice* this is a position which Shylock sustains for much of the play, and in doing so he is the instrument through which Venetian values are exposed, stripped of their ideological efficacy.

Significantly, Shylock's first appearance in the play occasions a dispute concerned with the reading of Scripture. The difference between Antonio and Shylock is a religious difference, but it extends into an area of juridical and social practice which sharpens the distinction between the two adversaries. The moment of Shylock's acceptance of Antonio's 'bond' is carefully juxtaposed against his refusal of Bassanio's invitation to dine with them: 'I will buy with you, sell with you, talk with you, walk with you, and so following; but I will not eat with you, drink with you, nor pray with you' (I.iii.33–5). The legality of Shylock's transaction – which is, in effect, the only means he has of protecting himself – is, however, glossed on the occasion of Antonio's entry by a soliloquy which functions dramatically as a means of providing a motivation for the hatred that each bears to the other. Shylock's hatred of Antonio is reciprocal:

> I hate him for he is a Christian,
> But more for that in low simplicity
> He lends out money gratis and brings down
> The rate of usance here with us in Venice.
> If I can catch him once upon the hip,
> I will feed fat the ancient grudge I bear him.
> He hates our sacred nation, and he rails,
> Even there where merchants most do congregate,
> On me, my bargains, and my well-won thrift,
> Which he calls interest. Cursèd be my tribe
> If I forgive him.
>
> (I.iii.39–49)

The difference between them is that Shylock's own violation of the decorum of dialogue serves simultaneously as a justification of his hatred, at the same time as it edges his characterisation towards the position of the demonic. Moreover, Antonio, who for what will become clear *scriptural* reasons firmly resists Shylock's philosophy, begins by acknowledging the need for a practice that he despises:

> Shylock, albeit I neither lend nor borrow
> By taking nor by giving of excess,
> Yet to supply the ripe wants of my friend
> I'll break a custom.
>
> (I.iii.58–61)

It is difficult to gauge precisely how disingenuous this claim is, since Venice needs Shylock even though it despises him. But what this exchange does do is initiate a process of gradual exposure of the way in which Venice articulates Shylock. The latter's scriptural justification of his usurious practices is not challenged simply on the grounds of interpretation, but on those of a much deeper motivation – 'Mark you this, Bassanio, / The devil can cite Scripture for his purpose' (I.iii.94–5) – and it is one for which some evidence earlier on in the scene has already been forthcoming. Thus, when after pointing up the contradictions in Christian practice, Shylock formulates his 'merry bond' (I.iii.170), its carnivalistic excess smacks of the subversive who operates from within the very discourse of demonisation that Venice ascribes to him. Bassanio's 'I like not fair terms and a villain's mind' (I.iii.176) crystallises that process of counter-identification through which Shylock evinces a familiar kind of behaviour, while at the same time exposing those contradictions in which Antonio and Bassanio are now caught, and against which their ideologically loaded responses can offer them no real protection.

In this context Shylock's rejection of Venetian social rituals represents a rejection of courtesies which are not contingent upon the latter's economic practices, but rather are constitutive of them. It is clear that dining, and male friendship, as well as romantic entanglement, are the socially constituted means through which Venice conducts both its interpersonal *and* public economic life. From the very outset the 'friendship' between Antonio and Bassanio effectively subsumes money into its aegis: 'My purse, my person, my extremest means, / Lie all unlocked to your occasions' (I.i.138–9); for him his 'person' is an extension of his 'purse', yet this is underwritten by an already extant friendship, and serves, in effect, to contain, while at the same time shadowing, a bawdy, carnivalesque meaning.[44] It is worth contrasting this utterance with Solanio's later account of Shylock's response to Jessica's elopement with Lorenzo where essentially the same formulation is made to produce a different, far more reductive effect, even though what is clearly at issue is the crucial question of patriarchal authority, that is in essence no different from that exercised by Portia's father, and accepted reluctantly by her. Here it is the *contents* of Shylock's 'purse' with which he is preoccupied, rather than with the purse as a facilitation of the practice of human multiplication:

> I never heard a passion so confused,
> So strange, outrageous, and so variable,
> As the dog Jew did utter in the streets:
> 'My daughter! O my ducats! O my daughter!
> Fled with a Christian! O my Christian ducats!
> Justice! The law! My ducats and my daughter! ...'
> (II.viii.12–17)

Parody here functions to expose Shylock's behaviour as the practice of the 'bad subject', hinting at sexual excess as opposed to the legitimised sexual practices of Venetian society, and as such it augments Antonio's ascription of demonic tendencies to his adversary. Conversely, Shylock's parody of Venetian practices functions to expose the extent to which they are not so much essentially natural and hence humane, but rather irreducibly social constructions invested with powers of exclusion.

The vehemence of Antonio's response to Shylock's semitic identity – 'A goodly apple rotten at the heart. / O, what a goodly outside falsehood hath!' (I.iii.98–9) – which is sustained throughout the play, is one of its most disturbing features. The image which Antonio produces of Shylock (which the latter's behaviour does little to invalidate), augmented with a cumulative rhetorical force, is that of the infernal patriarchy whose very existence threatens to deconstruct the faith and practice of Venice. That in the play Shylock is given a 'family' of his own, that its own internal interpersonal, psychic, and emotional relations are directly represented, and that it is shown to be a divided unit – 'My own flesh and blood to rebel!' (III.i.32) – articulates in dramatic terms precisely that 'transgressive mimesis' which demystifies even as it imitates, and which is positioned in Venetian discourse as a demonic form, a challenge from below, a 'family' in the devil's name, so to speak. Let us pursue this question of patriarchy a little further in the play.

The debate between Antonio and Shylock about usury follows immediately upon the scene between Portia and Nerissa, set in Belmont. Here the emphasis is upon Portia's acceptance of the constraints imposed upon her by patriarchal law, but it is clear that this prescriptive restraint is a rational masculine response to the subversive potential of an irrational, feminised 'blood':

> I can easier teach twenty what were good to be done than to be one of the twenty to follow mine own teaching. The brain may devise laws for the blood, but a hot temper leaps o'er a cold decree: such a hare is madness, the youth, to skip o'er the meshes of good counsel, the cripple. But this reasoning is not in the fashion to choose me a husband. O me, the word 'choose'! I may neither choose who I would, nor refuse who I dislike; so is the will of a living daughter curbed by the will of a dead father. Is it not hard, Nerissa, that I cannot choose one nor refuse none?
>
> (I.ii.15–26)

Portia is here caught in a double bind, accepting the rationale for control, but agonising over the uncertainty of its consequences. The whole issue is handled more circumspectly in the case of Jessica, where some justification for her rebellion is cautiously provided, but where the emotional effects upon her 'father', though contextualised parodically, as we have seen, imitate the frustrations consequent upon the loss of patriarchal authority. Nerissa's response to Portia's question illuminates for us the hermeneutic significance of the episode with the caskets as one involving the choice of one from a determinate number of 'meanings' – a domestic, gender-specific analogue of the discussion between Antonio and Shylock in the following scene – which reinforces the patriarchal notion of authority which prevails throughout the play; Nerissa responds:

> Your father was ever virtuous, and holy men at their death have good inspirations; therefore the lott'ry that he hath devised in these three chests of gold, silver, and lead, *whereof who chooses his meaning chooses you*, will no doubt never be chosen by any rightly but one which you shall rightly love.
>
> (I.ii.27–32; emphasis added)

In both cases the challenge to the dominant patriarchal order from below, characterised in Portia's case as a rebellion of the (female) 'blood', and in Shylock's case literally as a rebellion of his 'own flesh and blood', which Solanio mocks as a demonically Judaic excess – 'Out upon it, old carrion! Rebels it at these years?' (III.i.33–4) – threatens a division in the ideology of patriarchy, and proposes that in certain circumstances rebellion is justifiable.

Shylock's repression of his own 'flesh and blood', augmented with the evidence in the play by the escape from captivity of Lancelot Gobbo, becomes for the mocking Solanio the site of a hermeneutical conflict: 'There is more difference between thy flesh and hers than between jet and ivory' (III.i.36–7). But by this point in the play Shylock has accumulated a number of identities; what is now an infernally hermaphroditic Shylock, who is both 'the dam' and the devilish instrument through which Jessica will, 'if the devil may be her judge' (III.i.31), receive her damnation, is also puritanically antifestive in his disposition, a combination which marginalises him theologically *and* historically as the protean embodiment of all that is symbolically central to the play's dominant ideology.

The 'will' or law of Portia's dead father represents a secret meaning which it is the task of her prospective suitors to prise from the caskets;

this practice is underwritten by patriarchal goodness and virtue which resists the temptation to align itself with shows of material wealth. In a play where gold in its material guise figures prominently, the housing of secret meanings in a leaden casket affirms ideologically the non-material claims of Christian patriarchy. By contrast, Shylock's patriarchy is shown to be not one of provision, but rather one of tyranny and restraint. After his earlier refusal in Act I, scene iii, to eat with Antonio and Bassanio, Shylock accepts an invitation to supper, but goes 'in hate, to feed upon / The prodigal Christian' (II.v.14–15). Moreover, his exhortation to Jessica to 'stop my house's ears – I mean my casements: / Let not the sound of shallow fopp'ry enter / My sober house' (II.v.34–6) augments that initial counter-identification with a refusal to acknowledge that productive excess through which contractual obligations are celebrated in Venice.

In the case of Shylock, it is precisely the *failure* of this patriarchal power of constraint, embodied in Jessica's rebellion, which is emphasised. But this creates an additional problem in that Shylock feels her rebellion as a father; and the language in which he articulates his own agony is one which imitates the ethos of Christian humanism, even though that position is not sustained, and the project to which it becomes allied is one which directly challenges Christian judicial practice:

> I am a Jew. Hath not a Jew eyes? Hath not a Jew hands, organs, dimensions, senses, affections, passions; fed with the same food, hurt with the same weapons, subject to the same diseases, healed by the same means, warmed and cooled by the same winter and summer, as a Christian is? If you prick us, do we not bleed? If you tickle us, do we not laugh? If you poison us, do we not die? And if you wrong us, shall we not revenge? If we are like you in the rest, we will resemble you in that. If a Jew wrong a Christian, what is his humility? Revenge. If a Christian wrong a Jew, what should his sufferance be by Christian example? Why, revenge. The villainy you teach me I will execute, and it shall go hard but I will better the instruction.
>
> (III.i.55–69)

In what is a superb example of resistance through counter-identification, Shylock's simultaneous alignment with, and exposure of, the essentially violent underpinnings of Venetian humanism, exposes some of the ways in which he is himself constructed as a 'subject' in this social formation. If, as Barber has perceptively observed, Shylock 'can be a drastic ironist because he carries to extremes what is present, whether acknowledged or not' by the values of a 'silken' Venetian world, then it has to be said that the irony is double-edged.[45]

What draws Portia and Shylock together as particular foci of resistance is that they are both possessed of material wealth which Venice needs. What distinguishes them from each other in structural terms is that, while in Portia's case the institution already exists for making that wealth available, and constitutes a legitimate form of acquisition articulated through the discourses of romance and marriage, the stark necessity of Shylock's role in Venetian economic life can only be expressed negatively. Because he is engaged in an 'unnatural' and therefore unchristian practice, the sterile activity of making money breed, Venice can only admit him as a demonisation of its own social and economic practices, and as an obstacle, in the sphere of aesthetics, to comic closure. Only when he is coerced fully into the life of Venice by being forced to become a Christian, does he become a reconstituted subject who can then play a full patriarchal role in its affairs, transferring his wealth legitimately to his heirs, and replenishing the coffers of the state. To this extent the play historicises a key element of the genre, the obstructive father, by effecting what is actually a problematic transformation of its content. The transition for Shylock is, however, not an easy one; we should recall that, after being forced to accept Christian values, to be 'christened', in effect, he asks leave to depart the court of justice: 'I pray you, give me leave to go from hence. / I am not well' (IV.i.391–2). Instead of succeeding in his quest to deprive Antonio of 'an equal pound / Of your fair flesh to be cut off and taken / In what part of your body pleaseth me' (I.iii.146–8) – itself, as James Shapiro has argued,[46] a form of circumcision, and hence an attempt at conversion – Shylock is himself 'converted' and with that conversion comes an anxiety which he now shares with his adversary Antonio.

V

This moment marks the entry of Shylock into the Christian state, a process which enacts through its deployment of the metaphor of death and rebirth the history of Christianity itself:

> You take my house when you do take the prop
> That doth sustain my house; you take my life
> When you do take the means whereby I live.
>   (IV.i.371–3)

Prevented from owning land, all Shylock has is his money; his life is synonymous with the means by which he lives. He is, however, coerced into Christian patriarchy, and his entry into this religion also involves his entry into the institutions in and through which it sustains itself; as Machiavelli observed, 'every religion has the basis of its life rooted in some one of its main institutions', at the same time as it inculcates a belief in the abrogation of the responsibility for human action now displaced on to a superhuman force: 'the god who can predict your future, be it good or evil, could also bring it about'.[47] Significantly, part of Shylock's accumulated wealth is to pass on his death, 'Unto his son Lorenzo and his daughter' (IV.i.386), betokening a shift from what Freud, in *Moses and Monotheism* (1938), called 'the religion of the father' to 'a religion of the son'.[48] If we were to extend this into a full-blown Freudian reading of this moment then we might connect the symbolic 'killing' of Shylock's Semitic identity with what Freud called, in *Civilisation and Its Discontents* (1930), 'the killing of the primal father'.[49] Antonio's self-definition as 'a tainted wether of the flock, / Meetest for death' (IV.i.113–14) brings him into alignment with the emasculated Shylock whose identity at the end of the scene is reconstituted but under duress. For Antonio money 'breeds' in the sense that it permits him a vicarious pleasure in the amorous success of his friend, and yet there remains a vaguely articulated residue of guilt. With the 'conversion' of Shylock that guilt is given a much sharper focus; the symbolic 'killing' of 'the religion of the father' produces a psychic disability which is 'an expression of the conflict due to ambivalence, of the eternal struggle between Eros and the instinct of destruction or death'; for Freud, of course, this conflict is initiated when human beings form communities, and he goes on to insist that 'So long as the community assumes no other form than that of the family, the conflict is bound to express itself in the Oedipus complex'.[50] It is around the institution of the family, and the dispositions of power within its framework, that images of money, civilisation and psychic disability circulate in this play. But I want to draw back from a full-blown Freudian reading, and to seek to identify the psychic energies in play at such moments in the text of *The Merchant of Venice* as symptoms of historical rather than universal and timeless phenomena.

It is only to this extent that it is possible to see Shylock as Cohen sees him: 'a figure from the past – medieval, marginal, diabolical, irrational, anarchic'.[51] He is, of course, both the focus of Christian history, and that part of it that requires to be repressed and marginalised in order for Venice to continue to function economically. To this extent he represents that *real* history which Venetian representations overlay with social and cultural forms designed to displace their own anxieties. Indeed, the 'discontent' which Shylock feels as he enters the domain of Christian patriarchy is a registering of that political repression upon which a form of national unity is predicated. Shylock is part of Venice's own unconscious that it can only deal with either by repression, or by transformation into what we might call the Christian imaginary – that set of images and institutions in and through which Venice recognises its own cultural identity. Here a form of anarchy, positioned in the play's dominant discourse as a 'damned' patriarchy, is repressed through the very mechanisms of sacrifice and salvation upon whose structures and images its ideologically dominant 'other' depends for its own identity. Thus, Shylock's 'transgressive mimesis' turns out to be the means whereby Venice recognises itself and *experiences*, as Foucault would say, 'its positive truth in its downward fall'.[52] That process, however, decentres the human subject, splits him and forces him to live in the world, as it counsels him to disregard worldly practice: forced to accept a normative ethic of wealth accumulation whose operations are attributed to the determining force of a divinely motivated 'Nature', but committed by practical desire to secular intervention. By a subtle manoeuvre, the play first demystifies usury, and then discloses the mechanisms whereby it can be remystified again, transformed into a theatrical practice and dispersed through a series of symbolic representations which aligns the theatre itself with the non-theatrical production of cultural forms. But that mystification, once dismantled, is not easily reinstated. Shylock's 'illness' is the direct consequence of his entry into what is now a deeply decentred Christian patriarchy. His illness becomes, as it were, a form of self-hatred which can only be expressed in terms of a mechanism of displacement.

If Shylock's 'illness' is the condition of his entry into the patriarchal order of Venice, then Antonio's 'sadness' is a condition of his existence within it. The homily 'Of the Miseries of Man' counsels the open confession of 'our state of imperfection',[53] and ends with the exhortation: 'In the meane season, yea and at all times, let us learne to knowe our selves, our frailtie and weakenesse without any craking or boasting of our owne good deedes and merrites.'[54] Antonio, we may recall, is committed to accepting a causal link between mercantile success and divine providence, where the operations of God are articulated as the 'risk' which the Christian merchant must always undertake. Antonio suffers also from a 'sadness' which is inexplicable: 'And such a want-wit sadness makes of me / That I have much ado to know myself' (I.i.6–7); in other words, his unease produces in him a failure to recognise himself, and as a consequence, his own identity is unsettled.

Criticism has generally been receptive to W. H. Auden's reading of the cause of Antonio's 'sadness': the consequence of frustrated homosexual desire for Bassanio. Certainly the sublimated metaphors of sexuality would, as we have already seen, lend some support to this view. In an attempt almost to equate the sterile breeding of money with homosexuality, Marilyn French somewhat confusingly asserts that in this instance 'erotic love of man for man is repudiated because it cannot breed naturally'.[55] But at no level in the play is it possible to read such a negative image of male friendship. If the problem revolves around Antonio's 'friendship' with Bassanio, then it is important to understand what that relationship actually involves. Here friendship is deeply implicated in the process of wealth accumulation and distribution whose operations are subject to the vagaries of 'Nature', but whose practices can easily be displaced into the sphere of romantic pursuit. Bassanio plans to get rich by marrying Portia:

> If you please
> To shoot another arrow that self way
> Which you did shoot the first, I do not doubt,
> As I will watch the aim or to find both,
> Or bring your latter hazard back again
> And thankfully rest debtor for the first.
> (I.i.147–52)

For Antonio, this is not a matter of economics but 'honour', an honour that conflates, as we have seen, Antonio's 'purse' with his 'person', his identity with a capacity to inseminate. This is Shylock's 'Christian courtesy' (III.i.46), which he imitates himself when his daughter absconds with his wealth.

Antonio rejects the suggestion that his 'merchandise' should make him sad, since he has taken all human precaution against the vicissitudes of Nature:

> My ventures are not in one bottom trusted,
> Nor to one place; nor is my whole estate
> Upon the fortune of this present year:
> Therefore my merchandise makes me not sad.
> (I.i.42–5)

There is a sense in which Antonio as a Venetian 'subject' cannot admit *directly* to the need for money credit as a safeguard against failure. What Portia is later made to feel as a consequence of patriarchal constraint, Antonio anticipates as an experience which is unaccountably *in excess* of his own capacity to explain. That 'excess' is always present and threatens to undo those discursive formations through which Venice articulates its own mercantile practice; Venetian institutions convert the real mechanisms of financial exchange into a series of symbolic practices, such as the patriarchal bond between man and man, and the relationship between man and woman, where the two are not conflictual but complementary.[56] Any departure from that complex discursive formation of 'Christian courtesy' can only be admitted in textualised form as a demonic force. Shylock, therefore, comes to occupy that space in which Christian patriarchy seeks to efface through ideology the contradictions in its own practice of wealth accumulation. As Braudel observes of the Jews in the Renaissance generally: 'if they had not existed, it would surely have been necessary to invent them'.[57] In reality the presence of Shylock as a composite figure who challenges Venetian mercantile practice at the same time as he represents, within the genre in which the play is nominally cast, an anti-comic force, signals a practical need which cannot be openly acknowledged without radically transforming the ethical basis of Christian patriarchal ideology altogether. In this way commercial activity is never quite represented in the play as itself, and is forced to repress, not homosexual desire, but the reality of its own operations in the world. The result is precisely that 'alienation' or loss of identity which Antonio laments, and which Marx identifies in the 'Christian state' which has yet to become fully secularised:

> In the so-called Christian state it is alienation [*Entfremdung*] that is important, and not man himself. The man who is important, the king, is being specifically differentiated from other men (which is in itself a religious conception), who is in direct contact with heaven and God. The relationships which prevail are still relationships of faith. This means that the religious spirit is not yet truly secularised.[58]

There are no monarchs in *The Merchant of Venice*, but this is the 'state' which the cross-dressed Portia invokes when, disguised as a man, she lectures Shylock on 'mercy'. Indeed, the Duke arrogates to himself all of those patriarchal powers that elsewhere in Shakespeare are associated with monarchy.[59] Here in the most ironical of contexts, a Christian 'mimesis' is proposed that will supersede the dependency upon the letter of the law which Shylock invokes to protect his interests:

It blesseth him that gives and him that takes.
'Tis mightiest in the mightiest. It becomes
The thronèd monarch better than his crown.
His sceptre shows the force of temporal power,
The attribute to awe and majesty,
Wherein doth sit the dread and fear of kings;
But mercy is above this sceptred sway.
It is enthronèd in the hearts of kings;
It is an attribute to God himself,
And earthly power doth then show likest God's
When mercy seasons justice.
(IV.i.184–94)

From the outset, therefore, Antonio's 'sadness', and his lack of self-knowledge are, to a very considerable extent, the *subject* of The *Merchant of Venice*, although the play cannot speak its concerns directly except in terms of an intolerant, deeply nationalistic fear.

VI

Thus far our concern has been to situate the figure of Shylock in the aesthetic and historical structures of the text of *The Merchant of Venice*, to demonstrate the threat which he poses to the society which needs his services but marginalises him for providing them. He represents that part of Venice's experience that it habitually represses, although when that experience surfaces it challenges the stability of identity itself. Our discussion, therefore, has moved away from 'character', and from the presumption of a deep structural similarity between antagonistic forces in the play, to those *differentially* constructed mechanisms whose operations are disclosed at moments of disturbance in the text. Very often what is read in this text as 'sameness' turns out to be inflected very differently; when Shylock repeats Christian values, he does so at a distance from them, and the result is a kind of parody which serves to expose their investment in ideology. In this way the text can be read in such a way as to disclose those fault-lines in ideology which the play's own aesthetic emphases attempt to resolve. Here the theatre itself, charged with imitating ideology, also exposes its workings, and can thus be said to function as the 'mirror' of Elizabethan culture in so far as its function is mimetic, but also as the means whereby the ideological underpinnings of that culture are displayed. In other words, the theatre *represents*, but also exposes the constitutive features of representation itself.

Shylock's marginal position in the play, and the final recuperation of his subversive energies for the dominant discourse of Christian patriarchy, *presents* what was for Elizabethan society an 'insurmountable contradiction'.[60] This contradiction, involving Christian participation in usurious practice, receives its inscription in *The Merchant of Venice* in the form of what Macherey and Balibar would call 'a special language, a language of "compromise", realising in advance the fiction of a forthcoming conciliation'.[61] That conciliation is achieved aesthetically in the play through the presentation of Belmont as Venice's saviour; or to put the matter a little more tendentiously, what happens in Belmont ultimately guarantees the continuation of a Christian patriarchy which articulates its practices through a discourse of romance, friendship and human ideals. If Shylock is the agency through which Venetian institutions are demystified, then Belmont is the place where an attempt is made to reverse that process. Bassanio's success in winning Portia guarantees racial purity and opposes an essential moral worth against the deceptive surfaces of worldly show. But the process is itself contradictory, since the 'Gifts of rich value' (II.ix.90) that he deploys are part of a rhetoric of persuasion which he later denies in his choice between 'caskets' and 'meanings':

> In religion,
> What damnèd error but some sober brow
> Will bless it and approve it with a text,
> Hiding the grossness with fair ornament?
> There is no vice so simple but assumes
> Some mark of virtue on his outward parts.
> (III.ii.77–82)

It is not surprising, therefore, that Bassanio should deny the representational value of 'gold' and 'silver': 'The seeming truth which cunning times put on / To entrap the wisest' (III.ii.100–1), and, 'thou pale and common drudge / 'Tween man and man' (III.ii.103–4). Here in the form of a game, is an attempt to construct a 'centre', a 'meaning', but also a recognition that it can never be, as Derrida puts it, 'absolutely present outside a system of differences'.[62]

The object of Bassanio's quest is herself a 'meaning' inscribed within the law of Christian patriarchy *and* Venetian fiscal practice, but presented as a 'knowledge' secreted at the heart of the linguistic sign. The issue is rendered even more problematical by the fact that theatrical practice demanded that the role of Portia be played by a male actor, thus problematising even further the mimetic possibility that the character should be present to her/himself. Fixed thus ideologically, it is significant that while Bassanio chooses, Portia articulates in an 'aside' those very feelings of 'excess' which it is the function of the law of her dead father to constrain:

> O love, be moderate! Allay thy ecstasy,
> In measure rain thy joy, scant this excess!
> I feel too much thy blessing. Make it less,
> For fear I surfeit.
>   (III.ii.111–14)

At a purely psychological level, Portia's 'fear' here is, surely, the patriarchal fear of 'excess' internalised by the female subject as part of the mechanism of social and emotional regulation. Spoken by a male actor, its parodic potential is foregrounded to the point where it can be made to reinforce patriarchal constraint. To this extent both Portia and her more unruly counterpart, Jessica, are central to an understanding of the normative, regulatory practices of Christian patriarchy as the play represents them.

Both Portia and Jessica violate the constraints imposed upon their own gender by dressing as males. Portia and her maid Nerissa do so in order to reinforce the very laws that hold them in position as gendered subjects, and when Portia finally submits to Bassanio she does so as a subject who, as Althusser would say, works by herself; that is to say, she accepts her position and her identity. In the case of Portia, her cross-dressing is both a form of empowerment, *and* a disempowerment, where she freely consents to the assigning over of her power to her 'husband'. By contrast, Jessica's cross-dressing represents an act of usurpation of patriarchal authority; she seeks marriage with a Christian, but she takes responsibility upon herself for effecting it. Jessica's systematic *undoing* of a network of domestic power relations is both a challenge *and* an enabling strategy in that it contributes ultimately to the Christianising of Shylock, but at the same time it aligns the father momentarily with those very emotional structures which support the order of which his own example is, as we have seen, a 'transgressive mimesis'. Why, otherwise, should Shylock be given so powerfully emotional a voice at the moment when he is told of his daughter's prodigality:

> Out upon her! thou torturest me, Tubal. It was my turquoise. I had it of Leah when I was a bachelor. I would not have given it for a wilderness of monkeys.
>
> (III.i.113–16)

Shylock's ring, the symbol of his marriage, is exchanged by the iconoclastic Jessica for 'a monkey'. By contrast, Portia recuperates in her own gesture Shylock's domestic ritual for an act of Christian betrothal, one which, as we suggested, simultaneously asserts both her social superiority and her gender inferiority as she yields to Bassanio's masculine authority. Here, unlike in Jessica's case, patriarchal authority passes through the willing female subject from father to husband:

> Myself and what is mine to you and yours
> Is now converted. But now I was the lord
> Of this fair mansion, master of my servants,
> Queen o'er myself; and even now, but now,
> This house, these servants, and this same myself
> Are yours, my lord's. I give them with this ring,
> Which when you part from, lose, or give away,
> Let it presage the ruin of your love
> And be my vantage to exclaim on you.
>
> (III.ii.166–74)

If the power which this gives Bassanio is considerable – 'But when this ring / Parts from this finger, then parts life from hence' (III.ii.183–4) – it is also conditional. But the threat of female power which it contains is carefully circumscribed by the fact that Portia's 'self' is itself a social construct: she fulfils a series of roles, and they facilitate her willing 'conversion' from daughter to wife. By contrast, Jessica's status as an unruly woman, contradictory though it is in that she wants to marry Lorenzo, requires a different handling since the problem here is not the threat of female 'excess', but the identity of her father. Within patriarchy, if the daughter is an 'effect' of her father, and if her father inhabits a problematical identity, then it is *his* identity that requires to be changed. Shylock as infernal patriarch and comic obstacle becomes, therefore, the point at which the generic features of comedy are made to intersect with a determinate social history.

It is this troubled and complex history which virtually dictates the transformation of the 'insurmountable contradictions' involving fiscal 'excess' into a discursive terrain such as comedy, and female sexuality, where the possibilities of negotiation, if not containment, seem more promising. In Act V of the play it is left initially to Lorenzo, the Venetian 'son' through whom both Jessica and Shylock are recuperated for the integrated structures of Christian patriarchy, to refurbish masculine identity. He does so through a movement into the sphere of aesthetics, as a way of effecting a closure designed to produce an imaginary resolution to the various problems which have been raised in the play. The wealth which 'gilded' Jessica's subversive act of elopement at a purely materialistic level, is now aestheticised as a transcendent ideal: 'Sit Jessica. Look how the floor of heaven / Is thick inlaid with patens of bright gold' (V.i.58–9). What was earlier, for Bassanio 'The seeming truth which cunning times put on / To entrap the wisest' (III.ii.100–1), now becomes, through the pun on 'paten', a necessary alliance between 'wealth' and 'religion'. The 'paten' as the silver or golden dish upon which the Christian host is placed in the ritual of transubstantiation, heralds a victory for Christianity, but the attempt at transformation is beset by a history, that of Acts I–IV which can never expunge completely the dubious rhetoric of its construction. Faced with the problem that historical example, both theatrical and non-theatrical, foregrounds, the text is forced into the reiteration of a distinction between the material transience of life itself, moralised as Lorenzo's 'this muddy vesture of decay' (V.i.64), and the immortality of the soul whose musical pattern is heaven's inscription in human psychology of a safeguard against political subversion:

> The man that hath no music in himself,
> Nor is not moved with the concord of sweet sounds,
> Is fit for treasons, stratagems, and spoils;
> The motions of his spirit are dull as night,
> And his affections dark as Erebus.
> Let no such man be trusted. Mark the music.
>
> (V.i.83–8)

What has intervened in the space between Lorenzo and Jessica's alignment of their action with those of Troilus and Cressida, and Dido, and Lorenzo's metaphysical pronouncement is, of course, ideology. Indeed, it is as though having raised an issue for which, as yet, there exists no clear historical solution, the text makes a detour onto that terrain for which there already exists a range of formal resolutions already legitimised and authorised by the dominant ideology of patriarchy.

Thus, at the end of the play, and after all obstacles and doubts have been overcome, 'Nature' – in the form of a Christian providence – speaks to Venice, transforming Antonio from his role as 'th' unhappy subject of these quarrels' (V.i.238) into the happy recipient of 'life' from Portia: 'Sweet Lady, you have given me life and living, / For here I read for certain that my ships / Are safely come to road' (V.i.286–8). Here 'purse' and 'person', 'life and living', receive their composite inscription within the complementary economies of homo-social and heterosexual friendship in Venice. Neutralised within the joint practices of aesthetics and ideology, the 'fear' which interest as 'excess' generates, can be displaced onto an area of *difference* for which solutions exist socially, generically, and theatrically. But yet, even here something of a problem remains. Portia's fulsome confidence: 'Let us go in, / And charge us there upon inter'gatories, / And we will answer all things faithfully' (V.i.297–9), is shown to rest upon the mystified interrelationship of patriarchal authority, and the real mechanisms of wealth accumulation. Shylock's ring, which was a ritualised mark of possession and affection, is given a more specific inflection in the 'rings' which are the marks of fidelity and truth in Venice. Bassanio's parting with his token of fidelity to a disguised Portia, and Graziano's to a disguised Nerissa, draws the language of promises irreversibly into the domain of material signification. The removal of Portia's and Nerissa's rings from the fingers of Bassanio and Graziano respectively threatens to undermine sexual possession, and to introduce obliquely one of the persistent fears of masculine authority. Displaced on to the axis of gender ideology, the comic positioning of that 'fear' by the husband of Portia's social inferior, fails absolutely fully to contain the range of competing meanings which it releases: 'Well, while I live I'll fear no other thing / So sore as keeping safe Nerissa's ring' (V.i.306–7). The effect of this is to return the text to its own deeply flawed rhetoric.

The venality that the ritualised closure of marriage is designed to contain is shown here submitting to the aristocratic example of Portia and Bassanio. This resolution of the awkwardness which follows directly from the forsaking of gender roles is, however, not simply a reflection of 'historical reality', so much as an ideological product of it.[63] The ending of the play questions even the apparent fixity of gender identities since Graziano's bawdy couplet is delivered, in part, to a male actor *impersonating* a female character. All of this suggests that we should reject absolutely John Russell Brown's defensive suggestion that we should merely submit ourselves to the 'experience' of the play: 'Perhaps when the dance is in progress, it is undesirable to look too closely for a pattern'.[64] To abrogate this critical responsibility is to propose a complicity with texts such as *The Merchant of Venice* which lays the critic open to the charge of disseminating its prejudices. To discharge that responsibility is to acknowledge that such prejudices are the products of a determinate history whose partial and horrifying solutions cannot, and should never be allowed to, exert a permanent claim on our own historically constituted sensibilities.

From *The Merchant of Venice*, ed. Nigel Wood (Buckingham, 1996), pp. 23–53.

NOTES

[This is a revised version of John Drakakis's essay originally published in 1989 under the title '*The Merchant of Venice*, or Christian Patriarchy and its Discontents', which points up the essay's concern with the complex relations between religion and ideology in the play. But not just these. Drakakis's approach is, in fact, to question how we might read the play in the light of its discontinuities, its gaps, as well as its differences from the twentieth century. It is an approach that does not shy away from suggesting that, on one level, 'Shylock is not primarily a realistic representation, not a "Jew" in the strictly ethnological sense of the term, but both a subject position *and* a rhetorical means of prising open a dominant Christian ideology no longer able to smooth over its own internal contradictions'. In other words, the logic of the essay is to see Shylock not as a character at all but as a device, 'the agency through which Venetian institutions are demystified'. This, however, does not lead to a diminution of Shylock's significance in Drakakis's reading but almost the very opposite. By locating Shylock in a different critical practice Drakakis is able to draw together ideas about comedy, patriarchy and social history in a rich analysis of the play's problems and theatrical processes. All quotations are from the Oxford edition of *The Merchant of Venice*, ed. Jay L. Halio (Oxford, 1993). Ed.]

1. Moelwyn Merchant (ed.), *The Merchant of Venice* (Harmondsworth, 1967), p. 8.

2. Ibid., p. 9.

3. Ibid., p. 16.

4. **Ibid., p. 60.**

5. See James C. Bulman, *Shakespeare in Performance: 'The Merchant of Venice'* (Manchester, 1991), pp. 28–101; John Russell Brown, *Shakespeare's Plays in Performance* (London, 1966), pp. 71–90.

6. Bertolt Brecht, *Brecht on Theatre*, trans. John Willett (London, 1977), p. 190.

7. Ibid., p. 193.

8. Merchant (ed.), p. 167.

9. Theodor Adorno, 'Commitment' (1965), in Ronald Taylor (ed.), *Aesthetics and Politics* (London, 1980), p. 188. See also Theodor Ardorno, *Prisms*, trans. Samuel and Shierry Weber (Cambridge, MA, 1982), p. 34: 'To write poetry after Auschwitz is barbaric.' But see also Edward Bond, *The Fool and We Come to the River* (London, 1976), p. vi: 'What Adorno and Auden said about poetry and Auschwitz misses the point. They would have hit it only if Auschwitz had been the summing up of history – and of course it wasn't.'

10. Cf. John Russell Brown, *Shakespeare and his Comedies* (London, 1962), p. 74, where some residual guilt remains on the part of the critic that the aesthetic judgement he has himself made, savours of less than charity:

> Shakespeare does not enforce a moral in this play – his judgement is implicit only – but as the action ends in laughter and affection in Belmont we know that each couple, in their own way, have found love's wealth. We know too that their happiness is not all that we would wish; as they make free with Shylock's commercial wealth, we remember that they lacked the full measure of charity towards one who, through his hatred and possessiveness, had got his choice of that which he deserved.

11. Leslie A. Fielder, *The Stranger in Shakespeare* (London, 1973), p. 86. But see also James Shapiro, *Shakespeare and the Jews* (Southampton, 1992, The Parkes Lecture [see essay 4 – Ed.]), p. 3, who argues that there were Jews in England, though

> Virtually all those Jews practised their faith in secret – since most were of Spanish or Portuguese descent, *marranos*, they surely had had enough experience with disguising their beliefs because of their experience of the Inquisition, far harsher than any repression they might face in England.

12. Fielder, ibid., p. 111.

13. Ibid., pp. 117–18.

14. Ibid., pp. 166, 167.

15. Roland Barthes, *Mythologies*, trans. Annette Lavers (London, 1973), p. 142.

16. Ibid., p. 143.

17. Theodor Adorno, 'Reconciliation under Duress' (1961), in Ronald Taylor (ed.), *Aesthetics and Politics* (London, 1980), p. 160.

18. Julia Kristeva, *Strangers to Ourselves*, trans. Leon Roudiez (New York, 1991), p. 1.

19. Ibid., pp. 31, 95.

20. Stephen Greenblatt, *Learning to Curse: Essays in Early Modern Culture* (New York, 1990), p. 43.

21. Ibid., p. 41.

22. Ibid., pp. 55, 56.

23. Ibid., p. 43.

24. Fredric Jameson, *The Political Unconscious: Narrative as a Socially Symbolic Act* (London, 1981), p. 34. It is also worth remembering at a purely phenomenological level this battle was fought out in the institution of the Elizabethan theatre itself in connection with the reduction of the 'play' to the status of a printed text, with *The Merchant of Venice* not being printed until 1600, some three or four years after its first performance.

25. Barthes, *Mythologies*, p. 110.

26. Jean-François Lyotard, *Heidegger and 'the Jews'*, trans. Andreas Michael and Mark S. Roberts (Minneapolis, MN, 1990), p. 22.

27. E. C. Pettet, '*The Merchant of Venice* and the Problem of Usury', in John Wilders (ed.), *The Merchant of Venice* (Basingstoke and London, 1969), p. 100.

28. Walter Cohen, *Drama of a Nation: Public Theater in Renaissance England and Spain* (Ithaca, NY, 1985), p. 199.

29. Ibid., p. 202.

30. R. H. Tawney, *Religion and the Rise of Capitalism* (New York, 1947), p. 158.

31. Karl Marx, *Capital, Volume III*, trans. David Fernbach (Harmondsworth, 1981), p. 731.

32. Ibid., pp. 732–3.

33. Ibid., p. 745.

34. Martin Luther, *Works: The Christian in Society*, 6 vols (Philadelphia, 1962), vol. 2, p. 297.

35. Sir Thomas Wilson, *A Discourse Upon Usurye* (London, 1572), sig. D4[r].

36. M. Phillipus Caesar, *A General Discourse Against the Damnable Sect of Usurie* (London, 1578), sig N2ᵛ.

37. W. H. Auden, *The Dyer's Hand, and Other Essays* (London, 1963), p. 227.

38. Ibid., p. 231.

39. Ibid., p. 234.

40. Wilson, *Discourse*, sig D4ʳ.

41. Jonathan Dollimore, 'Subjectivity, Sexuality and Transgression: The Jacobean Connection', *Renaissance Drama*, ns, 17 (1986), 53–82, 59.

42. Ibid., 61.

43. Michel Pêcheux, *Language, Semantics, Ideology* (London, 1983), pp. 156–7.

44. *The Oxford English Dictionary* lists as one meaning of 'purse', 'The scrotum'. This raises the prospect of 'legitimate' as opposed to 'illegitimate' insemination; in mercantilist practice there is a legitimate way of making money 'breed', that of Antonio, which is closely aligned with friendship, contrasted with Shylock's illicit practice, articulated as a form of sexual licence.

45. C. L. Barber, *Shakespeare's Festive Comedy* (New York, 1959), p. 179.

46. Shapiro, *Shakespeare and the Jews*, pp. 14–15.

47. Niccolò Machiavelli, *The Discourses*, trans. Bernard Crick (Harmondsworth, 1970), p. 143.

48. Sigmund Freud, *The Standard Edition of the Complete Psychological Works*, ed. J. Strachey, 24 vols (London, 1953–74), vol. 23, p. 88.

49. Ibid., vol. 21, p. 132.

50. Ibid.

51. Cohen, *Drama of a Nation*, p. 202.

52. Michel Foucault, *Language, Counter-Memory, Practice*, trans. Donald F. Bouchard and Sherry Simon (Oxford, 1977), p. 34.

53. *The Book of Homilies* (London, 1594), sig B3ᵛ.

54. Ibid., sig B6ᵛ.

55. Marilyn French, *Shakespeare's Division of Experience* (London, 1982), p. 114.

56. Cf. sonnet 6, where the distinction is made between 'usury' and progeny:

Make sweet some vial; treasure thou some place
With beauty's treasure ere it be self-killed.
That use is not forbidden usury
Which happies those that pay the willing loan –
That's for thyself to breed another thee
Or ten times happier be it ten for one.

(ll. 3–8)

57. Fernand Braudel, *Civilisation and Capitalism: 15th–18th Centuries*, trans. Sian Reynolds, 3 vols (London, 1982), vol. 2. p. 166.

58. Karl Marx, *Selected Writings*, ed. David McLellan (Oxford, 1977), p. 50.

59. Cf. the role of the Duke in *Romeo and Juliet*, or, more problematically, the Duke in *Measure for Measure*.

60. See E. Balibar and P. Macherey, 'On Literature as an Ideological Form' (1978), in Robert Young (ed.), *Untying the Text: A Post-Structuralist Reader* (London, 1981), p. 88.

61. Ibid.

62. Jacques Derrida, *Writing and Difference*, trans. Alan Bass (London, 1981), p. 280.

63. See Pierre Macherey, *A Theory of Literary Production*, trans. Geoffrey Wall (London, 1978), p. 129.

64. John Russell Brown (ed.), *The Merchant of Venice* (Harmondsworth, 1964), p. viii.

10

Transformations of Authenticity: *The Merchant of Venice* in Israel

AVRAHAM OZ

Rarely has a dramatic piece haunted a whole nation for centuries as *The Merchant of Venice* has the Jews. Shylock has penetrated the Jewish collective identity so deeply that no reader or spectator sensitised to Jewishness can approach Shylock without some sense of personal involvement. Discussing the play in a Jewish classroom often sounds like discussing the lot of an accused person awaiting his verdict in the next room. A few days after my own Hebrew version of the play was first produced on stage (1972), the Israeli Open University applied for the rights to include some passages in one of its newly written courses. That course, however, formed part of neither the drama nor the literature programme: it was in Jewish history. More often than any other dramatic character, Shylock has visited the political columns of the Jewish press. A hard-line prime minister earned the name (by non-Jewish enemies) as a derogatory attribute; a Jewish guerilla fighter defended himself before a British court: 'I am not a Shylock; I am a freedom fighter!'[1] An Israeli reporter in London compared the British press, urging pardon for John Damianiuk (sentenced to death by an Israeli court for atrocities against Jews in a Nazi concentration camp), to the Duke of Venice asking Shylock to show gentle mercy for Antonio (IV.i.17–34).[2] The reporter's title was 'Legitimation for Antisemitism 1988', and her main concern was the production of

The Merchant of Venice by the Royal Shakespeare Company, which she had attended that same week:

> From the very outset of the play, under Bill Alexander's direction, it becomes clear that contending Judaism and Christianity are not perceived on equal terms. On the stage background one sees a yellow star-of-David, painted in coarse lines with dripping colour, beside a neat church window with stained glass depicting Christian saints. The Christians are handsome and clean, while Shylock is clad like an oriental Jew in dirty coloured robes, his hair and beard curled, his speech and accent grotesque and detestable, and even the town's kids chase him, abuse him and spit on him. Antonio spits on him immediately after receiving the loan, and both lender and creditor are obviously enemies and Shylock has good reasons to wish for revenge.[3]

The journalist admitted that the 400-year-old Shakespearean text 'does indeed present Shylock as a bloodthirsty, heartless persecutor', but she did not acquit the director of his responsibility for scenes prone to 'legitimise antisemitism'. She took particular note of the trial scene; Shylock (played by Anthony Sher, whom she did not forget to identify as 'a South African-born Jew') ecstatically donned a *Talit* when about to cut his pound of flesh, and muttered the Hebrew prayer, 'Pour thy rage over the gentiles who know thee not!' Knowing the Hebrew words, the journalist could not calm her own rage.

But whereas the reporter's rage sounded genuine, the same production was 'scholarly', attacked an Israeli academic, professing 'scientific objectivity'. The writer, Eli Rozik, had attended what he called 'an organised pilgrimage of the London Jewish community ... to take part in some inexorably recurring ritual ... to look again and again in the famous Shakespearean mirror and ask themselves again and again how are they reflected in the eyes of their host society'.[4] This anthropological observation did not stop at the audience: it was soon applied to Sher as well, who was identified as 'a Jew, born to a family of east European origin', who happens to be 'by a happy coincidence ... also of South African origin', showing solidarity with the sufferings of his newly adopted 'compatriots' (ironic inverted commas in text). Sher saw the production as an attack against apartheid, its silent accomplices (his own Jewish parents), and Jewish hypocrisy in general. 'The former victims of racism turned racists themselves at their earliest opportunity', Sher was quoted as saying, while Rozik reached his own conclusion: 'Surely the typical

English reader was delighted to read these words.' Having stereo-
typed the entire 'host society' in phrases such as 'the open consensus
of the English society regarding racism', he noted that 'the comparison with the Palestinians is not missing'.

But Rozik's main argument had to do with the legitimacy of theatrical interpretation. The director's 'line of interpretation' attempted to present Shylock as the victim of Christian racism, but
this 'is possible only if one abides by certain rules',[5] which Rozik un-
dertook to prescribe. Distinguishing between the presentation of
'the play as it is' (an essentialist position taken for granted) and the
director's deviations from it, he found the director guilty of 'redis-
tributing positivity and negativity between Christians and Jews,
mainly between Antonio and Shylock', and diverting the original
demonic, motiveless malignity of Shylock into a psychological reaction. The director chose, out of irrelevant historicist motivation, to
present Shylock as 'the oriental model' (namely, 'a Jewish merchant
of Turkish origin'). This anthropological model, Rozik argued, is
alienated not only from the Christian society on stage but also from
the audience: 'undoubtedly, in my opinion, the natural tendency of
the spectators is to identify with those who uphold the aesthetic and
not with those who discard it.' Thus the 'oriental model' chosen by
the director will not do, since racism cannot yield to psychological
argumentation. Rozik would have preferred the mythical antisemitic
stereotype to the insulting suggestion that 'any historical Jew could
act like Shylock'. But there is still a surprising ending to his story,
which seems to him bigger than life: contrary to all his theories, the
London Jewish spectators did not protest. 'Contrary to anything we
know about communication, we were witnessing a miracle. The
anti-racist message was taken in ... without resistance!' It never occurred to the writer that his 'rules' themselves contradicted 'anything we know about communication'; that perhaps even the
'oriental model' could raise some sympathy at Stratford. He opted
for another explanation, one which involves conspiracy and magic
at once: there is, he suggested, a silent agreement between audience
and artists, both of whom 'would experience the anti-apartheid
message to the point of neglecting [the rules of] theatre itself'.[6]

Authorial intention, so radically abused by our academic writer,
still frequently haunts directors and audiences in the theatre. It often
seems a convenient historical refuge from the high-handed dictates
of synchronic contemporary interpretations, into which a good
number of classical productions fall nowadays. Furthermore, it is

held by many to retain some inherent clue of authenticity which, set against the reality of the present, may capture the *kairos* investing 'the revolution of the times'.[7] Sought by both old and new historicists, intention is taken to shed some light on the particular discourse out of which a given work emanated.

It is against this background, then, that the question of 'how was Shylock intended to be' still matters to producers and audiences alike. This worn-out question seems to have embarrassed so many recent writers on *The Merchant of Venice*, that, if hardly able to escape its implications and consequences, they turn their backs upon its blunt wording whenever it awaits them at some dangerous corner. Others, who courageously address themselves to the question, are prone to blame Shakespeare for their own perplexities. Thus we are told by Francis Fergusson that 'perhaps Shylock turned out to be more powerful than Shakespeare intended, for at that moment in his career he was not quite in control of the great characters that were taking possession of his imagination'.[8] What this assertion suggests is that there exists a certain measurable model on which an ideal Shylock should rest, and of which the product of Shakespeare is an unintentionally inflated replica. The desirable proportions of a Shylock are dictated by the nature and properties of the play (in this case, mainly by the play's generic classification);[9] if the play as a whole, say, passes for a romantic comedy, then the character of the killjoy should spoil the fun only as far as the boundaries of romantic comedy will allow. Balance is all, as a good deal of the play's theatrical and critical history would seem to suggest: when Heine wishes to grant Shylock full tragic weight, he finds it necessary to attack fiercely every single member of Venetian society; and when M. C. Bradbrook describes him as a man reduced to a beast, she finds herself obliged to rehabilitate Bassanio from Heine's ferocious attack. This insistence on balance may of course be challenged by arguing for an intuitive attempt on Shakespeare's part to echo the imbalance characterising the time in which the play was written, foreshadowing the notes of melancholy evident in the dénouements of *Much Ado about Nothing, As You Like It*, and *Twelfth Night*, or the sober realism that dominates the problem comedies.

The foregoing samples of conflicting interpretations are commonly based, however, on the belief that Shakespeare's view of Shylock and the play can be retraced and is to be taken into account if one wishes to make sense of, and do justice to, *The Merchant of Venice* on stage or in a critical study. But this position is in itself questionable. Even if one assumes that the constraints laid by the text upon the production are definable, it does not necessarily mean that these constraints can be identified with authorial intention. This point is driven home particularly, for instance, by that trend in the hermeneutic approach of which Gadamer is a notable proponent: 'understanding means, primarily, to understand the content of what is said, and only secondarily to isolate and understand another's meaning as such.' The 'other' referred to is primarily the author, and it follows that

> The real meaning of a text, as it speaks to the interpreter, does not depend on the contingencies of the author and whom he originally wrote for ... Not occasionally, but always, the meaning of a text goes beyond its author.[10]

There are not many instances in dramatic history which may better illustrate the unbridgeable gap between 'intention' and interpretation than the case of the stage history of *The Merchant of Venice* in Israel. Shakespeare could hardly have anticipated the possibility of his play being performed for a Jewish audience, in Hebrew, in a Jewish state: for him, the probability of such a contingency would barely have exceeded that of an audience of fairies watching *A Midsummer Night's Dream* in fairyland (and, presumably, in fairytongue pentameters). It would seem that in such a context the whole question of the author's intention matters little, if at all. It did matter in Israel, however, as the public controversies surrounding each of the four major productions of the play since the establishment of the professional Hebrew stage in the twentieth century attest.

What lends particular interest to this case of stage history is the continuous dialogue taking place between a developing national consciousness – one which at no point could assume indifference towards Shylock – and a hypothetical original intention attributed to the text. The period concerned was, obviously, crucial for the development of such a national consciousness, and it may be a unique instance in the history of Shakespearean influence where a play readjusted its meaning to take an active part within the framework of a *kairos* totally different from the one in which it originated. For the significance of a Hebrew production of *The Merchant of Venice* clearly transcends the limited realm of the theatre in an age when a totally new national Jewish identity had emerged; in Israel the play is loaded simultaneously with the terror of extermination and the dilemma of might.

The first Hebrew production of *The Merchant of Venice* was mounted in 1936 at the Habimah Theatre (later to become the National Theatre of Israel). The director, Leopold Jessner (1878–1945), one of the major figures in the rich theatrical life of Berlin during the 1920s, achieved fame as the director of the Staatstheater and the Schiller Theater. A pioneer of German Expressionism, he exerted much influence with his productions of Schiller, Wedekind, and Barlach, as well as Shakespeare's *Richard III* (1920, with Fritz Kortner in the title role), *Othello* (which he directed twice: 1921 and 1932), *Macbeth* (1922) and *Hamlet* (1926, in modern dress).[11] He arrived in Palestine a Jewish refugee, intending to wander on to Los Angeles, after having started his enforced exile in London.

Fifteen years prior to his engagement at the Habimah, Jessner must have attended the colourful and vivacious production of *The Merchant of Venice* by his contemporary and compatriot Max Reinhardt at the Grosses Schauspielhaus, where Werner Krauss's flat-footed, boisterous, almost farcical Shylock retained almost no trace of dignity in the character of the Jew.[12] For Jessner, who always differed from Reinhardt in stressing the conflict of ideas inherent in the plays rather than their spectacular effectiveness, following Reinhardt's example would have been inconceivable, particularly in the Palestine of 1936. As he explained (and he had a good deal of explaining to do), the play was supposed to remain a legend, though one in which the legendary harmony was upset by the special weight of Shylock's role. His was not to be a patient Shylock, accepting his tragic lot quietly; rather he would be a long-struggling Shylock, who eventually falls victim to the treacheries of his adversaries. Not just one Shylock who was beaten in his battle with Christian society: he was to be The Jew.[13]

Much about the spirit of Jessner's production can be gathered from the musical instructions sent with the score by his composer, Karl Rathaus: the overture juxtaposed a decadent Renaissance world (Italian in colour), approaching its end, with a long-suffering Jewish one. In the opening scene, set in a lively café – the social centre of Venetian 'golden youth' – a tenor sang a tune associated with the 'Hep-Hep', the well-known antisemitic cry of abuse. As was his wont, Jessner made clever use of his famous *Jessnertreppe*, a stairway designed to connect various stage levels – an external parallel to the play's immanent structure. A typical employment of this device to stress a point of meaning in a theatrical manner occurred at the trial scene: the Jew, ridiculed by the entire court, his yellow badge attached to the back of his Jewish gaberdine, stood upright on a higher level than the judge, who sat below, speaking his lines in a thundering voice while everybody froze as if suddenly hypnotised.[14]

Predictably, however, the play roused a public controversy. 'In spite of Jessner's promises in all his speeches that his production was to stress only those points which will suit the Hebrew stage, most of the gentiles appeared almost as decent human beings', one critic typically complained. 'Even Antonio betrayed that touch of sombre decency invested in him by the author.' Attempting to guide his readers to a better understanding of the spirit of Jessner's production, the same critic added:

> Had our audience been more moderate and attentive, it would have sensed in Shylock something closer to us, to our feelings, and perceived that maybe even today (and perhaps *especially* today) the character of Shylock, as a symbol, is the expression of the Jew's contempt of those who despise him, be it for faults which are in him or such maliciously attributed to him. None of the many details in the play would overshadow the main point, namely that Shylock recognises his right to detest his enemies, that he realises his moral advantage over them ... When Shylock is deserted by his daughter, his last comfort in life, and when he leaves the courtroom, broken and wronged to the core of his being, one gets the feeling that in this very moment his rightfulness pierces the heavens. Yes, they have trodden him under their feet; they have wounded his soul. Helpless, unable to utter a word, to perform even one graceful gesture to fit fairly the tragic moment, his fire of spirit extinct in a moment, he learns that there is no hope and crashes into the abyss opening before him. But the fiery spirit of rage which has left this broken Jew is to haunt the world for ages to come. That is what Shylock symbolises – the humiliation of Israel, for which there is no pardon in the world for ever and ever![15]

While these were the words of one of Jessner's defenders, others voiced different views. In a mock public trial, organised by the theatre itself and in which Jessner took part as one of the three prosecuted (the author, the theatre, and the director), Shakespeare, though acknowledgement was made to his greatness as a writer, was accused of writing 'a play in which he invoked an anti-Jewish theme without being informed enough to treat his subject, in a way which produced a false, fictitious, impossible character, interpreted with a strong antisemitic approach, if not on purpose then at least erroneously'.[16]

One of the witnesses for the prosecution, the writer Avraham Kariv, a hard-line Jewish traditionalist, went so far as to deny the Shakespearean character its Jewish identity. Shylock was the 'hero of revenge ... [whereas] we, the Jews, in whom an ancient spiritual culture is coupled with the long experience of humiliation and suffering, cannot possibly be prone to such a wild and sadistic act of revenge as that which Shylock so wilfully wants to commit.'[17] Another witness for the prosecution, the well-known Communist poet Alexander Penn, reprimanded Jessner from a totally different stance:

> Shylock and society – that is the question which was so utterly blurred by Jessner's interpretation ... If in an age like ours a director such as Jessner wanted to shed a fresh light upon the Shylock problem, he had to shift his focus to the one real, substantial point in the play: Shylock the 'speculator'. This is the Shylock which was really to be defended. A pound of flesh – absurd! And absurd is being apologetic in front of the absurd! ... Instead of apologising, we have the full right to accuse ... 'You, who were angry at us for our success in accumulating money – *you* are to blame, because you never let us survive in any other way; you have turned us into usurers and profiteers.'

In the recent history of Palestine, the year 1936 marks the outbreak of the Arab revolt. Penn, happy with the moderate reaction of the Jewish community at the early stage of the hostilities, did not shy from seasoning his reaction to Shakespeare's play with topical references. Addressing Jessner directly, he went on:

> You have come to produce the play in Palestine! How did it not occur to you to disown hatefully anything which is fictitious in it? The way the Jewish community in this country behaved throughout these dangerous weeks, the very fact of its self-restraint is a decisive answer ... And if for the rest of the world a production of *The Merchant of Venice* should have served as a straightforward accusation ... for us, who came here in order to bring about a great spiritual –economical shift in our life, this show should have been a sharp reminder, an acute warning against all those petty Shylocks, those speculators and profiteers penetrating our country.[18]

The first production of *The Merchant of Venice* in Palestine, then, occurred at an heroic moment, where national pathos was a standard theme. Any attempt to deprive Shylock of at least some measure of his tragic pathos would have been self-defeating. On this occasion, reality proved stronger than the text in laying its constraints upon the limits of interpretation. The dictates of reality governed all facets of the production: the text bowdlerised, in the name of serenity, such vulgar references as Gratiano's 'stake down' conceit in Act III, scene ii and cut three-quarters of the same character's final speech at the end of the play, and the music and scenery served faithfully the director's solemn approach to its moral dilemma. So did the casting: the two rival leaders of the company, Aharon Meskin and Shim'on Finkel, alternated in the part, both denying the character of Shylock any trace of its inherent comic potential. Meskin was an heroic figure, making use of his commanding physical stature and resounding voice; Finkel emphasised Shylock's spiteful bitterness.

Twenty-three years later, the heroic pathos characterising Jewish reality in Palestine was considerably modified. The struggle for liberation over, the Israeli community was undergoing a process of stabilisation in its eleven-year-old state. And though the Israeli national character was still precarious and highly vulnerable, and the memory of the Jewish Holocaust still fresh, one could now more easily risk a presentation of *The Merchant of Venice* where Shylock was to be exempt from carry ing the full weight of Jewish history on his shoulders. This time it was a non-Jewish director, Tyrone Guthrie, who came over to the Habimah (where he had directed a much-acclaimed production of *Oedipus Rex* in 1947) to revive the controversial play. And although the same two actors again alternated the part of Shylock, a significant change of focus was generally expected. Said Meskin:

> When I first played Shylock, I stressed mainly the national, pathetic element. This time I shall endeavour to portray a more human Shylock: he has got a measure of fanaticism – but he has his weaknesses as well. Guthrie has told me that at the beginning of the play Shylock is a thriving merchant, a kind of Rothschild. This has given me much help. I have even obtained a picture of Rothschild.[19]

In Guthrie's modern-dress production, Shylock did indeed physically resemble 'a kind of Rothschild'. If Jessner's fame as a Shakespearean director rested mainly on his productions of the tragedies, Guthrie felt more at home in Shakespearean comedy, and his production attempted to coax the play as far as possible into that realm. In a busy Venice, he devised a lively and rapid succession of entrances and exits, with Salerio and Solanio portrayed as a pair of American businessmen holding their umbrellas in the rain while passing comments on city affairs, with Gratiano constantly on the move in a dancing step, humming merry jazz tunes – a persistent association of decadent Renaissance Italy with modern American life.

In his approach to Shylock, however, Guthrie remained pretty much faithful to the apologetic tradition. For him, the focal centre of the action is the duel between Shylock and Portia in the trial scene, at the expense of Antonio, who is saved from being a bore only when his homosexual relation to Bassanio (Guthrie used the term 'irregular' or 'tender') is carefully established. But even so, 'when all is said and done, in the theatre it is almost impossible to make Antonio dominate the play'.[20]

In spite of the particular emphasis laid on the Shylock–Portia duel, Guthrie's actress for the Habimah production (Shoshana Ravid) failed to become an equal partner to the Jew. Anonymously referring to her in his introduction, Guthrie later described how her ineffectuality made him realise how important the part was:

> Portia was entirely miscast – a sweet, motherly, young woman, the epitome of middle-class respectability. The more we stuck her with jewels and decked her up in pink satin, the more she resembled the Railway Queen of some remote junction; the harder she tried to be witty and sophisticated, the more she sounded like a hospital nurse reading a script prepared for somebody else.[21]

The scene, then, was left entirely to Shylock, and here Guthrie's excessive reverence for the Jew proved a major drawback. Guthrie's conception of Shylock in this production did not contradict his general view of the part, as his later commentary indicates:

> It is my view that Shakespeare's portrait is not antisemitic, that the pound of flesh wager was entered upon as a jest and only turns to vengeance after Shylock has been robbed and his daughter abducted by young Venetians of Antonio's set. In fact, after the trial, and after Portia's great invocation of mercy it is the Christians who lack all mercy toward their enemy. The sadistic vengeance taken upon Shylock is as offensive to Christianity as it is legally outrageous.

And yet, as he realises himself,

> to say this to Jews in the present epoch is as useless as to beg the rain not to fall. There is a rooted tradition among Jews that the play is an antisemitic document, and it is indeed true that many Jewish boys at school have, through generations, been taunted and execrated as 'Shylock' ... the remedy is ... to interpret it so that it becomes, *as its*

> *author intended*, a fantasia on the twin themes of mercy and justice ...
> in which none of the characters is either wholly good or wholly evil.[22]

Up to a point, Guthrie's colourful fantasia managed to work effectively. The problem of Shylock, however, proved recalcitrant: in appearance reminiscent of 'a liberal Rabbi, with a well-trimmed beard and a clever and pleasant expression',[23] neither of the two Shylocks could avoid the pathos presumably remaining with them from the former production. Shylock's pathos stood in awkward contrast to the air of romantic comedy informing the production as a whole, to the detriment of the sought-for balance. Some of the problems of Guthrie's production anticipated the emergence of similar problems in Jonathan Miller's 1970 production at the National Theatre, London: can a liberal, fairly realistic modern-dress production accommodate the weird story of the pound of flesh and remain liberal and fairly realistic? Guthrie's production could not. It was removed from Habimah's repertory after a few months.

The next production of *The Merchant of Venice* on the Israeli stage occurred after the most significant experience undergone by national consciousness since the founding of the state in 1948: the 1967 war, which had a dramatic effect on the nation's mentality. The prevailing sense of persecution and self-defensiveness, so far an infinite resource for rationalising any mistake made in the name of security or any moral conflict resulting from the rights, or 'positive discrimination', of Jews in Israel, from now on had to allow for the manifest reality of occupation and might. The euphoric period which followed the war (at least until 1973) was characterised by growing feelings of national pride up to the point of vanity, not unlike those of the Elizabethans in the years immediately following the victory over the Armada. It was now reasonably safe to assume that the self-confident audience would be able to stomach a totally different, non-apologetic approach to the play.

This was the situation when, in 1972, an Israeli-born director addressed himself to the play for the first time in Israel. The 'native view' permitted a portrayal of Shylock in the least favourable and most grotesque manner, as if coming directly from the heavily biased drawings of Jews in the Middle Ages. In Yossi Yzraeli's production of the play at the Cameri Theatre of Tel Aviv, everything was far removed from realism: Shylock, in a dark robe and a black bell-shaped hat, stood out among blonde Venetians, all clad in white, against abstract scenery consisting of a white back wall and a white rostrum. Tubal, in black, served only to underline the foreign look of the Jew, while Jessica (not unpredictably) wore a striped dress, with lines of black and white, following her conversion.

One of the major features which marked the production was its persistent departure from the individuality of character. I have dwelt elsewhere on one example of this practice, the experimental doubling of Morocco and Arragon, both played by the actor playing Bassanio, and thus lending a reinforced unity to the choice of the three caskets.[24] If this device might still have been accommodated within the boundaries of realistic characterisation (e.g., Bassanio eliminating alternatives in disguise), making all the Christians in Venice look alike transcended the boundaries of individuality to the point of rendering them, in some respects, as a collective entity. Typical of this approach was the treatment of Antonio in the trial scene: the stage was totally bare but for a black stool on which Antonio sat with a huge black cross fastened to his back. Thus made a type of Christ, Antonio himself did not become an object of empathy; the pathos and compassion evoked by the scene were directed to the figure of Christ beyond him rather than to Antonio in person.

The action was further circumscribed by a surrounding framework: the show opened with a Passion-like procession, with mummers in masks, and Shylock, his Jewish nose grotesquely prolonged, bending under the weight of the cross. Another symbolic procession followed the trial scene. But the most dominant element of this enveloping framework was the constant presence of a puppet theatre peering over the white back wall, reflecting, reverberating, and multiplying the action underneath by means of puppets in the likeness of the actual characters on stage. The puppet-show was used as a visual commentary on the action, sometimes comically imitating it, sometimes making visual interscenic connections, and occasionally even providing alternative action. The most outstanding example of the latter practice occurred when, as the background to Lorenzo's exhortation on music (Act V, scene i), the puppet-play enacted a symbolic ritual in which Shylock was baptised by the Christians.

The production, though in many respects lively and entertaining, was considered an artistic (and box-office) failure, its symbolism much too obvious and far from convincing.[25] Predictably, much of the critical controversy focused on the portrayal of Shylock. Even though, in the final analysis, Yzraeli's interpretation was meant to render Shylock as the victim of a sterile Christian society, his intentions were thwarted, for much of the audience, by the Jew's repellent appearance and mannerisms. Unlike Jessner and Guthrie, who chose for the part typically heroic actors, Yzraeli gave the role to a notable comedian, Avner Hyskiahu, whose style of delivery generally consists of a nervous staccato. Under the director's instructions, Hyskiahu played Shylock as 'a shrewd old Jew, his posture, his gait, his manner of speaking reflecting a life spent making shrewd, furtive money deals, a man accustomed to abuse. He delivers his key speech ("Hath not a Jew eyes")? Snarling at the two *goyim* [gentiles], practically spitting in their faces. He is a worm turned, but still a worm.'[26] The controversy over the production once again served to expose the age-old prejudices concerning the play:

> It is but natural that we Jews are practically allergic to a typical anti-semitic interpretation, which blurs Shylock's cry of pain and protest, stirring the heart of any human being, be it a Jew, a Christian, or other. In this the play was deprived of its tragic power and poetic flavour which are, in spite of the various amusing moments abounding in *The Merchant of Venice*, the very core of the play.[27]

This, however, was a fairly moderate reaction. Not surprisingly, the production in general, and the portrayal of Shylock in particular, were most fiercely attacked by the more radically nationalistic press.

Avner Hyskiahu repeated Shylock in yet a different production, in 1980, again at the Cameri Theatre, directed this time by a non-Jewish director from the Royal Shakespeare Company, Barry Kyle. In many ways Kyle's production was not distinguishable from any likely production of the play at his home theatre in Stratford. Set in no specific locality or period (Portia was dressed as a typical Renaissance lady while Launcelot Gobbo appeared on stage riding an ancient motorcycle), Christopher Morley's impressive scenery subtly captured the symbolism of the three caskets: a golden back wall (made of shutters typical of Tel Aviv verandahs) and golden bridges, surrounding waters of silver hue, and a lead-coloured central platform.

In his programme note (entitled 'Two Outcasts of Society: Shylock and Antonio') Kyle stressed the allegorical significance of the play, as his interpretation attempted to communicate it:

> The money world, though bound by contracts and stamped by passion, must depend on friendship.

Kyle marked value as binding together the two stories of the plot: the value of friendship, of marriage pledge, and of money. Time has turned Shylock into a racist stereotype; yet in the play Shylock is condemned not because of his Jewishness but because he lets money rule him. This condemnation has nothing to do with anti-semitism, says Kyle, since it also applies to the Prince of Morocco and Arragon, as well as to the young Christians of Venice, including Bassanio. Shylock, whose world is stamped by gold and silver, ignores the quality of mercy. Once wronged, Kyle said in his initial talk to the actors, Shylock easily falls prey to revenge in succumbing to the logic and mentality of terrorism. Triggering one of the most charged terms in the life of the Middle East, Kyle allowed the tokens of local topicality to penetrate his conception of the play.

Such an attitude towards 'a fellow countryman', however, proved an obstacle even for actors who took part in the production itself. At a certain point during rehearsals, Kyle was persuaded by some of the actors (though not before a thorough argument with many of the others) that in order for the message of concord and love to be accepted by the target audience, Antonio's first stipulation regarding Shylock's conversion had better be dropped. Thus, while in 1972 the ritual symbolising Shylock's baptism was virtually enacted on stage, no mention of his possible conversion was made to the audience of 1980, polarised between cultural assimilation with the west and a fervent, often fundamentalist search for traditional roots. It was the radically nationalistic part of the audience who failed to notice Kyle's conception of Shylock as 'succumbing to the logic and mentality of terrorism'. Social, economic, and political circumstances in Israel in the 1980s, a second decade of occupying another people's homeland, have had their effect on the national consciousness. Looking back on the long history of Jewish suffering up to the Holocaust, many in Israel have made it a flag 'not to be made a soft and dull eyed fool, to shake the head, relent and sigh, and yield to [gentile] intercessors' (III.iii.14–16). For those, Shylock's cry of defiance, 'My deeds upon my head' (IV.i.202) was justified in context, since 'Jewish' and 'the logic and mentality of terrorism' had become mutually exclusive concepts. This strange mixture of resenting Shakespeare's alleged antisemitism and identifying with Shylock's motives lent special significance to a topical image of a terrorist act, which, in the political context of the Middle East, is hardly confined to any one-sided allegorical interpretation.

Even though Kyle's production failed to make its political point, it was a crucial step towards setting the play in the contemporary Israeli context. Kyle's attitude towards Shylock surely would have antagonised the old historicist school, for the term 'terrorism' could enter neither the discourse nor the supposed 'master narrative' of the Renaissance. But there is another, more basic difficulty. From the stance of normative social order, terrorism must signify crime. Terrorism may not necessarily be politically motivated; but Shylock convinces neither the Venetian court nor the majority of Shakespeare's critics in his motiveless malignity. What is he, then? A political dissenter? And if so, what would be the moral position of a political terrorist in the Renaissance? Within the discourse of crime, the term 'political terrorism', meaning the use of violence to press individuals or society to meet political demands, may betray a peculiar sense of moral (if not legal) legitimation. As Uri Eisenzweig argues, the physical reality of terrorism 'appears to be dramatically unquestionable', whereas its actual legal content is missing from most judicial systems.[28] While terrorism must emanate from a logical procedure which stands outside the normative order, it draws for its validity on a different, meta-normative order, which recognises the dominant ideology as only one of several orders competing in the sociopolitical consciousness. Such an extra-official validity has no place in any legitimate code of values, and thus it may exist exclusively in the realm of text. The performative nature of the terrorist text thus becomes indispensable in this process. It is the word of Shylock's bond which becomes the symbolic, hence the essential, meaning of the terrorist act he performs. The consummation of the act of terrorism is not the actual deed (such as the cutting of the pound of flesh), nor is its author's real identity (as a Jew, a moneylender, or a Pantaloon) of necessary significance at the crucial moment. This may explain the discrepancy between Shylock's prominence in the play and his relatively brief presence on the scene, as well as his much-debated absence from the play after the trial scene.

And yet the legal content of terrorism, missing from most judicial systems, does reside in Shakespeare's Venetian book of laws. Any play composed during the reign of Elizabeth could not ignore the constant danger of contrivance by strangers, which may explain the peculiarly anti-alien nature of Shakespeare's Venetian legislation that otherwise pretends to be liberal and egalitarian. There is no sense in which such a private assault contrived by one individual against another should be distinguished ethnically or nationally, unless that distinction between alien and citizen implies an act of political subversion, or, in other words, political terrorism.

Shylock does not belong with those precursors of modern terrorism, such as Brutus, who use violence against tyranny. Yet if Shylock does not take hostages illegally, his act of appropriating the law itself is not entirely devoid of ideological grounds. Hardly an Iago-like 'motive-hunter', Shylock provides some solid reasons for his stubborn insistence on his bond, none of which has to do with ideology; and yet some tokens of ideological motivation are still betrayed in his behaviour. To cite but one example, whether or not we are to believe Jessica's evidence concerning her father's initial intentions to harm Antonio, her reference to Tubal and Chus as Shylock's 'countrymen' (III.ii.284) is telling. We do not know which is their common 'country' of origin, but this expression, together with Shylock's repeated references to his 'nation' and 'tribe', casts an ideological shade on his attitude throughout the play.

Beside the particular case of his Jewishness, Shylock represents a more generally subversive element within the dominant Christian, capitalist order in Venice. Together with Othello he belongs in the company of 'aliens', whose danger to the ideological integrity of the Venetian ruling class is so menacing that special legislation had to be issued to curb their rights and activities within the liberal state. Shylock is no self-styled machiavel like Marlowe's Barabas, who defies the law entirely. Thus his complaint cannot find any institutional outlet until his specific function within the trade-capitalist process which moves Venetian economy is directly addressed. Significantly enough, this opportunity occurs when emotion is mixed with business: the financial implications of courting Portia belong to the subversive parts of 'pure' love in the same way that Shylock the alien is a necessary constituent of the Venetian economic system. Once Shylock is allowed to interfere with the financial operations of Venice's prince of merchants, the subversive process of rebellion is set in motion.

Throughout the play Shylock is consistently urged to adopt a 'gentle' attitude ('We all expect a gentle answer, Jew'). This is but another way of demanding that he embrace a 'gentile' ideology, a demand which is finally imposed on him legally with the verdict of the trial, which suddenly turns out to be his own. Shylock's perception of the law of Venice is indeed 'alien', since the use he makes of the Venetian constitution rests on the word of the law but contradicts its spirit. It is, in fact, the very essence of Shylock's terrorism: he consciously subverts the soul of Venetian order, namely its book of laws, and turns it upon itself. The only counter-measure Venice could take against Shylock's act of legal terrorism is to subvert the spirit of language on which the law rests in order to re-establish the normal procedures of justice and social order by which Venice's mainstream ideology abides. And it is significant that this is brought about by an 'alien' of a different order, a woman disguised as a man, a country feudal who comes from afar, in order and in time.

Unlike his modern counterparts, Shylock never dreams of instituting a new order, where the ruling authorities will emanate from below, equally representing all the town's residents. His imaginary example of abolishing slavery (IV.i.90–8) remains a parable, without anybody knowing his own opinion on the matter. We do not even know for sure whether he would have pursued his murderous act to the very end, had not Portia's 'tarry' stopped him at the last moment. Nor is it crucial for us, or even for Shakespeare, to know, since, as we have noted before, the terrorist act performed by Shylock is consummated on the textual or symbolic level. As Grant Wardlaw is not alone in arguing, 'terrorism is primarily theatre'.[29] The gist of this notion is nothing but an extension of the textual identity of the terrorist act, as it is often expressed by a note or a telephone call which brings it to public attention, into the performative ritual of the theatrical gesture. Shylock need not act further, since, as the play as a whole shows us, his function in the plot is nothing but that of a catalyst. It is, in other words, the reaction of normative society to an extraterritorial act that the play is about.

Without resorting to the critical fallacies of traditional historicism, *The Merchant of Venice* may still be made to show us the ways in which, by temporarily taking hostage the Venetian law, and while the entire audience of the theatre of terrorism hold their breath, Shylock manages to bring forth the very target of political terrorism, exposing the moral fragility of the dominant ideology. His act succeeds in undermining the notion of reality as integrated and rational, as appropriated by the dominant ideology. In his *Geschichtsphilosophische Thesen* Walter Benjamin tells us that only from the stance of the victors is history viewed as a unitary process. In this respect Shylock is a loser. But as a political terrorist he celebrates the loser's victory in naming the name of the game. In this he disappears as a Jew, or a Pantaloon, or even as an 'alien' in the general sense. As the author and perpetrator of the 'terrorist' text of his bond he coerces the legal system to produce a counter-terrorist text of a similar nature, whereby it exposes itself, at least for one cathartic moment, to its own ideological limitations.

It is hard to predict to what extent the future stage history of *The Merchant of Venice* in Israel will reflect sociopolitical developments in the way it has been doing in the past century, or what course it may take. I believe that the intricate view of Shylock as representing the ideological complexities of terrorism, initially propounded in Barry Kyle's production, may shed new light on the age-old apologetic approach to the play, adopted in its stage and critical history by Jews and non-Jews alike. The easy transformation of Shylock from one form of minority affiliation to another renders the ideological content of the play more general. In a very peculiar way it is expressed in Rafi Bokai's film *Avanti Popolo* (Israel, 1986), which depicts the escape of two Egyptian soldiers through the Israeli lines in Sinai in the attempt to reach the Egyptian border. When captured by a group of Israeli soldiers one of the two Egyptians starts to recite Shylock's 'hath not a Jew eyes' speech. An Israeli soldier comments: 'He has changed the parts!' Has he, indeed? Portia, clad as a young male judge, opens the process of justice in the Venetian court, asking: 'Which is the merchant here? and which the Jew?' (IV.i.170). It is the very question that any judicious reading of the play must attempt to leave open.

From *Foreign Shakespeare: Contemporary Performance*, ed. Dennis Kennedy (Cambridge, 1993), pp. 56–75.

NOTES

[Avraham Oz's essay (reprinted in his study, *The Yoke of Love: Prophetic Riddles in 'The Merchant of Venice'* [Newark, DE, 1995]) strikes a different note from the others in this volume in so far as he is concerned with productions of the play and in so far as those productions take place outside the cultural boundaries of the English language (Oz has translated the play as well as writing about it and has also been involved in productions of it). The essay thus functions as a reminder of the cultural significance of Shakespeare in a world-wide context and also of the way in which productions of *The Merchant of Venice* constantly transform the play both through staging and interpretation. This is a topic pursued in more historical detail by James C. Bulman in his excellent book *Shakespeare in Performance: The Merchant of Venice* (Manchester, 1991), but there is obviously a significance that is hard to measure about the staging of the play in postwar Israel. At the same time Oz's essay seeks to show how the play does not in the end have a stable meaning, a stable identity against which productions can be measured. The essay throws a searching light on the way in which pre-conceptions can get in the way of a more subversive approach to the play, but also on how the play has a particular resonance which is unlikely to diminish in the future. Ed.]

1. Anshel Spielmann, member of the Stern Group fighting against British mandate of Palestine.

2. Citations from Shakespeare are from the New Arden editions, unless otherwise specified.

3. Dalia Sharon, 'Legitimation for Antisemitism 1988', *Davar* (27 May 1988), 28 (Hebrew). For a detailed account of Alexander's production, see James C. Bulman, *The Merchant of Venice*, Shakespeare in Performance (Manchester, 1991), pp. 117–42, and Russell Jackson and Robert Smallwood (eds), *Players of Shakespeare, 3* (Cambridge, 1993).

4. Eli Rozik, 'Apartheid in Venice', *Bamah*, III (1988), 74 (Hebrew).

5. Ibid., 75.

6. Ibid., 84.

7. The present usage of the term *kairos* follows, e.g., that of Kermode; see Frank Kermode, *The Sense of an Ending* (New York, 1967), p. 47.

8. Fergusson, in the introduction to the Laurel (1958) edition of the play; reprinted in his *Shakespeare: The Pattern in His Carpet* (New York, 1971), p. 113.

9. See Northrop Frye, in whose view the play 'seems almost an experiment in coming as close as possible to upsetting the comic balance': *Anatomy of Criticism* (Princeton, NJ, 1957), p. 165.

10. Hans-Georg Gadamer, *Truth and Method* (London, 1975), pp. 262, 263–4.

11. See Herbert Ihering, *Reinhardt, Jessner, Piscator oder Klassikertod* (Berlin, 1929); also Ernst Leopold Stahl, *Shakespeare und das deutsche Theater* (Stuttgart, 1947), pp. 608–14 and *passim*. For a recent ap-praisal of Jessner's work, see David F. Kuhns, 'Expressionism, Monumentalism, Politics: Emblematic Acting in Jessner's *Wilhelm Tell* and *Richard III*', *New Theatre Quarterly*, 25 (1991), 35–48.

12. Stahl, *Shakespeare und das deutsche Theater*, p. 592. See also John Russell Brown's introduction to his New Arden edition of the play (London: Methuen, 1955), p. xxxvi.

13. Leopold Jessner, 'On the Theatre in the Land of Israel and Its Vocation', *Bamah*, 10 (1936), 6 (Hebrew).

14. *Bamah*, 11–12 (1937), 31 (Hebrew).

15. Ya'akov Fikhman, 'On the Classical Theatre', *Bamah*, 11–12 (1937), 8 (Hebrew).

16. *Bamah*, 11–12, 24 (Hebrew).

17. Ibid., 25. A similar line of argument was adopted, forty years later, by the Israeli Embassy in London, when given an opportunity by the *Sunday Times* to answer thorough research carried out by the paper's reporters into the practice of torture of detainees in the territories occupied by Israel. Rather than refuting the accusations point by point, the Embassy issued a statement to the effect that 'the Nation of the Bible' was morally prevented from, and therefore unable to perform, acts of torture.

18. Ibid., 26–8. Penn's is a typical reaction of a member of the pioneer groups who came to Palestine during the early 1920s, many of them strongly influenced by the ideals of the Russian Revolution, contrasting with the later 'bourgeois' immigrants.

19. In an interview with Michael Ohad, *Dvar Hashavu'a* (Hebrew: February 1959). Guthrie himself opens his introduction to the play in *Shakespeare: Ten Great Plays* (New York, 1962) in the same spirit: 'Who is the merchant of Venice? Shylock's part is the most striking and effective, and he is arguably a merchant.' Reprinted in Guthrie, *In Various Directions: A View of Theatre* (London, 1965).

20. Guthrie, *In Various Directions*, p. 101.

21. Ibid., p. 102.

22. Ibid., pp. 102–3 (italics mine).

23. Avitam, *Davar* (Hebrew), 6 Mar. 1959.

24. See Avraham Oz, 'The Doubling of Parts in Shakespearean Comedy: Some Questions of Theory and Practice', in *Shakespearean Comedy*, ed. Maurice Charney (New York, 1980), pp. 175–82.

25. Originally, Yzraeli planned to set the play within a large cathedral, somewhere in Europe, where the townsfolk were mounting a Passion play with the local Jew forced to play the villain of the piece. This was abandoned during rehearsals, giving rise to a somewhat patched-up framework which eventually circumscribed the actual production.

26. M. Kohanski, *The Jerusalem Post*, 24 Mar. 1972.

27. Hayim Gamzu, *Ha'aretz* (Hebrew), 20 Mar. 1972.

28. See Uri Eisenzweig, 'Terrorism in Life and in Real Literature', *Diacritics* (Fall 1988), 32.

29. Grant Wardlaw, *Political Terrorism* (Cambridge, 1982), p. 38.

Further Reading

The first section below lists the standard single editions of the play. The books in Section 2 cover a range of approaches and include, for example, both the original Casebook edited by John Wilders, which contains much thought-provoking material, as well as more recent collections of essays. By contrast, the individual essays and articles in Section 3 largely focus on the modern critical debate about the play. The final section on recent books on Shakespeare and Renaissance drama, though not specifically on *The Merchant of Venice*, gives details of some of the most influential criticism of the last few years.

1 EDITIONS

The Merchant of Venice was probably written around 1597. The first edition (Q1) appeared in quarto form in 1600. (Quarto refers to the size of the page on which the text was printed which is half of that of a folio; quarto editions are copies of single plays as opposed to folio volumes.) A second quarto (Q2) edition was printed in 1619. The play was then printed in the first edition of Shakespeare's complete works, the First Folio (F1), in 1623. Most modern editions are based on Q1 but also use Q2 and F1 to emend the text. They are thus 'eclectic' texts, that is, they combine different editions in order to arrive at what the editor considers the best text. The Shakespearean Originals series seeks to challenge this practice and the assumptions that lie behind it, especially the notion of a single authoritative text. The edition listed below by Annabel Patterson, like all the volumes in the series, reprints Q1 with minimal modernisation. The question of what we mean by 'Shakespeare's text' is part of the larger critical debate about what we mean by 'Shakespeare', issues taken up in particular by Margreta de Grazia and Terence Hawkes (albeit from very different angles) but running through the whole of modern Shakespearean criticism.

The most recent editions of the play are:

John Russell Brown (ed.), *The Merchant of Venice*, The Arden Shakespeare (London: Methuen, 1961). A new edition edited by John Drakakis for the Arden 3 series is in preparation.

Jay L. Halio (ed.), *The Merchant of Venice*, The Oxford Shakespeare, World's Classics (Oxford: Oxford University Press, 1994).

M. M. Mahood, *The Merchant of Venice*, The New Cambridge Shakespeare (Cambridge: Cambridge University Press, 1987).

Moelwyn Merchant (ed.), *The Merchant of Venice*, The New Penguin Shakespeare (Harmondsworth: Penguin, 1967).

Annabel Patterson (ed.), *The Most Excellent Historie of The Merchant of Venice*, Shakespearean Originals: First Editions (Hemel Hempstead: Prentice-Hall, 1995).

2 BOOKS AND COLLECTIONS OF ESSAYS ON *THE MERCHANT OF VENICE*

James C. Bulman, *Shakespeare in Performance: The Merchant of Venice* (Manchester: Manchester University Press, 1991).

Lawrence Danson, *The Harmonies of 'The Merchant of Venice'* (New Haven, CT: Yale University Press, 1978).

John Gross, *Shylock: Four Hundred Years in the Life of a Legend* (London: Vintage, 1994).

Graham Holderness, *Shakespeare: The Merchant of Venice*, Penguin Critical Studies (Harmondsworth: Penguin, 1993).

Joan Ozark Holmer, *The Merchant of Venice: Choice, Hazard and Consequence* (Basingstoke and London: Macmillan, 1995).

A. D. Moody, *Shakespeare: The Merchant of Venice* (London: Arnold, 1964).

Bill Overton, *The Merchant of Venice: Text and Performance* (Basingstoke and London: Macmillan, 1987).

Thomas Wheeler (ed.), *The Merchant of Venice: Critical Essays* (New York: Garland, 1991).

John Wilders (ed.), *Shakespeare: The Merchant of Venice*, Macmillan Casebook Series (Basingstoke and London, 1969).

Nigel Wood (ed.), *The Merchant of Venice*, Theory in Practice Series (Buckingham: Open University Press, 1996).

3 ARTICLES AND ESSAYS ON *THE MERCHANT OF VENICE*

Alan C. Dessen, 'The Elizabethan Stage Jew and Christian Example', *Modern Language Quarterly*, 35 (1974), 231–45.

Lars Engle, '"Thrift and Blessing": Exchange and Explanation in *The Merchant of Venice*', *Shakespeare Quarterly*, 37 (1986), 20–37.

Michael Ferber, 'The Ideology of *The Merchant of Venice*', *English Literary History*, 20 (1990), 431–64.

Keith Geary, 'The Nature of Portia's Victory: Turning to Men in *The Merchant of Venice*', *Shakespeare Survey*, 37 (1984), 55–68.

René Girard, '"To Entrap the Wisest": A Reading of *The Merchant of Venice*', in *Literature and Society*, ed. Edward W. Said (Baltimore: Johns Hopkins University Press, 1980), pp. 100–19.

Stephen Greenblatt, 'Marlowe, Marx and Anti-Semitism', in *Learning to Curse* (London: Routledge, 1990), pp. 40–58.

Lorna Hutson, 'Shylock: Why this Usurer has a Daughter', in *The Usurer's Daughter: Male Friendship and Fictions of Women in Sixteenth-Century England* (London and New York: Routledge, 1994), pp. 224–38.

Lisa Jardine, 'Cultural Confusion and Shakespeare's Learned Heroines: "These are old paradoxes"', *Shakespeare Quarterly*, 38 (1987), 1–18.

Coppélia Kahn, 'The Cuckoo's Note: Male Friendship and Cuckoldry in *The Merchant of Venice*', in *Shakespeare's 'Rough Magic': Renaissance Essays in Honor of C. L. Barber*, ed. Peter Erickson and Coppélia Kahn (Newark, DE: University of Delaware Press, 1985), pp. 104–12.

Sarah Kofman, 'Conversions: *The Merchant of Venice* under the Sign of Saturn', in *Literary Theory Today*, ed. Peter Collier and Helga Geyer-Ryan (Cambridge: Polity Press, 1990), pp. 142–66.

Carol Leventen, 'Patrimony and Patriarchy in *The Merchant of Venice*', in *The Matter of Difference: Materialist Feminist Criticism of Shakespeare*, ed. Valerie Wayne (Ithaca and Hemel Hempstead: Cornell University Press, 1991), pp. 59–79.

Thomas Moisan, '"Which is the Merchant here? and Which the Jew"?: Subversion and Recuperation in *The Merchant of Venice*', in *Shakespeare Reproduced: The Text in History and Ideology*, ed. Jean E. Howard and Marion F. O'Connor (New York and London: Routledge, 1987), pp. 188–206.

Steven Mullaney, 'Brothers and Others, or the Art of Alienation', in *Cannibals, Witches, and Divorce: Estranging the Renaissance*, ed. Marjorie Garber (Baltimore and London: Johns Hopkins University Press, 1987), pp. 67–89.

Lawrence Normand, 'Reading the Body in *The Merchant of Venice*', *Textual Practice*, 5:1 (1991), 55–74.

Marianne Novy, *Love's Argument: Gender Relations in Shakespeare* (Chapel Hill and London: University of Carolina, 1984), ch. 4: 'Giving and Taking in *The Merchant of Venice*'.

Marc Shell, 'The Wether and the Ewe: Verbal Usury in *The Merchant of Venice*', *Kenyon Review*, 1 (1979), 65–92.

Arnold Wesker, 'Why I Fleshed out Shylock', in *Distinctions* (London: Cape, 1985), pp. 155–62.

Frank Whigham, 'Ideology and Class Conduct in *The Merchant of Venice*', in *Shakespeare's Comedies*, ed. Gary Waller (London and New York: Longman, 1991), pp. 108–28.

4   RECENT CRITICAL BOOKS ON SHAKESPEARE AND RENAISSANCE DRAMA

Catherine Belsey, *The Subject of Tragedy: Identity and Difference in Renaissance Drama* (London and New York: Routledge, 1985).

Jonathan Dollimore, *Radical Tragedy: Ideology and Power in the Drama of Shakespeare and his Contemporaries* (Brighton: Harvester, 1984).

Jonathan Dollimore and Alan Sinfield (eds), *Political Shakespeare: New Essays in Cultural Materialism* (Manchester: Manchester University Press, 2nd edn, 1994).

John Drakakis (ed.), *Shakespearean Tragedy* (London: Longman, 1992).

John Drakakis (ed.),*Alternative Shakespeares* (London: Methuen, 1987).

Terry Eagleton, *William Shakespeare* (Oxford: Blackwell, 1986).

John Gillies, *Shakespeare and the Geography of Difference* (Cambridge: Cambridge University Press, 1994).

Margreta de Grazia, *Shakespeare 'Verbatim': The Reproduction of Authenticity and the 1790 Apparatus* (Oxford: Clarendon Press, 1991).

Stephen Greenblatt, *Renaissance Self-Fashioning: from More to Shakespeare* (Chicago: University of Chicago Press, 1980).

Terence Hawkes (ed.), *Alternative Shakespeares: Volume 2* (London: Routledge, 1996).

Terence Hawkes, *Meaning by Shakespeare* (London: Routledge, 1992).

Jean E. Howard and Marion F. O'Connor (eds), *Shakespeare Reproduced: The Text in History and Ideology* (New York and London: Routledge, 1987).

Lisa Jardine, *Still Harping on Daughters: Women and Drama in the Age of Shakespeare* (Brighton: Harvester, 1983).

David Scott Kastan and Peter Stallybrass (eds), *Staging the Renaissance: Reinterpretations of Elizabethan and Jacobean Drama* (New York and London: Routledge, 1991).

Kathleen McLuskie, *Renaissance Dramatists* (Hemel Hempstead: Harvester Wheatsheaf, 1989).

Steven Mullaney, *The Place of the Stage: Licence, Play and Power in Renaissance England* (Chicago: University of Chicago Press, 1987).

Kiernan Ryan, *Shakespeare* (Hemel Hempstead: Prentice-Hall/Harvester Wheatsheaf, 2nd edn, 1995).

Valerie Traub, *Desire and Anxiety: Circulations of Sexuality in Shakespearean Drama* (London and New York: Routledge, 1992).

Gary Waller (ed.), *Shakespeare's Comedies* (London: Longman, 1991).

Valerie Wayne (ed.), *The Matter of Difference: Materialist Feminist Criticism of Shakespeare* (Ithaca, NY: Cornell University Press, 1991).

Robert Weimann, *Shakespeare and the Popular Tradition in the Theatre* (Baltimore and London: Johns Hopkins University Press, 1978).

Richard Wilson, *Will Power* (Hemel Hempstead: Harvester Wheatsheaf, 1993).

Notes on Contributors

Catherine Belsey chairs the Centre for Critical and Cultural Theory at the University of Wales, Cardiff. Her publications include *Critical Practice* (London, 1980), *The Subject of Tragedy: Identity and Difference in Renaissance Drama* (London and New York, 1985), *John Milton: Language, Gender, Power* (Oxford, 1988), and *Desire: Love Stories in Western Culture* (Oxford, 1994).

Walter Cohen is Professor of Comparative Literature and Dean of the Graduate School at Cornell University. He has written *Drama of a Nation: Public Theater in Renaissance England and Spain* (Ithaca and London, 1985), and is one of the editors of *The Norton Shakespeare* (New York, 1996).

John Drakakis is Professor of English at the University of Stirling. He is the general editor of the Routledge English texts series and the New Critical Idiom series. His publications include *New Casebooks: Antony and Cleopatra* (Basingstoke and London, 1994) and *Alternative Shakespeares* (London, 1985).

Kim F. Hall is an Associate Professor of English at Georgetown University, where she teaches English and Women's Studies. She is the author of *Things of Darkness: Economies of Race and Gender in Early Modern England* (Cornell, 1995), and is currently working on a book on women, colonisation and luxury foods.

Graham Holderness is Professor of Cultural Studies, Dean of the Faculty of Humanities, Language and Education, and Director of Research Policy at the University of Hertfordshire. His publications include *D. H. Lawrence: History, Ideology and Fiction* (1982), *Shakespeare's History* (1985), *The Shakespeare Myth* (1988), and *The Politics of Theatre and Drama* (1992).

Karen Newman is University Professor and Professor of Comparative Literature and English at Brown University. Her books include *Shakespeare's Rhetoric of Comic Character* (Methuen, 1985), *Fashioning Femininity and English Renaissance Drama* (Chicago, 1991) and *Fetal Positions* (Stanford, 1996) as well as numerous articles on early modern culture and literary theory.

Avraham Oz is the head of the Department of Theatre at the University of Haifa. He is the general editor of the Hebrew edition of Shakespeare and the founder of the journal *Assaph: Theatre Studies*. His publications include *The Yoke of Love: Prophetic Riddles in The Merchant of Venice* (London and Toronto, 1995).

Kiernan Ryan is Professor of English Language and Literature at Royal Holloway, University of London, and an Emeritus Fellow of New Hall, University of Cambridge. He is the author of *Shakespeare* (Hemel Hempstead, 1989; 2nd edn, 1995) and *Ian McEwan* (Plymouth, 1994), and the editor of *King Lear: Contemporary Critical Essays* (London, 1992), *New Historicism and Cultural Materialism: A Reader* (London, 1996) and *Shakespeare: The Last Plays* (London, 1998).

James Shapiro is Professor of English and Comparative Literature at Columbia University. He is the author of *Rival Playwrights: Marlowe, Jonson, Shakespeare* (New York, 1991) and *Shakespeare and the Jews* (New York, 1996).

Alan Sinfield is Professor of English at Sussex University. His publications include *Faultlines: Cultural Materialism and the Politics of Dissident Reading* (Oxford and Berkeley, 1992), *Cultural Politics – Queer Reading* (London and Philadelphia; 1994), *Political Shakespeare: New Essays in Cultural Materialism*, with Jonathan Dollimore (new edn, Manchester and New York, 1994).

Index

DAVID GLENN HUNT
MEMORIAL LIBRARY
GALVESTON COLLEGE